STRIKING SILVER

The Untold Story of America's Forgotten Hockey Team

Tom Caraccioli and Jerry Caraccioli

SP
SPORTS
PUBLISHING
L.L.C.

SportsPublishingLLC.com

Publishers: Peter L. Bannon and Joseph J. Bannon Sr.
Senior managing editor: Susan M. Moyer
Acquisitions editors: Noah Adams Amstadter
Developmental editor: Travis W. Moran
Art director: K. Jeffrey Higgerson
Dust jacket design: Joseph T. Brumleve
Project manager: Kathryn R. Holleman
Photo editor: Erin Linden-Levy

Printed in the United States of America

Sports Publishing L.L.C.
804 North Neil Street
Champaign, IL 61820
Phone: 1-877-424-2665
Fax: 217-363-2073
SportsPublishingLLC.com

Library of Congress Cataloging-in-Publication Data

Caraccioli, Tom.
    Striking silver : the untold story of America's forgotten hockey team /Tom Caraccioli and Jerry Caraccioli.
        p. cm.
    ISBN 1-59670-078-5 (hardcover : alk. paper)
    1. Hockey teams—United States—History—20th century. 2. Winter Olympic Games (11th : 1972 : Sapporo-shi, Japan) I. Caraccioli, Jerry. II. Title.

GV848.4.U6C37 2006
796.962'66—dc22
                                2005034972

This book is dedicated to Pete Sears,
who was not only a member of the 1972 United States Olympic silver medal-winning
hockey team, but to a generation of kids in Oswego, New York
—a leader, a teacher, a friend, and a role model
who will never, ever be forgotten.

And to our parents, Ed and Barb, our greatest role models,
whose love and support fueled our dreams and gave us the strength
to persevere in order to pursue—and now live—those dreams.

CONTENTS

FOREWORD

There are three mementos that I proudly display in my office: a painting of my father, Gordie Howe—the greatest father and hockey player of all-time; a picture of my brother, Marty, my father and me as we lined up for a face-off while playing together as members of the Houston Aeros of the WHA; and the silver medal that I earned as a member of the 1972 United States Olympic hockey team.

Reflecting back to when I was just 16 years old and given an opportunity to represent my country in the Olympic Winter Games in Sapporo, Japan—it was a dream come true.

To watch, learn, and play alongside such gifted players as Henry Boucha and Tim Sheehy. ...

To witness the spectacular goaltending of Mike "Lefty" Curran. ...

To learn from the leadership displayed by Huffer Christiansen and so many others. ...

And of course, the guidance provided to me by my roommates—Robbie Ftorek, Dick McGlynn, and Stu Irving—stays with me today after playing 22 years of professional hockey.

Some of the players from this team were able to go on to distinguished professional careers in the WHA and NHL. Others retired soon after and became teachers, lawyers, coaches, and businessmen.

Being 16 years of age and playing ice hockey in the Olympics—and being the son of Gordie Howe—may have brought a lot of attention my way, but I was only a small cog in the wheel. We played halfway around the world, and this team's success has not been recognized or celebrated until now—34 years later.

Striking Silver: The Untold Story of America's Forgotten Hockey Team is a book about the players and coach who came together as one and took home the silver—a team that wasn't supposed to win a game, let alone win a medal. The story of this team, and the individuals who represented the United States in Sapporo, is the story told within these pages.

And it is a vital part of USA hockey history.

Finally, I would be remiss not to thank my terminally ill mother—and to all the hockey mothers for their love and dedication. Without them, none of us would have had the opportunity to play the great game of hockey that we all love so much.

—MARK HOWE

AUTHORS' NOTE

After all these years, we still remember the sequence.

"Legs shoulder-width apart, hands together, right hand over left and reach down to the right for the ground to the outside of your foot ... one, two, three, four ... 10. Up. Switch hands. Now the same thing to the left side ... one, two, three, four ... hold it ... 10. Up. Keep your legs apart and touch the ground with your palms ... one, two, three, four ... holding ... don't bounce ... 10. Up. Now arch all the way back and look up to the sky."

Thus began many of our days doing summer off-ice training for hockey. Stretching always lasted around 30 minutes and was taken as seriously as any drill. Each day was different. One day would be circuit training with various stations of weights, dumb bells, a broom handle with a brick hanging off it, push-ups, sit-ups, squat-thrusts, dips, wall-sits, and other exercises all designed to work out a certain muscle or reflexes that were used in hockey.

On other days, we alternated between interval and Fartlek training, where we would run sprints, somersault, duck walk, crab walk, stop and do push-ups, wheel-barrel races, piggy-back races, and all kinds of different motions and exercises around the park in a big circle. On other days, there was the dreaded hill. We hated that day most. That day, running seemed like all we did—up the hill and down the hill—simulating killer drills from end boards to the blue line and back; to the center ice and back; to the far blue line and back; all the way down and back, but in much hotter weather, for far longer distances, and on much steeper inclines. Onlookers had to wonder what we were doing—sometimes we wondered, too.

"This will help you come winter," was the only explanation we needed.

The weights made us stronger; the broom handle with the brick helped develop our wrists after rolling and unrolling it; the push-ups and sit-ups, squat thrusts and dips enhanced our strength and coordination. And whoever Fartlek was, we just figured that sprinting, duck-walking, and wheel-barrel racing would help us in the winter. Little did we know that we were doing things the Russians devised in order to become better hockey players—the same training methods that were learned and passed on to our coach while playing for the 1972 U.S. Olympic hockey team.

When we were finished, we were dead tired, but not too tired for the finale—street hockey. That was the payoff. We got to play, and we manifested all of our spirit and enthusiasm in those games. They were heated battles, literally and figuratively, and none of us hesitated to play competitively, roughly. We were brothers and friends—the best of friends. While we may not have realized it then, we now know that we were the type of friends that would be friends forever. Some are the five-finger kind, but most remain open, inviting, and no matter how much time separates us, reuniting is the easiest thing in the world.

Some of us first heard of Pete Sears when he was an All-American goalie for the Oswego State hockey team in the late 1960s and early 1970s—or as a silver medalist on the 1972 United States Olympic hockey team. Others knew him as the Pee-Wee Road team coach in the Oswego Minor Hockey Association. A stint in the Vietnam War interrupted his college career, but he then returned to Oswego, where he finished his college career and then began pursuing an Olympic dream. We remember when he came back from the 1972 Olympics in Sapporo, Japan, and spoke at our brother's Minor Hockey Association banquet. He recounted his experience, generously answered questions, and posed for photos with all of the kids along with his silver medal. We laugh about that now, but even then—as six- and seven-year-olds—Pete started to inspire us.

My brother and I remember the first time that we really saw that silver medal up close. Pete and his wife, Kay, lived next to our aunt and uncle, where we often went to swim. On several occasions, we would knock on Pete's door and ask if we could see his silver medal. He kept it displayed in a study/living room surrounded by a framed blue jersey with "USA" emblazoned on the front, which he wore in the Olympics. Other memorabilia such as photos of the team marching into the Olympic Stadium during the Opening Ceremony and him standing on the podium receiving his medal surrounded the medal, which was smaller than we imagined, with a dullish-gray hue and what appeared to be a squiggly-snake design on it, but it was huge. Until the USA hockey team won the 1980 gold medal in Lake Placid it never dawned upon us that, up until then, very few men had ever won an Olympic medal in hockey for the United States—and Pete was one of them.

Along with our parents, Pete Sears was one of the most important role models in the young lives of a certain generation of kids growing up in upstate Oswego, New York. We never really questioned what he asked us to do—we just did it. To this day, and to a man, we probably would all still do whatever he asked us to do—and we all probably could rattle off a half-dozen or so of the motivational messages that he hung in his classroom, on our locker-room walls, and peppered in his speech. We were teenage kids, and we would've literally gone through a brick wall for him if he asked. Such blind faith in someone at that age can be both dangerous and glorious. For us, it was glorious. He was our coach, our friend, and for some of us in school, our seventh grade social studies teacher. He inspired us with his sayings, enlightened us with his knowledge and experience, and motivated us through discipline and a lasting will to "do one more when you think you can't do anymore."

We all wanted to play hockey for him—and we would do anything to prove that we were good enough, strong enough, and tough enough to do so once the weather turned cold.

ACKNOWLEDGMENTS

Our greatest thanks to the members of the 1972 United States Olympic hockey team for their time, encouragement and support in letting us tell their story: Kevin Ahearn, Larry Bader, Henry Boucha, Charlie Brown, Keith Christiansen, Mike Curran, Robbie Ftorek, Mark Howe, Stuart Irving, Jim McElmury, Dick McGlynn, Bruce McIntosh, Tom Mellor, Ron Naslund, Wally Olds, Tim Regan, Frank Sanders, Craig Sarner, Pete Sears, Tim Sheehy, head coach Murray Williamson and team manager Hal Trumble.

Special thanks to Mr. Hockey® Gordie Howe®, Mike Eruzione, Curt Gowdy, E.M. Swift, Steve Zipay, Del Reddy, Aaron Howard, Kay Sears and Tana Curran.

We'd like to extend an extra special thanks to Lesley Visser, and to Andrew Blauner—we could not have made our way as smoothly without him at our side shepherding us through the process of publishing this book and beyond.

For their encouragement, support and keen advice, our thanks to members of the CBS family including Armen Keteyian and Dick Enberg, as well as Sean McManus, LeslieAnne Wade, Robin Brendle, Jennifer Sabatelle, John Filo, Gil Schwartz, Dana McClintock and Kelli Raftery. As well as members of USA Sports: Gordon Beck, J. Kevin Landy, Steve Dinkes and Deenise Rebeiro.

To the professionals at Sports Publishing, LLC, especially Travis Moran for his time and patience, Scott Rauguth, Noah Amstadter, David Hulsey, Courtney Hainline, Mike Hagan, Randy Fouts and Maurey Williamson.

For their help in our research, thanks to Cecil Bleiker, Dave Fischer, Harry Thompson and Chuck Menke, as well as the *Minneapolis Star Tribune* archives and the New York City Public Library.

Thank you to Todd Rucynski, Charles Young, Bill Hancock, Dave Daigle, Dr. N. Scott Adzick, Dr. Michael Bebbington, Dr. Mark

Johnson, Dr. R. Douglas Wilson, Susan Miesnik and Jane Wright for their advice and support.

To those who first had a hand in launching the trajectory of our careers, including Tim Mead, Dick Bresciani, Ed Carpenter, Jim Small and Mary Jane Ryan.

Our deepest thanks to those who have contributed in ways too profound to fully mention, including our parents Edward and Barbara, our sister, Mary Anne, and brothers Mike, Paul, John and Kevin, who is always generous and quick with counsel, especially with this book, as well as Rudy, Elaine, Jeff and Pam.

To my wife, Marcela, for her love and inspiration—*Te quiero siempre.*

—*JC*

To my wife, Mary, whose unconditional love and support helped steer this rudderless ship nearly three years ago toward a future of endless possibilities and whose suggestions helped provide me the impetus to begin writing—I treasure you. And to my daughter, Olivia, whose bravery and strength are the personification of courage, you are the greatest gift I've ever received and my source for inspiration.

—*TC*

And finally, to all who "played for the Cup" at the "Caraccioli Gardens," "Seventh Street Spectrum," and "Albany Street Omni."

INTRODUCTION

"Many people say that we were the team that time forgot. I say that we were the team that nobody ever knew about. That's why everybody forgot us—they didn't know about us in the first place."

—PETE SEARS

Having done the math prior to Sunday's final games, the United States players knew exactly what needed to happen in the final two games in order to realize the best-case scenario—a silver medal. However, they were also mindful of the worst-case scenario—no medal at all.

In games pitting bitter rivals against each other, Finland and Sweden faced off in the morning; and Czechoslovakia took on the Soviet Union that afternoon to determine the gold. After computing the math, if Sweden defeated Finland and Czechoslovakia upset the Soviets, then the Czechs would take home the gold, the Russians the silver, and the Swedes the bronze. If Sweden lost, the United States was assured at least a bronze—if the Russians beat the Czechs, as most predicted, then the Americans would be striking silver.

༺ ༻ ༺ ༻ ༺ ༻

As the seconds ticked away in the third period, and the horn finally sounded, the seesaw battle between Finland and Sweden ended, and a sudden realization overwhelmed the Americans.

"The game got over, and we looked at each other and said, 'We just won a medal!'" remembered U.S. defenseman Bruce McIntosh.

As had been the nature of the tournament in the closing days, the unexpected happened as the Finns upset the Swedes, 4-3. With

Finland's win, the Americans had realized their dream of winning a medal.

The U.S. players all went to the final game hoping and rooting for the Russians to do what they were expected to do all along—win the gold medal. The Russian players realized that a victory secured the gold medal, of course, but a win also vaulted their young American friends to a silver medal past their hated rival, Czechoslovakia. Because of the tie-breaking system, a Czech loss would give them a 3-2 medal-round record, tying them with the Americans. Since the Americans had defeated the Czechs head to head, the silver medal would go to the United States.

CRSO   CRSO   CRSO

From the beginning, no one had any reason to believe this United States hockey team would do any different from its 1964 and 1968 Olympic predecessors. In '64, the U.S. team finished in fifth place with a 2-5 record. Four years later, they placed sixth at 2-4-1. Moreover, the U.S. national teams that participated in the World Championship tournaments of 1969, 1970, and 1971 did even less to sway the opinion of the international and American hockey experts.

Yet, with a core group of players from the '71 U.S. National team—Mike "Lefty" Curran, Dick McGlynn, Tom Mellor, Jim McElmury, Tim Sheehy, Henry Boucha, Kevin Ahearn, Charlie Brown, Keith "Huffer" Christiansen—gaining invaluable international experience, the ground work for the 1972 United States Olympic hockey team in Sapporo had been laid.

CRSO   CRSO   CRSO

Northern Japan's largest city, Sapporo originally was selected to host the 1940 Winter Games, but Japan's 1937 invasion of China forced it to resign. Thus, in 1972, the XIth Olympic Winter Games in Sapporo—located 10,000 miles and 10 time zones away from the United States—became the first conducted outside of Europe or the United States.

To some 1972 Olympic team members, holding the Winter Olympics in Japan seemed odd.

"When Murray Williamson asked me if I wanted to play on the team I said, 'Well, where are they going to be held?'" remembered McIntosh.

"He said, 'They're in Sapporo, Japan.' I'd never heard of it and didn't know anything about it. It was kind of like, 'Geez, this isn't going to be very interesting to anybody.' There was a general lack of knowledge of where Sapporo was and what was there. The fact that they actually had great skiing, had arenas and hockey teams in Japan— I don't think anybody really knew that. Certainly, nobody on our team really knew that. I went home and read about it. To me it was surprising. Instead of having [the Games] in the Swiss, Italian, or French Alps—those romantic ski villages where they'd all been held before—they were going to be in Japan. I looked at it as if it would have been nice to go to Cortina, St. Moritz, Oslo, or somewhere in Europe to play these Olympics. Instead, we were going to Japan, and that was fine."

cʒ୫ɔ   cʒ୫ɔ   cʒ୫ɔ

The mighty 1972 Olympic hockey team from the Soviet Union, made up of what many deemed "professional amateurs," was favored to win their third-straight gold and fourth out of five since fielding an Olympic ice hockey team for the first time in 1956. International hockey tournaments and the Olympics, particularly since '56, had become virtual battles for second place to the Soviet juggernaut, which turned opposing teams into mere pylons.

Czechoslovakia always competed with the Russians—and beat them on occasion. Sweden and Finland each played a wide-open, free-skating style with some of the most skilled players in the world. Canada, always a threat in international hockey, decided to protest the Eastern Bloc's use of what they deemed "professional amateurs," by boycotting the hockey tournament in Sapporo.

As in 1960, the U.S. team had its moments. However, the U.S. had shown nothing to contradict that the Russians were international hockey's preeminent superpower. That Soviet dominance, combined with low expectations of the U.S. team, deflated the priority that television and print place upon Olympic hockey today.

CR80   CR80   CR80

To match the lack of television coverage from Sapporo, very little was written about the team during the Games. Low expectations contributed to disinterest as well, but to U.S. head coach Murray Williamson, everything was unfolding according to plan.

Williamson, who coached the 1968 U.S. Olympic hockey team in Grenoble, France—as well as the 1967, 1970, and 1971 U.S. National teams—understood that the round-robin format of this Olympic hockey tournament pinpointed all the pressure on winning a one-game qualifier in order to play in the round-robin medal round. The U.S. team had finished last in "Pool A" of the '71 World Championship and was scheduled to play that year's "Pool B" champion, Switzerland, in the qualifying game.

"It was about one game," explained Williamson. "We played Switzerland, and if we lost, we were done—dropped into "Pool B" and playing for pride with no chance at a medal. There was a tremendous amount of pressure."

With that pressure in mind, Williamson decided to shelter his team as much as possible.

"Our strategy was to reduce the pressure on the guys, play for fun, and not risk a big buildup with the potential for disaster. To hype any Olympic hopes and face that one game was more than I wanted to expose these guys to. It was like, 'Let's low-profile this thing and get by that first game.'"

Williamson's low-lying tactics succeeded so well that when *Sports Illustrated* reporter Mark Mulvoy followed the team for a week and a half during their pre-Olympic tour, he couldn't find anything exciting to cover. When the magazine's Olympic preview issue hit newsstands, Mulvoy presented this in-depth analysis:

"In the U.S., meanwhile, it is the same old story: a young, inexperienced, unpredictable team. For the first time in 10 years, the club is made up mostly of American collegians with no naturalized Canadians. Three of the strongest players were lost to the NHL last year; now the team's average age is under 22. They could be ready, but an upset like the one that stunned Squaw Valley in 1960 seems unlikely. Fifth place is more like it."

The U.S. team didn't have endorsement contracts. No press corps followed them from city to city. Aside from sending out statistics to each player's local newspapers, no public relations guy pumped out press releases every day—all according to Williamson's strategy.

"We didn't have the media coverage. We just played for ourselves. We knew exactly what we wanted to do. We didn't want the press to hype us. We didn't need it."

Their 47-game pre-Olympic tour consisted of about three or four "home" games and the rest on the road—again by design. Williamson wanted his team to get used to playing on the road and hearing the crowd cheer for the other team. When the team played what most considered a "home game" against the University of Minnesota, Williamson's point was reinforced. For former Minnesota alumni McIntosh, Wally Olds, Frank Sanders, and Craig Sarner—as well as Twin Cities residents Charlie Brown, Jim McElmury, and Ron Naslund—often hearing cheers being drowned by boos was disheartening as well.

Subtle resentment amongst the USA hockey community also seemingly led to a lack of recognition for some of the '72 team. The USA hockey hierarchy resented the fact that Williamson, a Canadian, withheld his team from the decision-making committees that were commonplace.

"I told them, 'If you want a politician for a coach, find another man,'" Williamson explained. "I was not a politician. Herb Brooks faced a similar situation in 1980, but Herbie controlled it. He gave them a voice—then went behind the door and ignored them. I never did that. It created a closed band of guys that had great chemistry, by design. We didn't share. We didn't have people that communicated with the press and gave away free tickets in each city we played. We didn't have any of that."

Ultimately, Williamson maintained the lack of media coverage that allowed the team to approach the Olympics unnoticed.

"I just don't think it caught on," remembers NBC's host of the 1972 Winter Olympics, Curt Gowdy. "It sort of caught everybody by surprise. There wasn't any big story or headline blaring 'U.S. Team Does This or That.' It was a surprise, and it caught everybody by surprise. We'd been so bad before. I think people just expected that. And the Russians were so good—I think people just thought, 'Oh well, the Russians are just going to win it again.'"

⟨჻⟩⟨჻⟩⟨჻⟩

NBC had paid $6.4 million for the rights to broadcast the 1972 Olympic Winter Games. The network ended up broadcasting just 37 hours from Sapporo. It was a far, far cry from their most recent broadcast of the Winter Games in 2002 from Salt Lake City, Utah, where they had paid $545 million for the rights to broadcast in prime time and through various cable outlets for a total of 376 hours.

Due to the 10-hour time difference from Sapporo to America's East Coast, NBC executives faced some very tough programming decisions. Many of the events took place when Americans were sleeping. Therefore, the network taped them and delayed showing them. In some instances, what had taken place in Japan almost 20 hours earlier was shown on tape delay in prime time. Sometimes, if the timing was right, they went live with an event. Thus, much of the news about the U.S. hockey team was shown in sporadic taped segments of maybe 15 or 20 minutes and aired around three or four in the morning. For the most part, only families and friends, if they didn't fall asleep, were monitoring what was happening in Sapporo. Many of the players would check back home with calls to their parents, wives, or friends to ask them if they were following what was happening. Many of the responses were the same.

"People would say, 'We tried to see it, but we couldn't stay up until three o'clock in the morning. They just had it on for a couple of minutes, and that was it.' That was basically the interest that was presented at that time," said back-up goalie Pete Sears. "Many people say that we were the team that time forgot. I say that we were the team that nobody ever knew about. That's why everybody forgot us—they didn't know about us in the first place."

Seemingly, the entire U.S. Winter Olympic team had been overlooked as a whole—perhaps due to an unimpressive total of eight medals. The hockey team, which had overcome impossible odds and low expectations to win America's first hockey medal outside the U.S. since 1956, felt particularly frozen out by an apathetic press. Even as they approached their crowning Olympic moment—receiving their silver medals following another Soviet victory over Czechoslovakia—NBC added insult to injury by pulling the plug on their broadcast just as officials readied the flags and podiums for the presentation. They were the only American male athletes to take a medal home from these Olympics.

"Maybe if we had won the gold it would've been different," said star center Henry Boucha, one of the U.S.'s most talented players and leading scorers throughout the Olympic schedule. "In the United States nobody really recognizes anybody that comes in second. They don't like second best. It's unfortunate in this country, but that's the way it is."

Having won the silver medal between the 1960 gold medal victory and the "Miracle on Ice" gold medal win in 1980, fate also had a way of shadowing the accomplishment of the 1972 team.

"Even if the coverage had been similar to the present-day coverage of all the Olympic venues, I still think that you're naturally going to be forgotten a little bit finishing second between two gold medal-winning teams from the U.S.," said goalie Mike "Lefty" Curran. "That's normal. People don't ask who finished second in big events. It's always first. No one cares about second. However, we care."

A year after the 1980 team struck gold in Lake Placid, Craig Sarner remembered visiting with his friend, Herb Brooks—his former college hockey coach at the University of Minnesota and the coach of the 1980 team.

"We were sitting one day catching up when Herbie said, 'When you look at it, what you guys did was probably a helluva lot tougher than most people ever realize.' Coming from him, that's all the recognition I need."

1

THE TEAM

"The bond I formed with the Tommy Mellors, the Dickie McGlynns, Frank Sanders, Peter Sears, Timmy Sheehy and the rest of the guys, those are the things that are much more important than anything else."

—CRAIG SARNER

The word "chemistry" is often used to describe a team. The word "love" is applied just as often when describing a family. Thirty-four years later no better words could define the 1972 United States Olympic hockey team.

Bonds almost instantly formed between the young men who would become their country's Olympic hockey ambassadors. Composed of players who were all shapes and sizes, from all locales, from all backgrounds, from big-time eastern schools in Boston and western schools like the University of Minnesota, from smaller schools such as Colgate, Oswego State, and Bemidji State, the team reflected the fabric of American hockey.

The eclectic group of young and old also sported a wide range of personalities—from comedians such as Dick McGlynn and Tom Mellor to the studious Wally Olds, and Pete Sears to the intense Robbie Ftorek, Stu Irving, "Huffer" Christiansen, and "Lefty" Curran. This lunch-pail group came to work each day understanding that the sum of their parts was greater than any individual. Ever mindful of their teammates, each knew that if he weren't prepared to leave everything he had on the ice each day, he would be letting down 19 of his brothers and a father-figure coach who were sure to be doing just that.

Although common in American hockey at the time, no East-West rivalry existed between the players—except for occasional sibling rivalries in spirited scrimmages, playful verbal jabs, and jokes. No star egos, harsh words, or bad feelings ever created a wedge between this band of brothers. Instead, they were motivated by mutual respect and a common goal—the exact result head coach Murray Williamson intended when designing his blueprint for success, which began its development with 22 guys training at Bemidji State.

A constant tinkerer, Williamson fretted daily over his lines and defensive pairings, experimenting with many different combinations, switching players between offense and defense to discover the perfect chemistry. He realized that the best talent didn't necessarily produce the best chemistry. Williamson often brought in different players for tryouts to keep his players on their toes, but aside from some late additions, the team that came to Bemidji began to click, and the roster formed itself.

"The whole thing started in training camp," remembers defenseman Mellor. "Getting us up in Bemidji in that isolated area where they had tennis courts, a golf course, a really beautiful facility right on Bemidji State, was where it all started. We were a bunch of kids, and Murray had us up running, up playing tennis. We ran right to the end—even in Sapporo. We would go out for runs on the days of the games."

ᘓᕉᕟ ᘓᕉᕟ ᘓᕉᕟ

Several of the players knew of each other while growing up playing with or against each other on school teams, in tournaments and summer leagues. Irving, from Boston's North Shore, knew of South Shore schoolboy-phenom Ftorek from all the Boston records he was breaking. Mellor and Sears crossed paths in Lake Placid during an all-star tournament when they were 14. McGlynn and Kevin Ahearn went to high school together in Milton, Massachusetts. Craig Sarner and Frank Sanders grew up playing on the ponds of St. Paul, Minnesota—and Tim Sheehy and Henry Boucha were fierce Minnesota high school rivals.

Although many players knew of each other already, success depended on them getting to know each other inside and out. They had to be able to rely on each other.

"There was no East-West rivalry because Murray wouldn't allow it, and the players didn't allow it," remembers Ftorek. "We had some real spiffs on the eastern side. I mean how could you not like Dickie McGlynn? He wouldn't allow people to get off-center, same with Lefty and Huffer. It developed into a liking of one another, and that's how we created a team—we grew as one."

As time passed, the bonds between the teammates began to grow even stronger. The foundation group of guys, those considered the stars, blended in with those considered the grinders.

"We had guys who were really good hockey players—like Robbie Ftorek, Henry Boucha, Huffer Christiansen, Tim Sheehy, Craig Sarner, Mike Curran, Wally Olds," said the oldest player on the team, Ron "Daddy Nas" Naslund. "These were the core guys. They were really good hockey players. Then we had a lot of other guys like Stuart Irving and me. We just had to work really hard and felt very fortunate to be on the team. But you had to have the other guys fill in to make the team really work."

CR80   CR80   CR80

Williamson continued to keep everyone on edge by bringing in players for tryouts, right up to the final day. Even though the roster seemed set, Williamson made two key additions about three weeks before the team left for Sapporo, both recognizable to their teammates.

Mark Howe, son of hockey legend Gordie Howe, was quiet, tough, and had great hockey genes. Thick and muscular with a heavy shot like his famous dad, he was only 16 years old, but he had the body and the presence of a 22-year-old. And Mike "Lefty" Curran, a U.S. National team veteran goaltender known for his swagger and confidence, was one of the old-timers on the team. Because of his international experience, Curran almost immediately became one of the leaders of the team.

Both Howe and Curran were accepted by their new Olympic teammates, but not before dealing with their own intruding feelings. Howe felt like he had taken someone else's spot because of his famous last name. Ftorek, Irving, and McGlynn took the young Howe under their wings—but it was Ftorek, out of high school just a year but mature beyond his years, who really helped set him straight.

"Mark was in a tough spot," explained Ftorek. "First of all, he was 16—a great kid. I just knew that he didn't think he should be there. First and foremost, he didn't think that he earned it like everybody else because he took someone else's spot late. I had to try to explain to him he did deserve it because he was very talented. I told him, 'Yeah, your dad is someone very special. However, your dad may have gotten you an opportunity, but you made the team because of your skill and your ability.'"

Things became even tougher for Howe when they arrived in Sapporo because the team that no one knew anything about suddenly had an angle for the media to write about and report.

"We were over in the Olympic Village and Curt Gowdy wanted to talk to him," remembers Ftorek. "Mark was rooming with Stuey, Dickie and me, and he didn't want to go. He didn't want to go because he couldn't understand why the media didn't want to talk to the other guys. He thought they should be talking to the other guys. I said, 'Yeah, you're probably right, but you're the guy they want to talk to and you've got to do it.' I made him go and I went over with him. We had a lot of talks. It was tough for him. Nobody understands how tough it was. Out on the ice it was easy, but it's all the other stuff that happens off the ice. People probably thought he loved to do all that crap. He didn't. He was very concerned with the team and the individuals and was really kind of embarrassed."

On behalf of Williamson, intermediaries stepped in about a month before the Games to end an ongoing feud between the coach and the fiery 26-year-old veteran international goaltender.

"Murray and Lefty got into some type of row after the '71 World Tournament," recalled team captain Christiansen. "As the captain, before the Games I went to talk with Murray. He had called me in and we talked about what was happening. We had good goaltending in Pete but I told Murray, 'We need Lefty Curran. He's a guy that can stand on his head and turn it around for us.' Plus, it wasn't like we were bringing in a complete unknown."

Williamson concurred—he had been keeping tabs on the fiery goalie during the months leading up to the Games. He was straight with the other goalies in explaining his plan when the time came to add the wildcard Curran.

"We always kept an eye on him," admitted Williamson. "All coaches, no matter who they are—if you're Bill Parcells or Herb Brooks—all coaches are going to have a player or two that you can get to, and he can get to you, and there's going to be a clash of personalities. Lefty was always a part of my thoughts, but he was older, and I wasn't sure his intensity level that he played at would have been good for the team the whole year. Lefty had the experience and skill. Pete had the skill but not the experience that was needed to get the job done. Either of them could've, but Lefty was the guy at the time. There also was a learning curve with this team, and he could've blended in at any time because everybody loved Lefty."

At first, though accepted by others, the team's other goaltenders gave Curran a less-than-warm reception. He knew he was going to be given a shot to prove himself. And he also knew that he had to perform.

"I didn't feel as though I was going to walk in there and have the job handed over to me," said Curran.

Questions lingered in his mind from his days on the other national teams he had played on. Was he prepared? He had been there and done it. He played against the mighty Russian and Czechoslovakian teams. Curran knew how difficult it was going to be. And then there was the fact that there were still three other goalies on the team besides him.

"Quite frankly, when I joined the club at practice the first day, I felt as though I was an interloper," admitted Curran. "They had a nucleus put together. They had worked so hard. They were a bunch of young guys. I looked at the three goalies, and the three goalies looked at me—they didn't welcome me. I didn't blame them one bit. I went to practice with the club, and they made a quick decision with Kim Newman. They let Kim go. He talked to me before he left. He said, 'Good luck. I wish you the best Lefty. Do well.' I said, 'Thank you very much.' He left, and I felt bad about that. That left the three of us.

"Pete wasn't real happy about the situation, either. I know that Regan wasn't. It was very challenging. They gave me a couple of exhibition games. We played the Saginaw Stars, the North Stars minor league club. I believe I played in two or three exhibition games, the last one being in Fort Worth [Texas]. I wasn't really happy with the way I was playing. I felt like I was physically ready but wasn't real good at that time. It wasn't like, 'Okay, I'm here. I'm ready to go.' I didn't go out there and light it up. It wasn't like that. But Murray had probably already made up his mind about it."

During the exhibition games, Curran saw something in the young team that he hadn't seen before in the other teams he had played for in international competition.

"I saw a spark in their eyes," remembered Curran. "I saw an innocence and optimism that I had never experienced on other clubs that I had played on. The other clubs I played on all recognized their capacity, just how untalented they might have been. How difficult it was going to be because they were more mature. This group, even though they had lost five exhibition games to the Soviet Union—it was as if they never played those games. That was one of the things I looked for when I first strapped on my pads and went out to practice. It was a combination of optimism and innocence. It was like a young soldier going off to war thinking he's going to go off and win the war for his country but comes back in a bag. I knew that once we got over to the Olympics, it was going to be a very similar venue to the World Championship, but the stakes were even higher."

When the time came for them to go to Sapporo, Curran, who had only been with the team for a couple of weeks, further remembered thinking, "I don't know what's going to happen when we get to Sapporo, but these guys are geared up. It seemed like some of them were still drinking mother's milk. Marky Howe was 16 years old and a junior in high school. I knew what we were getting into. I was thinking Stockholm, where we lost every game. But he didn't know the difference, and I wasn't going to tell him—neither was Murray."

CᏚᏰꝜ   CᏚᏰꝜ   CᏚᏰꝜ

To this day, Williamson's scouting report of the members of his 1972 U.S. team reads as if he was still patrolling his practices with a clipboard in hand, trying to figure out who would match up the best playing together on a line or a defensive pairing.

CᏚᏰꝜ   CᏚᏰꝜ   CᏚᏰꝜ

Years later, when the time came for reflection and each was asked about his most vivid experience of the 1972 Olympic Winter Games, each player—without hesitation, some choking back emotion—said one word: "Team."

For the members of the 1972 team today, the urge to check in with one another throughout the course of the year is as strong as it was in Sapporo. Sarner, Sanders's boyhood friend from their playing days on the ponds of St. Paul, ultimately put the proper perspective on this forgotten team.

"The bonds I formed with the Tommy Mellors, the Dickie McGlynns, Frank Sanders, Peter Sears, Timmy Sheehy, and the rest of the guys—those are the things that are much more important than anything else."

COACH'S SCOUTING REPORT

KEVIN AHEARN

Class guy, a Boston College blue blood with lots of pride. Probably one of the hardest working guys on the team, Kevin was always there after practice. He could shoot like crazy—a good player who played better than his capabilities.

LARRY BADER

Larry was a different kind of guy, but a very dedicated hockey guy. One of the dangers you can have is if your 20th guy is a whiner, complainer, bitcher. I learned from that in 1968. That's why he was there—he was a dedicated guy who wasn't going to create problems for anybody if he wasn't playing.

HENRY BOUCHA

Everybody loved Henry. He had skill coming out of his ears. Totally dedicated, he was one of our horses. Great skill, he was our leading scorer and was tough. Guys loved to play with him. He had the admiration of everybody. He and Sheehy used to go at it—both great players. They used to scrap every once in a while. Both were from Northern Minnesota and played for rival high school programs.

CHARLIE BROWN

The Silent One. Totally involved. Totally intense. Charlie would throw his body in a fire if that's what it took for the team to be successful. Quiet, very reserved, and the guys loved him. He never said much. He never had a complaint and was always positive. He would go through a brick wall if that's what you told him to do.

KEITH "HUFFER" CHRISTIANSEN

Huffer was one of the "oldies." He and Naslund were there to blend in with the experience. He was a total team guy. He was one of our captains and the leader. Cockier than hell. He was a star anywhere he went. He was spectacular. Huffer liked his beer and cigarettes. He and

I established the ground rules. I said to him one time, "You're finely tuned. You don't pour bad oil into a racing car, so you have to give up that stuff." He did. He was probably the most skilled player of all. Boucha was right up there. Sheehy was a power forward and Robbie Ftorek was highly skilled, but Huffer had the most of all of them.

MIKE "LEFTY" CURRAN

Everybody loved Lefty. He was a major contributor—skill-wise and with his fiery competitive spirit. But he was just another piece of the puzzle.

ROBBIE FTOREK

Someone came up to me at the New England tryout and said, "This kid Ftorek is the top soccer player in the state of Massachusetts." I said, "I have to take a real close look at him." He was skating around, this little guy with ragamuffin pants and hair sticking out of his helmet. He was a little bit of a loner. Very intense. A very, very intense kid. He was young at the time. Stubborn as hell but he gave 100 percent all the time.

MARK HOWE

We picked Mark up, and he played some exhibition games with us. We needed a left-winger. He was on our list for skill and attitude. The maturity level of this kid was overwhelming. He was a big part of the team. He was tougher than hell. Vaclav Nedomansky of Czechoslovakia nailed him in a preseason game, and he didn't know where he was, but it didn't bother him at all. I used him as a forward, and he became a Hall of Fame defenseman.

STU IRVING

Stuey was the glue of the team. This guy was the greatest. I would have to rate him No. 1. I say that because, like Peter Sears, this guy set the tone. He worked his ass off because he didn't want to go back to Vietnam, but he had a great attitude. He was really a great kid. The guys who went into the NHL right after the Olympics—Sheehy, Boucha—were so far ahead of the teams conditioning-wise. Stuey set the tone for the physical conditioning of our team. He just never quit.

His work ethic was unbelievable, and the guys loved him. His skill level was good. His size and power were a little bit of a handicap to be able to play in the National Hockey League.

JIM McELMURY

Jim wound up playing in the NHL. Low key, low profile, last guy in the line to get accolades, first guy in line when punishment had to be dished out. Team player. Winner. But a low-key player. He took the good and the bad in the same vein.

DICK McGLYNN

Dick was our "keep it loose" guy. Dedicated. The guys loved him. He kept everybody loose. He was kind of the pep 'em up guy. When things were down, he'd jack up the troops. He had that confidence and that "We can do anything" attitude. It was a big factor.

BRUCE McINTOSH

Bruce didn't get in to any games, but he was one of our top guys before getting injured. I had made the promise that everybody would get some ice time. I was fully prepared to get them all some action, but he said, "Hey, team comes first. We're rockin'. Don't sacrifice the team."

TOM MELLOR

A great skill player, Mellor was a toughie. He didn't go around as a tough guy, but when he gritted his teeth, watch out. He whipped Dave Schultz in a scrap. Ned Harkness, who was coach of the Red Wings when Tommy was playing right after the Olympics, told me the story.

"Schultz asked one of his teammates, 'Who's this guy?' The teammate replied, 'He's a rookie who just played in the Olympics for the Americans.' Schultz licked his lips and said, 'Well, here's another rookie that's going to get taught a lesson.' Tommy whipped him." He never went looking for it, never paraded himself as a tough guy, but he could handle himself. He was the guy who organized the street hockey games when guys were lying around. He was the one who made it fun for everybody. A great player. He could've played today in the NHL and been a very good player.

RON NASLUND

They called him "Daddy Nas." He was our experience. He had a great attitude and brought a fatherly look to our team. Nas had a lot of experience. He kind of replaced Herbie in terms of that older, experienced, mature guy. You had to have that type of guy in the locker room.

WALLY OLDS

Very dependable. Very smart.

TIM REGAN

He was a great guy. He made many great sacrifices for the team. He didn't get to play, but he was a big part of the program. We went over there with three goalies. When we had to declare the roster, he wasn't a part of that roster. He was part of the team, but not on the roster that was declared. All credit to this guy. He came to me and said, "I'm not going to be able to help anybody here, but I can go back and help my Boston University team. I'll be with you in spirit and go back and fulfill my commitment to BU." His presence on the team had a major impact because he kept everybody honest. We had some people in the wings for us to say, 'If you let down and lose sight of the goal, you ain't going to be here.' He kept everybody honest, but Pete was ahead of him. And Lefty, of course, with all that experience.

FRANK SANDERS

Big Frank. Frank got three goals in the Olympic Games. I think he had five goals all year in 47 games, then came up big in the Olympics. A big strong guy with muscle and skill. He wouldn't back down from anyone. He didn't go looking for it, but when he got into it, watch out. He got us through all of the pro games when they wanted to test the 'Young American upstarts.' He gave our team a lot of confidence. And we had to have that. He was the backbone of the muscle part of our operation.

CRAIG SARNER

He was another journeyman pro. A team player. Good defensive player. He was the type of guy who could blend in and play with anybody. He would do whatever I asked of him.

PETE SEARS

He was a great sobering effect. We had a bunch of wild guys, conservative guys, guys with a lot of intensity, and Pete was an integral part of that team. His dedication and passion were unbelievable. He was a real good goaltender but whether he was ready for the real big shooters, experience-wise, I didn't know, but he was always there. He was always going to be a part of that team no matter how many goaltenders were there. If we had 10 goaltenders, he was number one or two at all times without any question. Never below that. He was there. He served as a very sobering effect on anybody who took his duties lightly. Not vocally, but by the way he handled himself. His dedication was great.

TIM SHEEHY

He was our other captain. He too had skill coming out of his ears. Very prideful. He clashed with Henry. They were good for each other. They were both from Northern Minnesota and high school rivals. Strong, tough, with many skills. The Boston College boys had a lot of class there. He was a big part of our team. He had a bad knee injury but we got him back just in time, otherwise we would have had trouble.

2

VIETNAM

"It always stood out in my mind that Murray knew there were about five of us in the Army, or had been in the Army, and he told us—either you make the team or you go to Saigon. There was plenty of incentive for us to do well. There was no guarantee."

—TIM SHEEHY

As team members convened in the fall of '71, the nation's collective conscience was engrossed by radical events at home and abroad. The winds of change blew through all corners of the country. The revolutionary ideas of the 1960s began to gain wider acceptance through advances in civil rights, including affirmative action and desegregation—as well as a rising women's movement and problems with lingering environmental issues. Growing disillusionment with the government led to a galvanized college-student populace who

15

strongly voiced its dissent toward the Nixon Administration's handling of the Vietnam War. The military draft remained in effect, and America's boys were still being summoned into an increasingly unpopular and deadly war.

In 1971, the United States was in its 10th year of involvement in the Vietnam War. Despite the fact that the number of troops fighting in the jungles of Southeast Asia had decreased to nearly 157,000 from the 334,600 troops there in 1970 (and the 475,000 who were there in 1969), many Americans had grown to resent that the United States was still involved at all. Public sentiment against the war was at its apex in March, as U.S. Army Lieutenant William Calley was found guilty of the premeditated murder of 22 villagers at My Lai—later known as the "My Lai Massacre"—and a massive anti-war march in Washington, D.C. followed a month later.

Veterans were scorned and labeled "baby killers" upon their return home. Some veterans actually joined the anti-war movement, citing the atrocities that they had witnessed, and at times, unfortunately administered.

If veterans of World War II are recognized as the "Greatest Generation," then the young men and boys who fought in Vietnam are the "Forgotten Generation."

ଓଞ୍ଚ   ଓଞ୍ଚ   ଓଞ୍ଚ

None of the future '72 Olympians—whether they were playing hockey on the ponds of Minnesota, in New England prep academies, for Eastern colleges or Midwestern universities—could predict how global events would affect them in the years to come.

The United States' direct involvement in what was then categorized as the "Vietnam Conflict" began in 1961, when South Vietnam signed a military and economic aid treaty with the United States. That aid led to the arrival of U.S. support troops and the formation of the U.S. Military Assistance Command, Vietnam (MACV) in 1962. In November 1963, Duong Van "Big" Minh engineered a military coup over the Ngo Dinh Diem-led government in South Vietnam. Diem was executed. As fighting and casualities escalated, at President Lyndon B. Johnson's request, U.S. military aid to South Vietnam grew after the U.S. Senate passed the Tonkin Gulf resolution on August 7, 1964. The Tonkin Gulf resolution authorized the president to take "all necessary measures to repel any armed attacks against the forces of the United States and to prevent further aggression."

Now actively engaged in fighting, the U.S. provided further aid and support, helping to establish control of South Vietnam—which had suffered a power vacuum created by competing coups—under the premiership of Nguyen Cao Ky in 1965.

In March 1965, the United States began a systematic bombing of North Vietnam known as "Rolling Thunder." By 1966, 190,000 U.S. troops were in South Vietnam, while North Vietnam was receiving armaments and technical assistance from the Soviet Union, among other countries. Aside from sporadic pauses, "Rolling Thunder" continued until October 1968.

Johnson's demands for increased support led to the draft lottery, which brought the horrors of Southeast Asia into the living rooms of many American families. Most future members of the '72 U.S. Olympic hockey team during this time were ripe for the draft. Had they not taken notice of what was happening in Vietnam, their attention was drawn immediately by the nationally televised draft. As ping-pong balls labeled with birthdates spun around a large, plastic bubble, families shuddered with their eyes on their 18-to-22-year-old sons. Each birth date was assigned a number, which was followed by a letter from the Selective Services of the United States, notifying the nation's young men that they would be sent to war.

If your number was low, you were most likely headed to hell—if your number was high, you might escape.

"That was quite a night, and I'll never forget it," remembers defenseman Dick McGlynn. "It was the absolute height of the Vietnam War. It was a long night watching the draft on television. I had draft number 104. I was pretty sure I was going to go at some point in time. My friends and I all met up later, and of course, the bars were packed. One-third of the guys were delighted; one-third were extremely upset; and one-third were confused."

By the time the '72 U.S. Olympic hockey team had been formed in 1971, few members were spared from the events of the world as it happened before them. Teacher and student deferments, along with high draft lottery numbers, were saving graces for some. Others were forced to trudge Vietnam's treacherous and deadly jungles before skating the ice in Sapporo—a situation goalie Pete Sears and forward Stuart Irving soon found themselves living.

CR   CR   CR

Sears had been attending Oswego State University when he left school to try out for the '68 Olympic team. After four days of tryouts, coach Murray Williamson was impressed with the 19-year-old's play, but informed him that the team had been selected. The coach arranged for Sears to play in a more competitive semi-pro league in Green Bay, against some older players that included Olympic veterans, and others whom Williamson wanted to keep tabs on for future Olympic consideration.

In December 1967, after four months of bagging groceries by day and playing hockey by night, Sears received his draft notice. Upon returning home to Lake Placid, he reported to the draft board. He was sent to Albany, then on to Fort Dix, New Jersey, for basic training.

"That was a real bummer for me," remembered Sears. "I was doing something that I loved to do. I had my dreams that I wanted to move on with my hockey; then I was suddenly in the Army. I didn't really know if hockey was ever going to be a part of my life anymore."

After his basic training in Fort Dix, Sears went through Advanced Infantry Training in Fort Jackson, South Carolina, and then received his orders for Vietnam.

In May 1968, just weeks between the assassinations of Civil Rights leader Reverend Martin Luther King, Jr. and Senator Robert F. Kennedy, Sears was deployed to Vietnam. Stationed in the mountainous jungles of the central highlands, Sears served in the infantry, carrying a .60-caliber machine gun as the squad leader for a dozen men. Walking point on most patrols, Sears and his men often faced North Vietnamese mortar showers as they signaled coordinates to their firebase camp above for artillery support. After a year on the front lines, Sears returned to the States, reporting to Fort Knox, Kentucky, where he stayed for three months to complete his tour of duty. He then applied for an "early out" so he could go back to school.

കൈ   കൈ   കൈ

After failing to make the 1970 U.S. National hockey team—which would've kept him Stateside—Stuart Irving's Olympic dreams represented a beacon of hope after he was shipped to the steamy jungles of the Mekong Delta in October 1970. The Mekong Delta region encompassed a vast portion of southeastern Vietnam where the Mekong River empties into the sea. The marshy, farmland region of 75,000 square miles saw fierce fighting between Viet Cong guerillas and U.S. forces operating from river swift-boats.

Irving, 22 when tryouts began in 1971, was his company's clerk, but it wasn't all about mail calls during his tenure in the jungle. Though often quiet about his experience, he mesmerized 16-year-old Mark Howe—too young for draft consideration—with his tales of Vietnam.

"I remember one night he was talking about being over there," recalled Howe. "I remember him saying how he was on a chopper one time running out to grab somebody, and the guy right next to him took one, and it blew his leg right off. I heard these things, and it hit home especially for me because I was 16. The draft was still going on, and I was a year and a half away from the draft. It was scary stuff. I was thinking I was pretty lucky."

One particular parcel, sent to the company clerk from his father, helped Irving maintain his focus and hope during the war. That package contained several hockey sticks and pucks, allowing him to continue fueling his drive to one day play hockey again. Day after day, as Vietnamese villagers looked on in bewilderment, he trained by running laps around the camp, playing tennis, and practicing his shooting skills off a wooden pallet against sand bags in a foxhole.

CRBO   CRBO   CRBO

Other players, such as forwards Henry Boucha and Tim Sheehy and defensemen Dick McGlynn and Charlie Brown, also served in the U.S. Army. Through cooperation with the Pentagon, U.S. coach Murray Williamson and team manager Hal Trumble were able to have the players assigned to temporary duty under Williamson's command. Before that agreement was finalized, however, each young man had his share of worries.

Eighteen-year-old star center Boucha had played on the 1970 U.S. National team in Bucharest, Romania, and the World "B" Championships before going back to his Canadian junior team to finish the season. He then returned to his hometown, Warroad, Minnesota, to work during the off-season when the arrival of the daily mail brought a change in his life as he knew it.

"One day my mail came, and I was standing there in shock as I read this letter that said I was lottery number 32, and that they were going to be drafting up to 280," remembers Boucha. "I was expected to go probably in December. I didn't know what the hell to do. My first thought was, 'I gotta get a hold of Murray right away.' I thought my career was over right there."

Boucha called Williamson. And after the coach told his young star not to worry, he and Trumble started making calls to their contact at the Pentagon.

"The Army wouldn't excuse anybody for anything other than the Olympics," recalled Trumble. "And that's what we were doing—preparing for the Olympics. We had several players who had been subject to the draft, and part of my job was to see if I could get them released and sent to us."

As part of the process, Trumble would send letters to the Pentagon through a liaison at the Olympic Committee signifying which players could be playing on the Olympic hockey team for the United States. He would then travel to the Pentagon in Washington, D.C., to fill out some applications and talk to the Army hierarchy involved in the process.

"They took over and did whatever paperwork was necessary to get those players released to us," Trumble further explained. "After the Olympics, they had to go back to the service. It wasn't an overly complicated process. It wasn't only for the hockey players. At that time, both the Winter and Summer Olympics were held in the same year, so there were other sports doing the same thing. I went down to Washington three times. I got Boucha, McGlynn, Brown, and Sheehy, and later on, Irving. We knew that Stu was a possibility, and it was up to Murray to name the guys he wanted. He told me to try to get Stu free. It was a case of how the team developed and where we thought we needed some help."

"The U.S. Army took great pride in their people representing their country by participating in something other than war," said Williamson. "If you were in the Army, we would get these guys and say, 'Here's a guy who could be playing on the Olympic hockey team, and we'd like for him to be assigned to the Minneapolis barracks.' They would cut papers and assign the players to the base in Minneapolis. The Army was very cooperative and would release that person to us for an extended period of training and the Games. As long as they were still with the team, they didn't have to report back to whatever duty they were assigned to—that was their assignment."

Before Trumble could help with the others, Williamson returned Boucha's call a few days later with a plan. Williamson arranged to have his star player go through boot camp in Fort Knox, Kentucky, in August as a volunteer draftee. By November, Boucha was back in Minnesota with the U.S. National team playing in a 51-game schedule in preparation of the 1971 World Championship in Bern/Geneva, Switzerland.

"I was still in the service but was basically able to play all my time," explained Boucha. "I was on temporary duty to the United States National hockey team, at no expense to the government other than my base salary. We were allowed to receive some per diem living expenses from the team."

After the 1971 World Championship in Switzerland and a brief visit back home in the summer, Boucha returned to the service. He was stationed in Georgia at Fort Gordon going through Military

Police training when he found out he'd been drafted again—this time by the NHL's Detroit Red Wings. After a couple of weeks off following MP training, his orders came in to report to Germany.

"There were 250 guys, and 25 of us got to go to Germany—the rest went to Vietnam," explained Boucha. "I was very fortunate not to have to serve over there."

Boucha served in Germany as a military policeman for a couple of months, then happily rejoined his U.S. Olympic teammates for fall hockey training camp in Bemidji.

                       ০৪৪০   ০৪৪০   ০৪৪০

After plans to play in South Africa and training camp with the St. Louis Blues fell through, Dick McGlynn talked his way into a tryout for the 1971 U.S. National team, which he made as the eighth defensemen. Then he found himself in a situation he couldn't talk his way out of.

Due to his low draft number, McGlynn figured he'd be going all along. After his number was called, he was able to put off reporting until January 1971, when, while in the middle of a break from a 51-game domestic schedule, McGlynn found himself on a slow, lonely ride to Seattle for military induction.

"Murray and Hal had arranged for me to be inducted into the service during the middle of the season," explained McGlynn. "Gary Gambucci, who later played for the Minnesota North Stars, dropped me off at the train station. It was one of the worst times of my life. The train took three days to get to Seattle. I didn't know anyone. I slept in a sleeper car and took my meals in one of those domed cars. It was awful. My mental state was not good. First of all, I was going to be inducted into the service for two years. Secondly, it was the height of the Vietnam War, and you knew if you were cut from the team you were going to end up right in the middle of the Mekong Delta with Stu Irving. It was a depressing ride out there. When we finally got there, the harassment started, and they cut our hair, which took about 12 seconds per man. But I kept my mouth shut and never told anyone what the scoop was."

If McGlynn intended to get noticed by Murray Williamson during the 1971 U.S. National team tryout, it was the exact opposite when he was called by the Army. He knew that some of his teammates, such as Henry Boucha and Tim Sheehy had served, or were serving, in the Armed Forces before joining the national team. Armed with the knowledge of what to expect when he reported for induction during the 10-day break, McGlynn heeded the advice of his teammates about keeping a low profile and remaining anonymous by answering, "No," to all questions.

"Henry told me to be anonymous because they went after anyone who stood out in any way. Any question, say no," explained McGlynn.

When McGlynn got to the barracks, the advice he got couldn't have been more accurate.

"The drill sergeant started to ask questions.

"'Do you smoke?'

"If you said yes, they'd make that person take the pack out and smoke all 20 at once.

"'Do you have a license?'

"If they knew you had a license to drive, they'd make you take the lawnmowers and drive them all around the company area and make you do extra details.

"'Do we have any Catholics?'

"I was, but I kept my mouth shut.

"'Do we have any Protestants? Jews?'

"Again, I didn't raise my hand for anything. After about eight questions, the drill sergeant came down to me and said, 'Kid, you didn't raise your hand for anything. You don't believe in God?'

"I said, 'I'm an agnostic.' He looked at me, and I looked right back at him. I don't know whether I had a cat-ate-the-canary look on my face, but I didn't admit to anything. I just kept to myself."

For the one player from the 1972 team remembered as the chatterbox and the character of the team to this day, that was a tough assignment.

After 10 days, the drill sergeant walked into the barracks and asked, "Do we have a McGlynn in here?"

After finally figuring out who McGlynn was, the drill sergeant called him over and asked, "What the hell is this TD Ride to Minneapolis stuff? You've got orders from the Pentagon saying you're going to Minneapolis tomorrow."

Of course, McGlynn knew exactly what that meant, but he remained true to his silence and didn't say anything to anyone. Ten days later and 10 pounds heavier from all the potatoes he was fed at each meal, McGlynn returned to the U.S. National team.

CREO   CREO   CREO

Following the 1971 World Championship, McGlynn reported back to Fort Lewis in the Seattle area for eight weeks of basic training. Before he left, Williamson assured him that he'd take care of everything and get him assigned to special services. McGlynn graduated basic training and got his orders: AIT—Advanced Infantry Training. Though a bit surprised, McGlynn reported for eight more weeks of AIT as a mortar man in the infantry. The ever-growing anxious McGlynn wondered what was next. He knew Williamson had assured him of getting re-assigned, but he also knew that time could run out—as it did on Stuart Irving a year earlier. As the eighth week of AIT ended, McGlynn once again received his orders. This time his orders read: RVN. Not knowing exactly what that meant, McGlynn asked a buddy next to him. His buddy answered bluntly:

"Vietnam."

Not knowing what to do, when his company was dismissed from ranks, McGlynn ran to a nearby payphone and put in a call to his coach. McGlynn spoke with Williamson's wife and found out his coach wasn't in the country—he was visiting his friend Anatoly Tarasov in Russia. His next call was to team manager Hal Trumble. As he spoke with Trumble's wife, McGlynn learned that Trumble also was out of the country on a fishing trip in Sweden. With a growing sense of urgency and nerves, McGlynn took a deep breath and took matters into his own hands as he made his next call.

"I figured at that point I had nothing to lose," explained McGlynn. "At worst, I was going to be sent to Vietnam, so I called the Pentagon."

"Give me Major Johnson."

"Who's calling?" asked the voice on the other end.

"Dick McGlynn."

He failed to mention it was Private Dick McGlynn.

Major Johnson, who was the head of personnel for the Olympic Games and Pan Am Games, got on the phone. "Dick, how are you?"

"Not too well, sir," McGlynn said with growing frustration. "I just got orders for Vietnam. Murray Williamson said I was supposed to be getting re-assigned."

After calming him down, Major Johnson assured McGlynn he had his orders, as well as those of Tim Sheehy, Henry Boucha, Charlie Brown, and Stuart Irving, for special assignment to the United States Olympic hockey team right in front of him.

The day before McGlynn was to be shipped out to Vietnam, an officer once again walked into the barracks looking for him. Finally, his orders read: TDY—Temporary Duty—Minnesota; Commanding Officer: Murray Williamson.

"One of the most difficult things was the day I was leaving to come back to the '72 U.S. Olympic team," remembers McGlynn. "I was driven again to the airport by the staff car and dropped off at the commercial side of the airport. All my buddies were driven to the airport in yellow school buses or cattle cars and dropped off in the military side of the airport. They were going to Vietnam. I was going in the other direction. I was very conflicted. It was heart-wrenching waving goodbye to the guys in my unit who were heading off to the military optical. A few of my close buddies knew I was headed back to Minneapolis, but I generally didn't make it well known. It wasn't a good situation. These guys were going to Vietnam, and I was going back to Minneapolis. It was a very, very tough, emotional thing to do. It's kind of like a team, except in the service, you're even closer than a team, because you have to sleep in the same barracks with them. You eat with them. And when you do your Vietnam training and jungle training, it was scary. These guys were regular army. In those days, they kind of looked down on the National Guard and Reservists. They used to make you yell it out in the mess hall—'Regular Army, National Guard, Reservist ...' Now, it's different."

CRBO   CRBO   CRBO

Tim Sheehy was an All-America hockey player at Boston College in 1970. He also had a draft number of 49, which made him an All-America candidate for induction into the United States Army. Upon graduation, that's exactly what happened to the star college athlete, as he ended up in Fort Leonard Wood, located two hours west of St. Louis and an hour east of Springfield, Missouri, to begin a two-year hitch in the Army.

In the middle of Basic Training, Sheehy found himself excused to go try out for the 1971 U.S. National team, which would be playing in Switzerland.

"The captain of Alpha 3-2 couldn't believe I was getting out for a tryout," remembered Sheehy. "But it was just for the weekend. I went back to basic training after the tryout."

In July, Sheehy received orders to go to Fort Ord, California, which was the shipping area to go to Vietnam. But Sheehy was on Williamson's list of Olympic hopefuls, so after a call to the Pentagon, he was reassigned. Even though Sheehy was still at Fort Leonard Wood during the spring, summer, and part of the fall, he would get out in the winter to play hockey, assigned to special services and play for the U.S. National team and the U.S. Olympic team the following year.

Despite the fact that the number of elite U.S. hockey players was scarce, and Sheehy was certainly one of them, he never lost sight of where he could end up if he wasn't playing hockey.

"It always stood out in my mind that Murray knew there were about five of us in the Army, or had been in the Army, and he told us—either you make the team or you go to Saigon. There was plenty of incentive for us to do well, and there was no guarantee."

CRITICAL   CRITICAL   CRITICAL

Charlie Brown's draft number was 007. Due to a student deferment while he was attending Bemidji State in Minnesota, he was not called upon to serve. But upon graduation, he knew not even James Bond could keep him from having to report to the Army sooner than later. In the summer of 1971, Brown was at training camp for the California Golden Seals when his draft notice came. Like Boucha and McGlynn before him, he promptly put in a call to his U.S. Olympic team coach. Brown made his way from the Seals training camp to the Olympic training camp in Bemidji.

"I came back and called Murray at Bemidji," explained Brown. "I went up there and played with them until my induction at Fort Leonard Wood, Missouri."

Brown knew that despite his having to report to Fort Leonard Wood, the mechanism for him to be re-assigned was already in place by the time he made it to Bemidji.

"I went there for one week, got inducted, then returned to Minneapolis. I knew I was going to be at Fort Leonard Wood for a week because Hal Trumble called Washington to let them know I was playing with the Olympic team. It was funny because when I got there and they were giving haircuts, I told them I wasn't going to be there long, and they said, 'Sure, sure.' They had heard it all before. They wouldn't believe me, so I still had to get my hair cut. But after a week, I reported back to the Olympic team at Bemidji."

By the time Brown was set to return to the service, he had played for the 1971 U.S. National team, the 1972 Olympic team in February, and the 1972 U.S. National team a couple of months later. By April 1972, after exhausting his hockey-playing options, which put off reporting to service, Brown finally made it to Basic Training. However, by that time, a new draft bill had been passed stating that one couldn't be sent to Vietnam unless he volunteered. He also had time on his side since he had served on special assignment for six months already. By the time he would have completed basic and advanced training, there wouldn't have been any time to send him over to Vietnam, so he managed to fulfill his duty and miss going to Vietnam.

CR80   CR80   CR80

Though others did not actively serve, all were affected by the times in which they were living. As the 1970s dawned, college campuses became a focal point of dissent across the country in protest of the Vietnam War and the policies of President Richard Nixon. After Ohio National Guardsmen gunned down four unarmed students on the Kent State campus in May 1970, opposition to the war had crystallized.

For Larry Bader, who was his senior class vice president at the University of Pennsylvania in 1971, campus unrest and world politics threatened to hit home directly.

"There were sit-ins and other demonstrations," remembers Bader. "As vice president, I would meet with the administration, and they would ask, 'What should we do about these demonstrations?' They were blowing up our ROTC buildings. I had to move out of my apartment. I was housed in a room that was part of the athletic complex, and the third floor of that building was the ROTC building. They had just blown up one of the ROTC buildings at Temple, or somewhere like that. So I had to move out because they thought I would be in danger."

Others—like Sheehy's Boston College teammates Kevin Ahearn and Tom Mellor, Brown's Bemidji State teammate Jim McElmury, University of Minnesota teammates Wally Olds and Craig Sarner, Boston University's Tim Regan, and Robbie Ftorek, who was playing at St. Mary's in Halifax, Nova Scotia—either had high draft numbers or student deferments that kept them out of the Army. Despite several having student deferments, ultimately that was no guarantee.

"Even though you knew you had the student deferment thing going for you and wouldn't have to go, you just never really knew for sure," said McElmury. "That was probably the most pressure that any one of us had to go through."

University of Minnesota teammates Frank Sanders and Bruce McIntosh each had low draft numbers of 31 and 33, respectively, but each had student deferments while they were in school. Both surely would have had to report into the service upon graduating in 1971, but ironically, both world-class athletes failed their physicals. Sanders was out due to a bad skin condition that plagued him every hockey season; while McIntosh, after dealing with several layers of government red tape, was out because of a bum knee.

"I was always concerned about being drafted," said McIntosh. "My brother was in Vietnam. He came home my senior year in college. He told me it was the worst place in the world, which at the time was true. Not that I didn't want to serve my country, but I didn't want to go to Vietnam because I had all these opportunities in front of me."

One day in March, McIntosh's brother showed up on campus with a letter for him from the Selective Service telling him to report for his physical.

"I thought, 'This can't be.' I had a student deferment. I'm a full-time student carrying a full load. I'm getting decent grades and passing everything."

McIntosh called the draft board, and they went to get his file. After several minutes waiting, they couldn't find his file.

"It was nowhere—it was like I didn't exist."

After finding his file at the bottom of a file drawer, the draft board called him back. McIntosh learned that a clerical snafu on his birth date had given him a draft number of 33 instead of what it should have been—333. After reiterating that he still had a student deferment, he was told they couldn't help him, and he was going to have to come in for a physical.

"I told them, 'You have to be kidding me. ... You're telling me that you made the mistake, and now I have to ruin my life because you made a typing error and put down in the box that I don't have a student deferment? I can show it to you.' They said, 'You're going to have to come in.'"

McIntosh called the draft board again and asked what would happen if he didn't show up.

"They said, 'If you don't show up, we'll call you again.' I said, 'Fine. I'm not going.'"

Two months later, they sent him another letter. By that time, the hockey season had ended for McIntosh, and he had a knee that would slip in and out once in a while with particles and cartilage.

"I had some letter written by the doctors stating I was reporting for my physical," said the big defenseman. "It was the most humiliating experience of my life. I went in and my knee would not hold up to the physical, so they deferred me from military service."

The doctor explained that the reason McIntosh was deferred was because there was such a great potential that he would need surgery on his knee, and that they didn't want to have to pay him disability for the rest of his life.

The old timers, such as 27-year-old Ron "Daddy Nas" Naslund, 26-year-old Mike "Lefty" Curran, and 27-year-old Keith "Huffer" Christiansen were beyond the draft age limit by the time the team came together. Curran had a teacher's deferment upon graduating from University of North Dakota in 1968, then went on to play on the U.S. National teams, Christiansen was deferred, while Naslund served in the Air National Guard from 1965-71.

૮૩➹૦   ૮૩➹૦   ૮૩➹૦

Despite knowing that a decision to cut a player could have drastic consequences because of the Vietnam War, Williamson didn't feel any pressure to jeopardize his team for the sake of politics as he chose the Olympic teams in 1968 and 1972.

"There were people who came to try out from the Army who couldn't help or just didn't fit in," explained Williamson. "They were assigned to me and then released to go back to their other duty. We had Senator William Proxmire from Wisconsin in 1968 tell us he had a kid who was driving a vehicle for a general. The general said, 'Hey, this kid likes to play hockey. Let's get him assigned to the Olympic team.' The kid showed up, cocky as hell, and lasted one practice. We were doing conditioning drills where you start at the red line and push the guy while he's giving resistance. I told Doug Volmar, who was six foot two and strong as a bull, 'If this guy gets off the goal line, you're out of here.' I didn't want the kid to get hurt. We couldn't add somebody who hadn't paid the price. Playing on the Olympic team wasn't that easy. It was fun, but it was a helluva lot of hard work, travel, ups and downs, exhilaration of winning, then getting your butt whipped by the Rooskies in front of thousands of people."

Throughout the nearly seven months the members of the 1972 U.S. Olympic hockey team were together, the Vietnam War continued tearing the whole world and country apart. The country was in a state of change, and Vietnam was a looming presence every day in the collective minds of most Americans. The players were certainly aware of what was happening in the world, and nearly all of them were affected directly one way or another.

With protests and opposition to the war, daily body counts of soldiers who died—as well as news of the Nixon Administration's handling of the war garnering daily headlines and being broadcast each day on the nightly news—the times completely overshadowed anything that a bunch of no-name, hockey-playing kids were doing thousands of miles away in Sapporo, Japan.

"The overall world was not as concerned with athletics at that time as they are now," said Sanders. "There was such tension in the world at the time because of the nuclear possibilities. I'm sure we didn't get the type of press that we would've gotten today."

Ultimately, as most of the media were unaware of the 1972 U.S. Olympic hockey team, most of the young Americans trying out were merely concerned about making the team.

"I don't think we discussed Vietnam or world politics much like we would as adults now," said Bader. "It was almost like it was something different, because your intensity and mindset had to be so dedicated to making the team and playing well; you kind of put all other things aside. It was something that we were totally aware of, but not."

Others not only had to worry about making the team, but also played with the added pressure that if they didn't, they could be shipped to Southeast Asia.

"I look back, and I probably should have felt more compassion for what was going on," reflected Mellor. "When Stuey joined the team, and he was telling us the story about how four days before joining the team he was over there shooting pucks into the sand bags—reality really hit. Pete didn't talk much about Vietnam. But when he did I thought, 'Here's a guy who's my peer, and he just happened to walk in one door and I walked in another.' He was facing life and death every moment. It was then that I realized what was going on and said to myself, 'Wow, this was amazing and pretty unbelievable.' I was in my little world, and it was kind of a wake-up call when Pete and Stuey said, 'Hey, this is where we were.'"

3

COLD WAR MELTING

"We had a very special relationship with the Russians. It was a huge thing. If you asked any of our guys, it was like they were the varsity and we were the junior varsity. That's how it was. There was not even a question."

—TOM MELLOR

Though far from a consensus in the international hockey community and many were loathe to admit it, by the time the 1972 Olympic Winter Games rolled around, the Union of the Soviet Socialist Republic had become the dominant team in international hockey.

No matter the protests by other countries, it was difficult to argue against the fact that the Russians were an international hockey juggernaut. In 1956, at Cortina d'Ampezzo—the first time they had a team participating in the Olympic hockey tournament—the Soviet Union promptly gave the hockey world notice that they were going to be a force to be reckoned with by winning the gold medal over the

United States and Canada, which took silver and bronze, respectively. From '56 to the eve of the 1972 Olympics in Sapporo, the Soviets' Olympic record on the ice was 20-3-1, with three gold medals and a bronze—including their gold medal in '56, a bronze behind the United States and Canada in 1960 at Squaw Valley, California, and gold medals in 1964 at Innsbruck, Austria, and 1968 at Grenoble, France. In addition, the Russians hadn't lost a World Championship or an Olympic tournament since 1963, a string of nine consecutive years with an Olympic or World Championship title. There was no reason to think that they would not make it 10 in a row at Sapporo.

Despite the Soviet Union's record in international play, the arguments and protests against the Russians came from all corners of the hockey world. Because the Soviet Union was state-sponsored, the government took care of the best players by providing them with a more comfortable living—including better housing, more household amenities, cars, and more money than the average Russian citizen. As some countries reasoned, the Russians and players from other Eastern Bloc countries were being paid to compete for their country on those state-sponsored teams—including the Olympics—and thus they were professional players.

The Canadians felt particularly strong about this issue and withdrew from international play in 1969. By 1972, the Canadians' protest continued as a boycott of the Olympic games, reasoning that they were unable to use their country's best players because they weren't pretending to be amateurs. They were playing in the National Hockey League.

Czechoslovakia, which had its share of success against the mighty Russians in previous meetings in the Olympics and World Championships, was not ready or willing to give the Russians their due no matter how many gold medals they'd won since 1956. The Czechs could not forget the Prague Spring uprising and the sight of Russian tanks rolling into Wenceslas Square during the Soviet Union's invasion and occupation of Czechoslovakia in 1968. The bullet holes in the buildings were daily reminders to every Czech of those deadly and bloody days at the hands of the Russian army. Thus, the Czechs' issues with the Russians were both political and personal. And, as was often the case, it spilled onto the playing fields—a dangerous mix that literally bled onto the ice and always led to some of the fiercest hockey games ever played.

Other countries, such as Sweden and Finland, had some of the toughest and most skilled players in the world and were certainly capable of playing with—and threatening—the Russians. And as was the case in 1960, the United States also had it in them to be a threat, but hadn't been since that golden moment 12 years earlier.

❧ ❧ ❧

Because the Russians had become so successful and were transforming the game with its style of constant movement at high speed, tic-tac-toe passing, skill, and conditioning, U.S. head coach Murray Williamson started taking notice and notes in the late 1960s and early 1970s.

"The Soviets at that time were the team to beat," said team manager Hal Trumble. "So the question we asked ourselves was, 'How did they get there?' There were all kinds of reasons why. Some things they could accomplish we were not in a position to do. The Soviet Union was Communist, and playing athletics was one of the few areas in which a person could raise his standard of living and gain recognition. So many others had to work in the factories and had no other choice. Obviously, that wasn't a matter for us to have any concern, but the other things we saw through the Soviet Union was how they played the game. Everybody was sort of on the same page as far as style of hockey—pass a lot, don't shoot until you can score and hold onto the puck. The Russians didn't dump the puck in. They didn't do much 'dump it in and chase.'

"That was the ideal program and the ideal we tried to meet. The other thing I noticed with the Soviets was that they always had three or four coaches on the bench. I always felt that one coach was there to watch the players to see if they were giving a full effort. They did everything—physically and mentally—and we learned from it. The other countries were doing the same thing."

A friendly exchange of hockey ideas started one night during the 1971 World Championship in Geneva, Switzerland while Williamson was speaking with Russian coach Anatoly Tarasov, the "Father of Russian Hockey."

"We were exchanging vodka shots one night at the World Championship in Switzerland and Tarasov said to me, 'You have to come to Russia and see what we do,'" explained Williamson.

The conversation led Williamson to visit Tarasov in the Soviet Union prior to the Olympics during the summer of 1971.

In mid-July, after arranging all the travel logistics including securing a visa, flight reservations, and prepaying for all the food and lodging while he was to be in Moscow, Williamson received his plane ticket, visa, and receipt for all room charges. However, he had no confirmation from the other end that the Russian coach or officials knew he was coming or would accept him on the conditions that were laid out six months earlier in Switzerland over shots of Russian vodka.

Two weeks later, Williamson had USA Hockey officials send the Russians a final telegram advising them of his itinerary and arrival time and took off for a planned stopover in Boston to talk with Tommy Mellor. Mellor was an All-America defenseman about to enter his senior year at Boston College. His college coach, Snooks Kelley, had advised him to stay in school, while Williamson was there to assure him he was not going to be cut if he decided to join the team. After spending more time in Boston than he had securing a definite commitment from Mellor, Williamson missed his flight. He was stuck in Boston on his way to Russia with no confirmation, no Russian telephone numbers, and no way to communicate with Russian officials when he got there. With the help of Pan-Am airline officials, Williamson arranged a flight to Russia that flew to Shannon, Ireland, with the hopes of connecting with the Russian plane that he scheduled originally.

"How I ever got there, I have no idea," remembers Williamson. "I had people sending telegrams back and forth. I booked a flight but there was never a confirmation on the other end. My flight was late getting into Shannon, Ireland, and the connection to Moscow changed. I didn't arrive when I said I would."

After wandering aimlessly in the airport, Williamson was approached by two Soviet policemen who took him by the arms and escorted him to a room where he met with a Russian official for several hours. Williamson was informed that Tarasov had been at the airport to greet him but departed when he was not on the plane. The Russian official then took the U.S. coach to his hotel, where they had dinner and he was "interrogated." Williamson quickly realized that the Russian official was more of a political interpreter, as the questions ranged from President Nixon's forthcoming trip to China to aspects of international hockey. After two days of visiting with various Russian sports officials and touring Moscow, Williamson looked up from his breakfast and saw his Russian friend Tarasov walking towards him with a paper bag full of dandelions and a bottle of vodka. Tarasov informed Williamson that he would be joining him that day to observe and be involved in all of the day's sessions and drills. The American coach quickly finished his breakfast, grabbed his notebook, and was taken to the army sports complex, where he was introduced to all of the players.

Williamson spent just five days observing the Russian coach's training camp and watching the Russian athletes train in the most primitive and unorthodox ways. But for the U.S. coach, it seemed like it was a year with all that he was learning—training techniques and conditioning methods including the often-overlooked importance of stretching, developing "hockey muscles" by playing other sports like basketball and tennis, aerobic and anaerobic conditioning, as well as developing coordination with various skills and systems through dry-land training.

"The greatest comment I ever heard about coaching that resounded with me was when Tarasov said, 'A good coach has to be a good orchestra leader. Everything has to have a rhythm and speed.'

"We watched from the stands when they were out doing dry-land with these primitive weights and medicine balls. If the pace was slow, he'd jump up waving his hand like an orchestra leader and yell, 'Pick up the tempo.' The Czechs figured it out because, every time they played the Russians, they would freeze the puck and slow things down.

It would screw the Russians up big time, because the Russians were a highly trained machine, and that would get them out of sync."

What Williamson had learned while observing the Russians began the creation of a new system for United States Hockey and the genesis of Olympic success for the United States in 1972 and beyond.

It also was the beginning of an unlikely friendship.

"We were close," said Williamson of his respectful but competitive relationship with Tarasov. "We had a big sauna bath there and talked. And when he came here, we did the same thing in the North Stars locker room. We got some branches, poured some beer on the coals, talked hockey, and enjoyed each other's company, though we always had to have an interpreter with us most of the time."

The relationship between the coaches eventually extended somewhat to both the American and Russian players, in which social boundaries eventually were crossed despite their respective country's world and political views.

CREW   CRED · CRED

Upon returning from his visit, Williamson was ready to put his plan into action. He held final tryouts in Minneapolis in early September, paring down the squad to 22 guys. Williamson went with youth, picking a young team that included teenagers like 19-year-old Robbie Ftorek, 20-year-old Henry Boucha, and 16-year-old Mark Howe, who was picked up later. By the time the team was finally picked and they traveled to Sapporo, they were the youngest U.S. Olympic hockey team ever assembled with an average age of 22 and had three of the four youngest players of all the teams—the other was a 19-year-old rookie Russian goaltender, Vladislav Tretiak.

"We were building and decided that the only way we were going to win it all was to do it with youth," reasoned Williamson. "You can't lose with youth. You may not finish first, but you can't lose with youth."

Following the tryouts in Minneapolis, Williamson brought the team up to Bemidji State University, about 250 miles northwest of Minneapolis. Bemidji was all new territory for the players since none of them had ever played on an Olympic team, and most certainly never trained and conditioned in that manner. The training camp gave them an opportunity to bond as a unit, as well as offering Williamson a better look at those players and others he was bringing in on a near-daily basis. The team began to incorporate much of what their coach had learned earlier that summer while visiting Russia, including off-ice training with lots of stretching, aerobics, running, lifting weights, playing soccer, basketball and tennis, as well as a two-a-day on-ice program with practices in the morning, and "spirited" scrimmages at night. There was an emphasis on staying busy, getting up and getting your blood moving—all done in order to trim the team down even further and get them ready to embark on an intense 47-game pre-Olympic tour in the months leading up to Sapporo.

C3800   C3800   C3800

After training camp in Bemidji, Williamson shaved the team to 20 guys, who returned to their home base of Minneapolis to continue more training and practicing. A typical day for the players would be getting up in the morning to be at the Decathlon Club in downtown Bloomington at 6:30 or 7:00 to do aerobics with Ron Hall, who was nicknamed "The Hawaiian Eye" by the players. "The Hawaiian Eye" put the players through ballet-type stretching, aerobics, and strength conditioning. After aerobics, they would go for a half-hour swim—but instead of swimming laps of the pool length-wise, Williamson would have his team swim its width. And when they reached the other side, they wouldn't flip-turn and go the other way. They would pull themselves out of the pool, dive back in, and begin swimming the other way doing the same thing on the other side. The players would do that for 15-20 minutes, and by the end, their arms felt like hanging pieces of meat. Following aerobics and swimming, they would take a little break before returning to the rink for one hour of on-ice practice doing drills, with 20 minutes of wind sprints. By that time, they were ready for lunch. Following lunch, they would come back for an afternoon practice on the ice consisting of another hour of scrimmaging with wind sprints at the end. Then, they'd pack up their gear and play that night.

"Most people didn't ever realize that, on a game day, we would typically work out," said forward Larry Bader. "We worked out hard. I never knew about aerobics and stretching. One of the things Murray talked about was how they had shoulder injuries the year before. We had one exercise where we held our arms straight out and did little circles holding our gloves. We never had shoulder injuries. He would always say, 'If you have an injury you can't play.'

"We conditioned our whole body. That was important to me because I knew if someone got hurt, I would get into the lineup, but nobody ever got hurt. Thirty-some years later, I still ask, 'Why didn't anyone ever have any shoulder injuries? Why was that so important?' Hockey players never put their arms above their heads. Why don't basketball players ever get shoulder injuries? It's because their arms are always above their heads. Their shoulders have been built up strong. We were so well conditioned, not only aerobically. I remember doing end-board-to-end-board sprints stopping and starting at each line— the '80 team called them 'Herbies'—for 25-30 minutes straight on an average day. Murray kept us busy that way. We never had any idle time. And then there were guys like Ftorek who would find time to go out and run 100 miles."

The training and conditioning regimen was not only in preparation for Sapporo, but also for getting ready to embark upon their four-month pre-Olympic tour, in which they took on all comers much like Williamson's 1968 Olympic and 1971 U.S. National teams did. Their schedule was peppered with games against college teams, semi-pro teams, and touring national teams from other countries— including the mighty Russian team.

CﬔED   CﬔED   CﬔED

Playing against the Russians was another major part of Williamson's overall plan.

"That was an eye-opening experience to see what a real world-class team could do," said defenseman Bruce McIntosh. "I know we all learned from it. Did we get better or not because of it? Sometimes, when you get your butt danced around the ice a little bit and realize how good the other teams are that you're going to be playing, you raise your game up another level, concentrate a little bit more, and work a little harder in practice. We worked on some things in practice that we hadn't worked on before. That made practice a little bit more fun, interesting, and easier to tolerate."

The U.S. team first met up with the Russians on December 27, 1971, in Colorado Springs, where their on-ice learning at the hands of the Russian team began and continued throughout a two-week period of their tour. For the young Americans—who were admittedly awed by the magically skilled, more mature, and physically stronger Russians—the results were unimpressive.

In the five games the U.S. team played against the Soviet Union, they were outscored 51-14 (13-3, 7-3, 11-1, 9-3, 11-4). As was Williamson's plan all along, his team was playing with an eye toward the day in February when it really counted. And because his team was so young, they never really felt as if any team was unbeatable. They also never backed down, even if they were playing against some of the world's greatest players like Valery Kharlamov, Boris Mikhailov, Alexander Maltsev, Yevgeny Mishakov, Anatoly Firsov, and the goaltender, Tretiak.

"I remember Mikhailov the first game we played in Colorado Springs against the Russians," said McIntosh. "It was the third period, and we were down 8-1 or something like that. We were shoulder to shoulder waiting for the puck to be dropped at a face-off. I was dog-tired, with sweat pouring off my nose. I looked at him just before the puck was dropped, and he was barely sweating. He looked as if he'd barely broken a sweat. I said, 'Don't you guys sweat?' He just looked and winked at me. That set something off, and I guess I took it wrong. He was probably just being nice. But as soon as the puck was dropped I tried to cross-check him across the back of the neck. He went down and was complaining to the referee. But it was 8-1, and they weren't going to call anything. After the game, we were going through the line shaking hands and I remember skating off the ice next to him. When I looked at him, he flinched in mock fear of me. I looked at him and kind of shrugged. He took his stick and made a cross-checking motion and shook his head no. I just kind of waved at him. He didn't like the fact that I had taken a shot at him, especially in an 8-1 game. He was a great player, and we were all a bit frustrated. It was a learning experience for us. At that point we all knew we had a long way to go."

C3EO   C3EO   C3EO

That learning experience ultimately would serve them well in Sapporo. Following their first game in Colorado Springs, where the Russians beat the U.S. squad, 13-3, the two teams met four more times within an eight-day span in late December 1971 and early January 1972. The U.S. team and the Russians crisscrossed the United States, playing each other in St. Louis, Minneapolis, Philadelphia, and New York City. Despite being beaten badly at each stop, with each game the U.S. team gained valuable experience and increased respect from the Russians both on the ice and off.

Like the teams' two coaches, a cordial, if not friendly, relationship started to develop with the players as they competed fiercely on the ice but found themselves being drawn to each other off the ice as well.

"We really developed this relationship where you knew everybody," said defenseman Tom Mellor. "You knew who they were, and you knew their names—they knew you. We had a very special relationship with the Russians. It was a huge thing. If you asked any of our guys, it was like they were the varsity and we were the junior varsity. That's how it was. There was not even a question. These guys were so much more refined, polished, and skilled. It was unbelievable. Every time we played them, we just tried to earn a little more of their respect and get a little bit closer."

The Russian players always considered the U.S. players below them, but suddenly a friendship developed, and the players were talking and getting together.

"We dang near knew the guys on a first-name basis," said team captain Huffer Christiansen. "It wasn't like playing against them once in your lifetime. We played against them quite a bit. I think they kind of liked us. There was a kind of bond there."

With each game, the bond between the two teams grew tighter—as did the respect, even if it did seem like a big brother-little brother relationship. When the two teams met in Minneapolis for their third meeting, the "little brothers" had had enough of "big brothers," and decided to show them they weren't going to be pushed around anymore. A bench-clearing brawl ensued after Henry Boucha was sucker punched coming out of the penalty box, and Christiansen was jumped by two of the Russian players.

"I was one of the bigger guys on the team, so when I saw Huffer get jumped by the two players, I was over the boards," remembered Bader. "I think that's what started it. I went flying down the ice, and I don't know who it was, but I clothes-lined a guy from center ice and slammed him to the ice. I just kept sliding towards their net. I remember getting up and having the point of a goalie stick right in my throat. It was Tretiak. He was a big guy, and as I stood up, I was almost going to get in a stick-swinging brawl with him. I was a big guy, and no one tangled with me at that point. Tretiak and I just glared at each other. But we stood up to them."

During their final meeting before the Olympics, the Russians were once again beating the U.S. team in front of 15,000 fans in Madison Square Garden in New York City. But this time instead of "big brother" beating up the "little brother," the Russians protected the U.S. team.

"We were getting bombed in New York, and Tarasov came to me and said, 'Williamson, come.' He was going to let up, huge crowd, sold out Madison Square Garden, I think they were leading 6-1 or 6-2," said Williamson. "I said, 'Don't give me that, Anatoly.' But he took me into his dressing room, and Kharlamov, Mikhailov, Maltsev, and Firsov all had their equipment off and were headed towards the showers. He shut down his top guys. They were finished after the second period. He didn't want to embarrass us in front of 15,000 people in New York City. It was very nice of him to keep it close.

"He admired the Canadians. He loved us. But he hated the Czechs because they hated him. They used to fire the puck at the bench over the boards at him during the game."

᎒᠍Ꭷ᠍Ꮻ   ᎒᠍Ꭷ᠍Ꮻ   ᎒᠍Ꭷ᠍Ꮻ

In Sapporo a month later, the United States and Russian teams were forced to put their mutually acquired respect aside as the stakes of each game escalated and each team further understood their jobs and knew they would do whatever it took to achieve success.

Despite that, both the U.S. and Russian players continued looking out for each other on and off the ice.

"One day our coach came over and said, 'I'm going over to see Tarasov. Anybody want to go over with me?'" remembered goalie Pete Sears. "A bunch of us went over, and we got together and talked with a bunch of the Soviet players like Tretiak, Kharlamov, and Mikhailov. They brought us to their rooms. They had their vodka off to the side and shared it with us. They could understand a little bit of English, but we couldn't understand much of anything that they were saying."

Several days later, the U.S. players understood all they needed as they watched the Russians win the gold medal by beating Czechoslovakia. When the game was over, the joyful American players stormed the ice to congratulate themselves and the Russian players, as well as prepare to receive their medals. Amidst all the hugging and tears amongst the U.S. contingent, the Russians had plenty of back slaps and handshakes for the Americans as well. They seemed just as happy that the Americans had won the silver medal and finished ahead of Czechoslovakia.

After the medal ceremony, with their silver medals hanging around their necks, some of the U.S. players once again found themselves celebrating with their Russian friends off the ice as well.

"There was this unbelievable moment that, when I think about it now, it still has an impact," reflects Mellor. "Stu Irving and I were lingering around after the medal ceremony, and we somehow dispersed. It was a long walk back, and guys were getting rides. There were courtesy buses running, but somehow Stuey and I ended up together, and we rode back to the Olympic Village on the Russian bus. We sat up front with our medals, and they were in the back still in their uniforms because they dressed back in their rooms.

"The Russian players really smelled because they would eat garlic, and they had this certain smell. I haven't smelled it in over 20 years—but I would recognize that odor. We were on the bus, and the whole team was sitting around singing Russian songs. Stu and I were just sitting there drinking it all in. It was an amazing moment. We felt like we were really a part of something. They had just won the gold medal, and they were all on the bus. The Russians are different. They kiss and hug each other. The U.S. guys were like, 'Uggh.' But they really embraced us. I don't think anybody would look you in the eye and say we were disappointed in winning the silver medal, because the Russians were so good."

Once the U.S. players got back to the village, the celebrating with each other and the Russians continued, and some of the guys found themselves eating caviar and trading vodka shots until the wee hours of the next day.

"It was late at night, and they were drinking vodka straight out of a glass with no ice and eating caviar and raw fish," remembers Bader. "I was the only American with them at the time. Kharlamov was there. I knew that because he was the guy that I had to play against and had to back-check a lot because he was a left wing and I was a right wing. Mikhailov was there. Tretiak was in and out. I just remember drinking vodka with them. They would pour a glass, then pour a double glass for me, and say, 'Here, drink this.' I would give it a try, but that was the best I could do. They were trying to get me drunk. We exchanged photographs and stuff like that."

And though the players' countries each represented opposite opinions in their political and world views, politics was far from the minds of the U.S. and Russian players as they celebrated their Olympic victories together.

Sears seemed to sum it up best in the end.

"Everybody knew about the Cold War, but they were just basically good guys."

4

LET THE GAMES BEGIN

The XIth Olympic Winter Games began on February 3, 1972, in Sapporo, Japan—the largest city in Northern Japan that is known as the home of Sapporo beer—located on the island of Hokkaido Prefecture. Sapporo, an Ainu aboriginal word, means "large dry land" or "important river flowing through a marsh." Originally scheduled to host the 1940 Winter Games, Sapporo had to resign the honor after its 1937 invasion of China. Thus, the 1972 Sapporo Games became the first Winter Olympics to be held in the East—outside of Europe or the United States.

As in most Olympics, controversy swirled around the XIth Olympic Winter Games. Although the Vietnam War garnered its share of attention, another issue threatened the core of Olympic-competition ideals—amateurism versus professionalism.

In the Winter Games' 48-year history, no topic had sparked more debate. Three days before the Opening Ceremony, retiring International Olympic Committee (IOC) President Avery Brundage threatened to disqualify 40 alpine skiers for professionalism. The controversy had taken root during the '68 Winter Games in Grenoble when Brundage demanded that all trademarks and logos be removed from competitors' skis—so neither the companies involved nor the athletes could benefit commercially or economically from the exposure. Although Brundage couldn't get the trademarks removed, he did succeed in having the skis taken away from the medal winners before they could be photographed with their equipment.

Four years later, in Sapporo, the IOC executive committee reached a compromise by voting 28-14 to make an example of skiing's most commercialized star, Austrian Karl Shranz, by banishing him from Olympic competition. Shranz, who some in the international skiing community considered a "professional," reportedly had earned over $50,000 a year "testing" ski equipment.

The issue spilled into the Olympic ice hockey world when Canada refused to send a team to Sapporo, protesting the Eastern Bloc's use of what they deemed "professional amateurs." Canada had already withdrawn from international play in 1969, and Sweden joined their boycott in 1976—both countries returned to competition in 1980. In 1972, the Americans were aware of the Canadian controversy but weren't concerned. Many understood Canada's position since most of its stars were playing in the NHL. Had the Canadians been allowed to send their best, they would've fielded an NHL All-Star team.

The Canadians' argument against Russian policies stemmed from the Kremlin's ability to place its athletes in undemanding positions within its army where they were paid to play hockey year-round. Only a handful of American players were in the NHL, so the U.S. didn't care if Canada came or not since America's best were amateurs anyway. Plus, they were too busy preparing for the teams that *were* going to be there.

"The way we looked at it, if the Canadians didn't want to play, it just gave us a better chance at a medal," concluded goalie Pete Sears.

ભ્ટ્ર૦   ભ્ટ્ર૦   ભ્ટ્ર૦

Despite the controversy, the XIth Olympic Winter Games began in front of a crowd of 54,000 on a clear, cold day as 1,006 athletes, 801 males, and 205 females from 35 participating countries filed their way into the speed-skating venue, Makomanai Stadium, for the Opening Ceremony.

The ceremonies included the entrance march of the athletes and the presentation of the Olympic flag to officials of the city of Sapporo from officials of Grenoble, France—host city of the 1968 Winter Games. Speeches by dignitaries, including IOC President Brundage and Japanese Emperor Hirohito, officially welcomed the world to Sapporo. As horns and trumpets blared, the Games of the XIth Winter Olympiad opened.

The pledge of the Olympic oath was led by Japanese speed skater Keiichi Suzuki, and cannons introduced a lone dream-like skater dressed in a flowing white dress gliding slowly around the oval rink, holding the Olympic torch high above her head. The torch was then passed to Japanese schoolboy Hideki Takada, who then ascended along a white line leading up nearly 100 red stairs before pausing to climb onto a podium and lighting the Olympic flame.

The U.S. Olympic team, dressed in what some team members described as "pilgrim outfits" and others as just "plain ridiculous," marched in the Opening Ceremony wearing a three-quarter-length navy blue leather coat, blue pants, a sweater, a six-foot, red-and-white-striped scarf, and leather "Santa Claus"-type boots rimmed with fur and topped off with a small blue leather hat. When the team went to pick up the gear a couple days earlier, they actually avoided potential embarrassment during the Ceremony. After acquiring the outfits and holding a pre-Opening Ceremony semi-dress rehearsal, members of the U.S. team immediately began falling down as they encountered the slick, ice-packed snow outside. Their brand new boots had soles made of a hard material that didn't gain any traction as they walked on the frozen ground. So U.S. officials had sandpaper spikes placed on the bottom of each boot so they wouldn't embarrass themselves by falling down in front of over 50,000 spectators as they marched into the stadium.

Two days later as they entered Makomanai Stadium amongst Olympic athletes from all participating nations, amidst the giant ice sculptures and snow-capped mountains of Hokkaido serving as a backdrop to all the pageantry, they felt anxious—not only because of the experience of the Opening Ceremony, but because of the next day's game as well.

"We walked in there, and we saw all the other athletes marching in, and it gave you goose bumps," remembered Sears. "We were not only marching in with other hockey players but all the rest of the winter athletes as well. But basically, your mind was getting set for the games. You were there but you weren't there, because in your head you were thinking, 'Geez, we have a game tomorrow.' We were trying to get ourselves mentally prepared to play. I knew I wasn't the starting goalie, but I knew if Mike got hurt, I'm in the game. I had to prepare myself as if I were going to play even though I knew I probably wasn't. It was tough because you had to have yourself totally ready to go mentally. A lot of my thoughts were more on the game the next day than on the ceremony."

Let the games begin.

CBEO   CBEO   CBEO

Despite Olympic successes during the formative years of the first Winter Olympics in 1924 and 1932—when the U.S. team captured a silver medal, and then struck silver again in 1952 and 1956—expectations for the 1972 U.S. team among the media and international hockey community were low. Privately, the team had set a goal from Day One in Bemidji to win a medal—it didn't matter what color. A dozen years had passed since the U.S. had struck gold in Squaw Valley, and their records from 1964 and 1968 incited little concern from competing countries.

However, this American team was too young and too naïve to know what they didn't know. It was all part of Murray Williamson's master plan of keeping a low profile and deflecting pressure from the players. "Win that first game in Sapporo, then see what happens," were his thoughts. Their primary focus was defeating Switzerland— win and they would advance to the medal round; lose and they would play for pride in the "B" Pool. Their final two exhibition games versus Czechoslovakia and Poland, played in Tokyo just days before the

Opening Ceremony, brought a stark realization to the American players.

"They weren't any better than we were," recalled defenseman Frank Sanders.

According to tradition and prerogative, the host country had the option of setting up the hockey tournament. The '72 tournament was set up as follows:

Excluding the Soviet Union, which won the 1971 World Championship "A" Pool, 10 of the 11 teams had to win a qualifying game in order to advance to the round-robin medal round.

Each team would face the team opposite them in the standings, as based upon its finish in either the "A" Pool or the "B" Pool of the 1971 World Championship.

Since the United States had finished last in the "A" Pool of the previous year's World Championship, they played the winner of the "B" Pool, Switzerland. Czechoslovakia played Japan; Sweden played Yugoslavia; West Germany played Poland; and Finland played Norway.

Assuming the U.S. and all of the favorites—Czechoslovakia, Sweden, Finland and West Germany—advanced past the qualifying game, Williamson and some of the veterans knew exactly where they stood in the pecking order of the top six teams: Soviet Union, Czechoslovakia, Sweden, Finland, United States, and West Germany or Poland. The U.S. team hoped that they'd be able to win a medal, but had no preconceived notions about their chances or how they were going to be able to pull it off.

They were heavy underdogs, and they knew it.

"I knew coming in, talent-wise at best we were fifth out of six," said goalie Mike Curran. "There were four teams that were better than we were, that had more talent than us."

QUALIFYING GAME
February 4, 1972—12:04 a.m. EST
USA 5 - SWITZERLAND 3

"There was no greater pressure. Fortunately, there was not any pre-Olympic publicity to build that up. It was an unbelievable game. It was close. Their goaltender was making saves that literally bounced off the knob of his stick. We were on the brink of a disaster."

—U.S. HEAD COACH MURRAY WILLIAMSON

Playing before a capacity crowd that included Japanese Emperor Hirohito and with all the pressure of needing to win, the U.S. team jumped out to a quick lead with a goal from Kevin Ahearn at 2:48 of the first period to make it 1-0.

Tim Sheehy, who was playing in his first game since severely spraining his ankle and knee in a freak accident where he hooked skates with Mark Howe and spent a week in the hospital, made it 2-0 for the U.S. just 1:46 later. The first period ended with the U.S. up 2-1 after giving up a power-play goal at 13:45 of the period and firing 32 shots at Switzerland's goal.

The Americans upped their lead to 3-1 at 1:59 of the second period as Ahearn scored his second goal of the game. The U.S. was seemingly in control but couldn't shake the Swiss despite peppering 45 more shots toward the Swiss goal. After a Swiss goal at 19:22 of the second period cut the lead to 3-2, frustration and panic started to seep in as Switzerland's goaltender, Gerard Rigolet, with 40 saves after two periods, was standing on his head to keep his team in the game. If the frustration level of the U.S. team was building after the second period, the third period would show them new heights.

With just 1:03 gone in the final period, the Swiss tied the game 3-3 with a goal by Francis Reinhard. Playing with the pressure and urgency of a must-win situation—and knowing that they were the better team—the Americans responded quickly as Sheehy notched his second goal of the game just 1:09 later, giving the U.S. a lead they would not relinquish, 4-3.

Although Rigolet continued to dazzle, with less than three minutes left, Stuart Irving, who just nine months prior was firing pucks off a wooden crate in a fox hole in Vietnam, iced the game for the U.S. by scoring the biggest goal of his life and giving his team an insurance goal and an insurmountable 5-3 lead.

When the final buzzer sounded, the U.S. had beaten Switzerland 5-3, but due to a hot goaltender who saved 54 shots on goal of the overall 99 shots that the U.S. team fired toward his net, it was a much closer game than U.S. coach Murray Williamson had wanted for his young squad.

"There was no greater pressure," said the U.S. coach. "Fortunately, there was not any pre-Olympic publicity to build that up. It was an unbelievable game. It was close. Their goaltender was making saves that literally bounced off the knob of his stick. We were on the brink of a disaster. The guys came through, but it was touch and go. We ran into a hot goaltender at the other end, so we really had to persevere."

———

As the pressure of the first game evaporated, and although they were focused on their task, the experience of being in the Olympics—living in the Olympic Village amongst all the foreign athletes and experiencing their different traditions and cultures, as well as the Japanese culture—was eye-opening.

The mingling and interaction with the other athletes was part of what they remembered most about the Olympic experience.

"You mingled with other athletes," said forward Ahearn. "There were stories that floated around about some of the European athletes like one of the Swedish players was involved in ownership of a radio station. And so, you heard all these colorful stories that related to other people from other parts of the world and it was very, very interesting. It was a story within the story inside the Village. We had a hell of a lot of fun with the Russians. There was a guy we played against and he kept popping over into our community room a lot and we exchanged gifts. They had mink coats and we had leather coats and I was trying to do an Olympic barter with him but he didn't want anything to do with it. It was an interesting thing because he came over, and he spoke pretty good broken English, and wanted to know how much we were paid. I remember after we were done he came over, knocked on the door, opened a bottle of vodka and threw back a few cocktails. I told him we didn't get anything. He laughed and pulled out a big wad of money, and clearly the Russians understood the difference between amateurs and professionals. There were stories about them having apartments and cars and their standard of living in Russia being far better than other people in Russia."

Whether it was interacting with other athletes, trying different foods, watching American television programs like *Bonanza* and hearing Hoss Cartwright speak in Japanese, or cartoons and hearing Donald Duck quack in Japanese, or just experiencing the little differences in culture like noticing on commercials for cereal instead of putting bananas or strawberries on top of their cereal like they did in the United States, they would put kiwis or some other fruit on top, it was all part of the Olympic experience.

MURRAY WILLIAMSON

HEAD COACH

1967 U.S. National Team (Vienna, Austria)
1968 U.S. Olympic Team (Grenoble, France)
1970 U.S. National Team (Bucharest, Romania)
1971 U.S. National Team (Bern/Geneva, Switzerland)
1972 U.S. Olympic Team (Sapporo, Japan)

"The satisfaction of having these guys still communicating and keeping in touch after 30-plus years is far greater satisfaction than being touted."

Some coaches, if they're any good at what they do, almost become second fathers in the lives of their players. Whether that father conjures love or animosity in the lives of his players-sons, without a doubt, strong emotion is elicited throughout the relationship. Such can be said about 1972 U.S. Olympic hockey coach Murray Williamson.

These days, it's hard to find one player among the 20 who comprised the silver medal-winning team who doesn't have deep emotional ties to his Olympic coach. While it's true some had their differences, mainly goaltender Mike "Lefty" Curran, they all realize that Williamson possessed a revolutionary hockey mind. As in any sour relationship, even Curran came to realize over time that, without Williamson, he and his Olympic teammates probably wouldn't have returned from Japan with the silver medal.

Williamson, like any good father, stands up for his boys more than 30 years later when he considers their forgotten accomplishments.

"In the public, I'm not a guy that likes the spotlight," says Williamson. "So, it really doesn't bother me. It did bother me when I saw that our team's picture was not hanging up amongst all these gloried teams at the USA Hockey building."

For Williamson, satisfaction comes in the form of knowing his 1972 U.S. Olympic team continues to share a bond that is as strong now as it was when they were grinding, training, and dreaming their way through Williamson's grueling dry-land training sessions or his three-a-day practices on the ice following a morning of training.

"The satisfaction of having these guys still communicating and keeping in touch after 30-plus years is far greater satisfaction than being touted."

Williamson got involved in international hockey almost by default. After coming out of college, where he was All-America for the University of Minnesota in 1959, Williamson played and coached in what was then the United States Hockey League (USHL). He recruited guys to form a team, and they would barnstorm on the road because of guaranteed money at the gate. Teams would pay other teams to travel and absorb that expense. Williamson didn't mind taking his teams on the road because they had success.

"We kept knocking off all the teams, and the U.S. National Team said, 'Hey, we need all your players for our national team,'" remembered Williamson. He told them no. Thus, the national team organizers, not knowing what else to do, told Williamson his team would become the national team.

"In those days, the national team was a shambles," explained Williamson. "They said, 'We'll fund you—barely—and go to the World Championships in 1967 and see what happens.' So we went and had a great group of guys. The characters and personality of that team were spectacular. We knocked off the Swedes, who were highly favored. We did it on guts and determination. Their skill players were Borje Salming and a few others who went to play in the NHL. That big victory made us look at things, and say, 'Wow, what's happening here?'"

What was happening was Williamson was becoming the prime candidate to become head coach of the 1968 U.S. Olympic team. His rough edges needed softening, and the U.S. Olympic hockey delegation told him in so many words that he needed to be a bit of a politician if he wanted the job as Olympic coach. True to himself, Williamson told them, "Well, you better find somebody else because you have the wrong guy—I'm no politician."

Williamson continued to hone his coaching craft as head coach of the 1970 and 1971 U.S. National teams that competed in Bucharest, Romania, and Bern/Geneva, Switzerland, respectively. He also formed a close relationship with the man who was turning the international hockey world on its head with a dominating style of skating and puck control—Anatoly Tarasov.

"I incorporated a lot of what I learned into our training," remembers Williamson. "Tarasov followed the principles of Ace Percival. He was the father of hockey conditioning, and that's where Tarasov based the Russian philosophy for off-ice training."

Conditioning was the key factor in how Williamson turned USA Hockey upside down and revolutionized how Americans would approach international hockey. If conditioning was to be one of the key factors in creating change, Williamson also knew the character of his players had to fit the objective. It always came back to his players. If their character didn't fit, they didn't have a chance.

"We wanted to test the guys with the most grueling schedule we could encounter," explained the U.S. hockey revolutionary. "We'd play in hostile rinks even though we were representing our country. We would go somewhere such as Long Island, play the All-Stars, and they were hacking us up. We'd beat them 10-1, take a beating but you had to hang tough. Your position on the team was at stake. Then we'd go play these universities like Brown and Princeton. Very seldom did we ever play in front of a crowd that was all for us except when we played the Russians."

The residue of Williamson's work is present throughout the history of USA Hockey since the late 1960s. He had his way of doing things, and he stood by it. Eventually, his way led to silver in Sapporo and later helped draft the map to discovering gold in Lake Placid.

Where is he now? Murray Williamson is now a retired businessman in Eden Prairie, Minnesota.

KEVIN AHEARN

Born: June 20, 1948 • Jersey No. 16 • Draft No. 360

"It was just a great, great experience in total. There isn't one part of it that didn't feel like a connected piece."

If the Russian hockey team shared a fraternal relationship with the U.S. team in 1972, the lessons taught by the Soviets to the young Americans were well-learned and well-served within the United States Olympic hockey family in the years that followed. Kevin Ahearn is unflinching in his belief that the 1972 U.S. Olympic hockey team served as an indication that the 1980 Miracle Team could dethrone the mighty Russian Bear of professional amateurs eight years later.

"I don't think there's any question—if the program had languished, after getting pretty well shellacked in 1968, and Williamson hadn't studied the international style, specifically the Russian style, the 1980 team wouldn't have had the success they had."

Though, don't think for one minute Ahearn or any of his other '72 teammates hold any resentment or harbor any jealousy toward their 1980 brethren. On the contrary, those who have played on an Olympic team or participated as an Olympian understand that only a small fraternity or sorority of people can consider themselves part of an Olympic family. And family is what drove Kevin Ahearn to realize his Olympic dream in 1972.

"My parents were very involved growing up," remembered Ahearn. "My father would pick me up and drive me to practice at five o'clock in the morning. My mom and dad both followed it, and the family was very much involved in the whole experience. They're both deceased now, but it was a big family thing for sure."

To Ahearn, family didn't only mean his five brothers and sisters. Like most members of big families, having more kids around the house, at the supper table, playing in the yard, or skating on the ponds, seemed like a natural occurrence when friends or teammates would often visit the Ahearn residence in Milton, Massachusetts. That was the case with fellow New Englander, high school teammate, and fellow Olympic teammate Dick McGlynn.

"Dickie and I went to Catholic Memorial together, and he played defense," recalled Ahearn. "We were very close, and he spent a lot of time at our home in Milton throughout high school."

In tight-knit, provincial Boston, the word "close" could almost be a substitute for family. Born and bred New Englanders stick close to their roots firmly entrenched in a familial upbringing that includes your own brothers and sisters, school pals, and teammates. Staying close to home is a life choice, and whom one lets into his family is tantamount in understanding what makes that person tick. Kevin Ahearn is no exception to that rule.

"I played hockey through all the pee wee programs and ended up going to Catholic Memorial High School, which is a private boys school that has a history and long legacy of very successful hockey," said Ahearn, whose schoolboy career at Catholic Memorial—a perennial state contender in the Boston Catholic League—was very instrumental in preparing him for a Division-I scholarship to Boston College.

In the late 1960s and early 1970s, Boston College was one of the most noted and respected college programs in the country. Known for always being competitive, when it came time to compete for national laurels, Snooks Kelley's teams didn't have quite enough firepower, talent, chemistry, or whatever that elusive element is that teams need to reach their ultimate goal. That's not to say they didn't have good teams.

"Timing-wise, it was pretty impeccable to be going from CM, to Boston College where we went to the Nationals and lost to Denver," remembers Ahearn. "On paper, we were far better than what we actually achieved at BC, for whatever reason. BU really had their way with us for the majority of time. We didn't win a national title. We really didn't get to the point where we should have with the talent we had. There was a lot of talent there."

What Ahearn did have at BC, which he also had at CM, and through his days of pee wee hockey, were familiar faces around him every step of the way. A spirit and history pervades through New England hockey programs. And when one favorite son shines, the entire community embraces him and lays claim to his roots.

"I started out very early in the hotbed of Boston hockey," said Ahearn. "I had a good career in high school and then had a good, but not a great college career. I had a decent career but wasn't All-America or that type. But for whatever reason, I kept improving."

That improvement is what caught the eye of 1971 U.S. National team head coach Murray Williamson—and the eyes of scouts from the storied NHL franchise Montreal Canadiens. The Canadiens were another family of sorts, who always seemed just a bit taller, stronger, faster, and slicker than any of their NHL competitors. And they had their sights set on the youngster from Milton, Massachusetts, by way of Boston College.

While in college, Ahearn was drafted by the Canadiens, and the perennial Stanley Cup champions invited the young left winger to training camp in 1971.

"They drafted me as an overaged junior and that allowed me to go to Montreal's training camp in August without losing my amateur status," remembered Ahearn. "You could play two weeks—14 games—and that was quite an experience. I got the chance to play with Henri Richard, 'The Pocket Rocket,' Yvan Cournoyer, Jacques Lemaire, Larry Robinson was a rookie, Serge Savard, Guy LaPointe, all of them.

"They offered me a two-way contract to go to the Voyageurs, or if I made it up to the big club I'd get x-amount of bucks. I remember it wasn't a lot of money. When they called me and said that I had been drafted, Sam Pollock, who was a legend, said he wanted me to go to training camp, and that I'd probably end up with the Voyageurs. I told them I would come to training camp, but I really wanted to play on an Olympic team. They were astounded, and told me it would be the wrong thing to do. It would retard my career. They thought I could play in the NHL and the level of competition in international play, in their opinion, was not going to be in the caliber of what I could play with the Voyageurs. Nonetheless, I told them that was my game plan, and they invited me up to training camp anyway."

Knowing all along he would not make the NHL club in 1971 after 117 players showed up in camp—15 left wingers and 25 roster spots available for a team that would go on to win the Stanley Cup—Ahearn set his sights on joining a waiting band of brothers in Minneapolis for the Olympic tryouts.

"Williamson and the others took a very professional approach to the environment of the program to try and excel at it after not doing so well in prior years," said Ahearn. "It was a close-knit group of guys. It was a balance in the ranks between East and West. I forget what the breakdown was, but I think it was pretty close to 50-50. That was very exciting."

Ahearn followed in the footsteps of fellow Boston Olympians John Cuniff, and Bill and Bob Cleary. Cuniff was a South Boston guy who was All-America at BC and played for Williamson in 1968, while the Cleary brothers led the U.S. to gold at the 1960 Squaw Valley Winter Games. Having nearly attended Harvard, Ahearn also was very familiar with the legend of the Cleary brothers.

"I knew a little bit about the Olympic program by watching and knowing guys like that."

When it came time to pull on the sweater with "USA" stitched across its chest, it was no less a thrill than when he wore the fabled Montreal Canadiens jersey of his boyhood dreams during the summer of 1971.

"All along, I felt that I would make the Olympic team," said Ahearn. "I was playing pretty regularly and bouncing between the second and third line, and sometimes they would pop me up on the power play. So I had the sense I was in their plans. But, it was big stuff, big stuff. It was a great feeling of accomplishment, and it really hit me."

And making that team, becoming a member of a brotherhood that would spend more than six months together eating, drinking, training, and striving toward a common goal was something upon which Ahearn thrived. He thrived to the tune of a team-high six goals during the Olympic Games, tallying nine overall points during his stay in Sapporo. But some of his most lasting memories came from the relationships he established in the Olympic Village.

"The Olympic Village was one of the things that I do remember vividly," recalled Ahearn. "For a purist, it didn't get any better. You checked into the Olympic Village, and the cafeteria dining rooms were populated by athletes from all over the world in different-colored national gym suits, and it was just mind-boggling."

When the Games were over, the lack of respect from the public for a job well done boggled him and his teammates—that complete and utter lack of recognition for accomplishing anything extraordinary.

"I can't pinpoint the reason why we were flying so low below the radar screen, but being across the world in Japan, with the different time zones for viewing purposes didn't help. You really had to want to follow it. It wasn't right up in front of you."

And if it seemed the only ones watching back home in the States were family members, it was probably true.

To this day, only a small fraternity of people really know what happened—how it happened, and what a Herculean effort it was to come home with silver. That is the bond that connects these players, coaches, family members, and friends of the 1972 team.

"I think being sandwiched between two golds—'60 and '80, with the '80 team captivating the world—it's no surprise to me why our team fell through the cracks even though we won the silver," admitted Ahearn. "It was just a great, great experience in total. There isn't one part of it that didn't feel like a connected piece."

And yet, this is not the classic case of the "middle child" looking for acceptance and more love. Ahearn and his teammates are far beyond a desire for recognition. In this hockey family, as in any family, public recognition would've been appreciated, but the stories of the journeys far exceed the accolades of the accomplishment.

Where is he now? Kevin Ahearn now works in real estate in Boston.

Born: September 3, 1948 • Jersey No. 15 • Draft No. 49

"Growing up, every kid wanted to play on the national team and then the Olympic team."

If San Pedro de Macoris, Dominican Republic, is considered the "land of shortstops" because of its reputation as a development ground for growing Major League Baseball shortstops, the same argument can be made that the little Canadian border town known as International Falls, Minnesota, could be known as the "land of Olympians" due to its fertile ground for the production of Olympic hockey players.

Before 1972, four former Olympic hockey players called International Falls, Minnesota, their home when declaring their hometown on rosters and personnel questionnaires: Robert Rompre '52, Dick Dougherty '56, Ed Sampson '56, and Dan Dilworth '64.

Growing up in the late 1950s and '60s, if you played hockey in the Falls, you undoubtedly knew those four names. The years next to their names shouldn't be confused with the year they graduated from college, but it does denote a special admission to an alumni team that is more exclusive than the University of Minnesota or any other of the famed hockey universities. Those numbers represent the year each man was a member of the United States Olympic hockey team.

When the time came for Coach Murray Williamson to find players interested in pursuing a chance to play international hockey and represent the United States in the late 1960s, he soon found the best route to International Falls, where he would find three of the most pivotal members of the silver medal-winning team of 1972—co-captain Keith "Huffer" Christiansen, goaltender Mike "Lefty" Curran and co-captain Tim Sheehy.

Sheehy starred at every level of the hockey landscape. And athletic role models always surrounded Sheehy, the nephew of football legend and Hall of Famer Bronko Nagurski.

During Sheehy's developmental years, International Falls was a family-oriented environment where the Boise Cascade, a huge paper mill that employed most of the Falls, offered job stability. People embraced the recreational aspects of winter with hockey, snowmobiling, ice fishing and hunting. Families didn't move around because work was steady and kids had plenty to do with four outdoor rinks.

"Everybody pretty much stayed together," recalled Sheehy. "We were part of the first group to come through the recreation program. We were very fortunate because we had two classes of teams that were back to back with outstanding athletes."

In 1961, Sheehy began his winning ways as a member of the city's Pee Wee team that captured International Falls' first state championship. That scenario would ring familiar as Sheehy grew up in the minor hockey association. Shortly thereafter, the city's high school coach Larry Ross wanted Sheehy to play for his team. As a 14-year-old freshman, the coach had to petition the school board in order for ninth graders to suit up.

"We had real good teams, and I was able to make the varsity team as a 14-year-old freshman," remembered Sheehy. "We got to play towards the end of the season and we lost in double overtime in the state tournament to St. Paul John's. We came back and won the next three years and had a 59-game undefeated streak at Falls High School, so we were known throughout the state as simply 'The Falls.'"

As nephew of Nagurski, the only man to ever make All-Pro at two positions (fullback and tackle), Sheehy had the guidance from someone who had made it by going to college.

"He always wanted me to go to college, as did my parents," said Sheehy. "That was the route I always wanted to go. The only way I was going to go was to get a scholarship. I was on a mission and I did not want to go Major Junior."

Sheehy's star continued to rise throughout high school—to the point that he was offered full scholarships to some of the top hockey schools in the country. At the time, the University of Minnesota was interested, as was North Dakota and Denver. In the end, Sheehy chose to head East to Chestnut Hill, Massachusetts, and the campus of Boston College.

At BC, Sheehy played for legendary coach Snooks Kelley. As a 17-year-old freshman, unable to play on the varsity squad due to a NCAA rule forbidding freshmen to play varsity athletics, Sheehy struggled on his freshman team through the first half of the season. At Christmas break, Sheehy had recorded just one goal as he headed home to Minnesota for the holiday break. Following the break, Sheehy settled in and ultimately set the school scoring record for freshmen. As a sign of his future, Sheehy's college career took him to the 1968 Frozen Four in Duluth, Minnesota, where the Eagles lost to Ken Dryden's Cornell Big Red in the national semifinal matchup.

Sheehy's hallmark college career ended after his three years on the varsity made him the Eagles' all-time leading scorer with 185 points. One other landmark occurrence marked Sheehy's four years in Boston— a draft notice from the United States Army. Upon graduation, with draft number 49, Sheehy went into the Army and reported to Fort Leonard Wood during the spring, summer and part of the fall.

"I was born in Canada, seven of our nine kids were born over the border from International Falls, so I have dual citizenship. I could've gone to Canada at that time or the Junior route and Vietnam would not have been a factor. But I wanted to go and figured I could make the U.S. Olympic team as well."

At Fort Leonard Wood, Sheehy was in Basic Training preparing for Vietnam when he was notified that he would be excused to try out for the national team. Upon his return from tryouts, Sheehy was selected as the platoon guide after noting that he was a college athlete on an application.

Knowing he had to make the team to escape Vietnam, Sheehy encountered more pressure when he actually received orders to go to Fort Ord, California—the shipping area to Vietnam.

"The sports department in Washington changed those orders," explained Sheehy. "The Pentagon knew at the time I was an Olympic athlete because Murray had gone to the Olympic Committee. They had some workings with the sports department in Washington and they were able to put that together."

Just the same, the threat of going to Vietnam always loomed for Sheehy and several of his mates.

Though the Army was part of his life directly following college, Sheehy never lost sight of his childhood dream of the Olympics. "Growing up, every kid wanted to play on the national team and then the Olympic team. That's the way I grew up. It was something that I always wanted to do."

The time to make his dream come true was at hand in Minneapolis. Having the unique experience of growing up in the "West" and playing college hockey in the East, Sheehy was aware of the potential personality conflicts that arose in years past.

"I think it was very big in 1960, '64 and '68," said Sheehy. "I guess we didn't think about it so much, though we had several players from the East—about five to seven. I was always looking out for the Eastern guys, as well as the Western guys. We never really had that problem."

By the time the team was selected, despite a dismal record against the powerful Russian team in their pre-Olympic exhibition games, Sheehy and his mates were ready.

"We had confidence in each other. It was a real team."

And yet, Sheehy's thoughts never strayed far from his hometown as he prepared to lace up his skates and don the sweater with USA embroidered on the front.

"I always thought about 1960 all the time—even when I played on my first U.S. team in 1969. In '69, I got to play with John Mayasich. We'd always heard his name in Minnesota, so I never forgot that image of the U.S. winning at Squaw Valley. When it happens—making the Olympic team—there is great jubilation on the inside. It was fun to experience everything with such an outstanding group of players."

But Sheehy's Olympic dream almost came to an end when he hooked skates with Mark Howe and severely sprained his knee right before the Olympic Games. After spending a week in the hospital, the International Falls native felt very fortunate to be able to play at all. Just like the rest of his lunch pail-carrying teammates, Sheehy did not let a sprained knee stop him from fulfilling his lifelong dream.

As the young, inexperienced U.S. team entered the Olympic tournament, international veteran players like Curran, Christiansen and Sheehy knew the odds were stacked against them to even reach the medal podium, yet alone get to the top.

"Anyone who played hockey in those days knew the Russians just dominated for so long and were truly outstanding athletes," admitted Sheehy.

That didn't stop the contagious aftereffects of a win in the first game against a stingy Swiss goaltender, which propelled the U.S. into the medal round of the tournament. Sheehy made it back to the lineup for that pivotal game after a severe injury, and with limited mobility, more than chipped in with two goals.

Following back-to-back losses to the Swedes and Russians, the U.S. hopes were dwindling as they entered their game against the Czechs. With a "nothing-to-lose" attitude, the young Americans trounced their Eastern Bloc foes, again reinvigorating their sagging spirits.

"I think everybody knew at the time we had an outstanding team, but the Russians overpowered everybody. We had the top amateur players, but they were real professional players."

That thought nags the former co-captain the most. Though the rest of the world knew what they were up against when it came to playing the Union of Soviet Socialist Republics, Sheehy is plagued but not beleaguered by what might have been if the impossible had occurred in 1972.

"I think about that often, if we could've surprised them like they did in '80, but we were on foreign soil, and the last two [gold medals the U.S. has won] have been won on U.S. ground. It was a dream that maybe could've been, but it didn't happen. We knew how good they were. Do I still think about it? All the time."

Following the Olympics, Sheehy "the can't-miss kid," who had been drafted by the Detroit Red Wings, decided to forego life in the National Hockey League and try his luck in the upstart World Hockey Association. Former Boston University head coach Jack Kelley offered Sheehy $100,000 to sign a contract with his New England Whalers franchise countering Detroit's offer of $8,500 to play in Ft. Worth in the Central League.

"I was a finance major at Boston College, so I didn't think it was a difficult decision to make—I went the World Hockey route. I signed with New England, but at that time I really hadn't planned on a professional career."

And while Sheehy's professional career was lucrative, his dream had always centered on playing and representing the United States at the

Olympic Games. His two sons—11 and 13 years old—carry that dream today as residents of International Falls, Minnesota to some day be included on that very special civic alumni team that includes Sheehy '72, Curran '72, and Christiansen '72.

Today, nine men from International Falls, a place described as a "winter wonderland with brief, joyous summers," have the distinction of being part of a very select group of talented hockey players with years next to their names—the year they graduated from the most exclusive program in American hockey.

Where is he now? Tim Sheehy is now a players agent in Southboro, Massachusetts.

STU IRVING

**Born: February 2, 1949 • Jersey No. 19 • Vietnam War
Veteran—served 1970-71**

"I was on temporary duty with the Olympic team. Those were my orders. I was with the Olympic team and if I got cut, I had to go back to 'Nam."

Following another loss to the mighty Russian juggernaut at Madison Square Garden, small-but-speedy forward Stu Irving knew two things for sure as he and Robbie Ftorek made their way to Coach Murray Williamson's suite after being summoned on January 7, 1972. First, he had scored two goals in the 11-4 loss against the world's greatest goaltender, Vladislav Tretiak. And second, the United States Olympic hockey team was traveling to Sapporo, Japan, for the Olympic Winter Games within two weeks.

The night before, Irving's Dad had asked if he had heard anything. Irving said he had not. When he and Ftorek arrived at Williamson's suite, the coach said with seemingly no emotion to the linemates, "When we get back to Minneapolis, you're going to get your passports."

At that moment, as cool and methodical as Coach Williamson was, Irving knew he had dodged his last bullet in Vietnam and would join the 1972 U.S. Olympic hockey team in Sapporo.

That cold January day in New York City seemed like a dream from where the 22-year-old Irving had been just months earlier. For that matter, it was a dream. Four months before, the native of Beverly, Massachusetts, was stuck in the hot and steamy jungles of the Mekong Delta in Vietnam as a member of another team—the United States Army.

It was 1969, and Irving was 19 years old. His skills had taken him from the ponds of Beverly—he didn't skate indoors until he was 10—to Beverly High and on to Quebec, where he played with a farm club of the Montreal Jr. Canadiens immediately after high school. After returning to New England and Newman Prep, the well-known hockey player from the North Shore still intended on playing and was trying to make a break for himself.

The New England Amateur League consisted of teams like the Braintree Hawks, the Concord Mudmen, the Manchester Black Hawks, the Framingham Picks, and the Lowell Chiefs—and its players were mostly guys who had played in college. Some were All-Americans trying to prolong their playing days for $25 a day.

"I was in prep school, and that day I tried out with Tim Taylor, who had just spent three years in the U.S. Hockey League playing for the Waterloo Black Hawks," said Irving. "He was going to be the assistant coach for Harvard, and we were trying out for this team. I was 19, and the rest of the guys were 25 or 26. Jimmy Logue was one of the goaltenders."

Jim Logue was a goaltender on the '64 and '68 U.S. Olympic hockey teams. Today, he remains closely associated with New England hockey as Boston College's goaltending coach. In 1968, Logue was another kid from New England hoping to duplicate the gold medal win of the 1960 U.S. hockey team and living out a dream as an Olympic goaltender. Logue would end up playing an instrumental role in Stu Irving's introduction to international hockey, and ultimately, his release from the jungles of Vietnam.

"I had a good season in prep and a good season in the New England Amateur League," Irving recalled. "So they made an all-star team from the New England Amateur League to go play an international tournament up in Lake Placid. I ended up making the all-star team and so did Jimmy Logue. We played Canada and one other team. I had a good weekend up there flying all over the place on the big sheet of ice; and Loguey said, 'Anytime you want to play international hockey, you let me know. You've got some talent for the big sheet of ice—ya know, skating-wise.' I didn't know what international hockey was. I knew Loguey played in the '64 and '68 Olympics and the coach in '68 was Murray Williamson. That was March of 1970."

At the end of the season, a banquet in Manchester, New Hampshire, brought all the guys from the New England Amateur League together, and Irving had a chance to catch up with his friends and tell them his news—he'd been drafted. Unbeknownst to him at the time, the date—May 14, 1970—turned out to be the beginning of Irving's Olympic odyssey—the same day that he reported to Fort Dix, New Jersey, for induction into the United States Army.

"Some time in March I got my number—164—and they brought in from 168," explained Irving. "I was four digits away from getting out of it. I'll never forget that number. I had to take the train to Boston and then the bus to New Jersey, and I was down there for eight weeks. I finished my eight weeks at boot camp in mid-July, and then I had to go to Advanced Training. We were starting to get our orders. Some guys were going to Texas. Some guys were going down South. The next thing I knew, my orders came in—Advanced Infantry Training right there at Fort Dix for infantry."

It was late July/early August when the New England tryouts for the 1971 U.S. National team were taking place. Jim Logue called Irving's house only to find out Stu had been at boot camp since the middle of May. Logue couldn't believe it and told Irving's father about the tryouts for the national team. Logue wanted Irving at those tryouts, so he told Irving's father he would make a few phone calls to see if he could get Stu to the tryout.

While Irving was preparing for Advanced Training at Fort Dix, Logue made good on his promise to Irving's father and made some phone calls. He called his former Olympic coach, Murray Williamson, who was heading up the U.S. National team that year and would be coaching the 1972 U.S. Olympic team—and team manager Hal Trumble.

Following a day of Advanced Training at Fort Dix in July 1970, Irving was summoned by his captain.

"They're having an Eastern tryout for the U.S. National hockey team. You play hockey?" the captain asked.

"Yes, Sir. I do, Captain," Irving replied.

"Well, I've got orders here to give you a 48-hour pass."

"The captain was kind of pissed, but he let me go," recalled Irving.

"I went down to the tryout and got on the ice, warmed up, had a skate, did some stick handling, and came back later in the day for a scrimmage," remembered Irving. "On Friday afternoon, we scrimmaged, and by Friday night, my groin was killing me. On Saturday, we had two more sessions, and I was icing them—I was a mess. But, we got those tryouts out of the way, and I then had to go back to Fort Dix for more Advanced Training."

Irving headed back to Fort Dix from the Eastern tryouts not knowing where he stood as far as making the U.S. National team. By the end of August, he finished Advanced Training and it was time to get his orders.

"Some guys were going to Germany. Some were going to 'Nam," said Irving. "And then came my orders: Advanced Infantry Training completed, 30-day leave, report back to Fort Dix—Vietnam."

Irving's worst nightmare had come true—Vietnam—but he had a 30-day leave first, so he went home to Beverly for his leave and imminent deployment.

"As soon as I got home, I called Loguey and told him to start making calls because I'm going to Vietnam," recalled Irving in a voice with as much urgency today as it had more than 30 years ago.

"I was on 30-day leave. I should have been getting shit-faced, and I'm on my mountain bike working out four hours a day, knowing they've got the next tryouts in late September for the national team. I called Loguey once a week and told him I hadn't heard anything yet. He told me they had my name on the list."

As time was running out on Irving, he desperately tried to gather information about his chances of making the national team. He again called Logue five days before they shipped him off to Vietnam to find out what he knew.

"I had to be on campus to get my tags, jungle fatigues and all that before they ship me," said Irving. "Now, I'm with all my buddies from boot camp, and we're in the barracks and we went to the movies that Sunday night. I'll never forget that. I told the captain I was supposed to be trying out for the U.S. National hockey team in September and could he check on that?"

The following day, the Captain found Irving and said he'd checked into it and that there was something to his story. So they put him in a holding barracks.

"It might have been a blessing, I don't know. I could've been sent over to 'Nam and been up North. Anyway, I was in the hold barracks and I stayed there for another four days."

The Captain came back to Irving and said they couldn't guarantee he was going to make the team. That's what they needed—a guarantee.

"Your orders are cut, and you're going to 'Nam," the Captain said to the exasperated Irving.

Irving arrived in Vietnam on October 3, 1970, and was stationed in a small village about 100 miles from Saigon in the Mekong Delta.

"There were a couple guys, and they said we needed a radio operator and a mail clerk," explained Irving. "I remembered from training, they said the first guys the Viet Cong try to nail are the machine-gunners and the radio operators. I said I don't want to be a radio operator, so I'll take the mail clerk. I ended up staying in the compound and doing the mail."

As Irving settled into his clerk duties in the compound—he was part of a team that helped train the Vietnamese how to fight guerilla warfare. He also took weekly trips in the skies of Vietnam to pick up mail in Can Tho.

"It was fun for a while, but then it got a little hairy. I'd have to take a C131, and we'd have to land in these small airfields. I'd get back in the late afternoon. I did that for a good nine months."

Even in the middle of the Vietnamese jungle, Irving held onto the hope that he would someday play hockey again.

"I did one crazy thing over there. I wrote my Dad and told him to send me over a box of pucks and four sticks. All of a sudden, I'm in Can Tho and I'm walking out of the post office with these sticks. People are looking at me and they don't know what to think. I'd go against the bunkers and sandbags and take a couple hundred shots a night, run every night, and hope something would happen when I got out of there. Maybe go back and play."

"When I was in the service you got a newspaper called *Stars & Stripes*," remembered Olympic teammate Dick McGlynn. "I read an article about this kid from Massachusetts who brought a dozen pucks and hockey sticks to Vietnam. In 120-degree heat, rain, he'd shoot off a board into sandbags in his foxhole. He's over there, and people are shooting bullets at his head—he's shooting pucks into sandbags in his foxhole. Come to find out, it was Stu, who was my roommate."

After nine months, Irving's tour of duty approached "short time" and he was offered an opportunity to re-up for another six months in 'Nam—meaning his final months would keep him away from the heavy action he'd already experienced and closer to the base, where he was relegated to performing inspections. Irving re-upped and became friendly with the doctors, officers, and the Colonel. Together, Irving and his new friends, two of whom were doctors from Harvard, spent the scorching afternoons playing tennis and staying in shape while the rest of the camp took the time to get out of the sun.

Irving fondly remembers those days with Dr. Chuck Winters and Dr. Major Joel Avery.

"I'd be out there playing tennis with the Colonel of the whole group, the doctors, and they kept me in shape. We had round robins on Saturday afternoons because everything shut down. I got to know these high-end guys, and they were great. Some of them were civilians and some of them were CIA. They took care of me. They gave me a going-away party when I left, and they were really great to me."

Having re-upped, Irving knew all along that if he held any chance of continuing his hockey career it might come from an Olympic tryout. He made sure to set it up so he could go on "R & R" leave in September. On September 2, his company captain called him into his office and asked, "Stu, do you play hockey?"

"I told him, 'I used to, but those days are over, Captain; why?'" said Irving.

"Well, I have temporary duty orders for you to report to Minneapolis, Minnesota, on September 15," the captain said.

With that, it all clicked. Irving told Major Joel Avery, who was one of his doctor buddies and tennis partners, that he had a real plane ticket for one way from California to Minneapolis. After almost throwing the ticket away because he wasn't sure if it was legit, Avery told him to hang on to it. Irving then asked his captain if he could process himself out of 'Nam. His captain complied, and the next day, September 3, he got all his money out of the bank and handed off his mail to the new clerk who took over. On September 4, he was in Saigon, where he turned in his weapon and continued the out process. He caught a flight out of Vietnam on September 5.

Irving knew he had another 10 days before he was due in Minneapolis, so he started skating in the old New England League with Mike Gilligan.

"I was only about 150-155 pounds, and some of those guys probably should've been going to the tryout before me, but I was just getting on the ice."

Irving persevered until time came to head off to Minneapolis and his date with destiny. Because he was flying with a military ticket as "active military personnel on temporary duty," Irving had to dress in his uniform as he made his way to Minneapolis. The next day, he put his uniform back on and reported to the Met Center, where the old Minnesota North Stars used to play.

"We all had to check in, and I was still in my uniform while everyone else was in jeans," said Irving.

The one-week tryout started right there. The team did some on-ice drills and then went right into scrimmaging. From there, initial cuts were made, and the team was pared down to approximately 22 guys—enough to at least be able to scrimmage when the next set of tryouts/training were conducted on the Bemidji State campus.

"I had no time constrictions because I was on temporary duty with the Olympic team," explained Irving. "Those were my orders. I was with the Olympic team, and if I got cut, I had to go back to 'Nam."

For the next five weeks or so, the team played exhibition games, and Williamson was keeping an eye on Irving. The small and speedy Irving was getting bounced around pretty good out there—especially when they played the pro teams. When the team made an Eastern swing, Irving ran into his Boston pals Logue and Taylor. They asked how Irving was doing. They told Irving that he looked good out there, but they could see he was getting knocked around a little bit.

Years later, when Irving told his story, he credited Logue with an Olympian assist.

"I think Loguey talked to Murray and asked him how I was doing," Irving modestly explained. "Murray told him I was struggling out there a bit and that he didn't know what's going to happen. I think Loguey said to Murray, in so many words, 'Murray, what are you going to do—send the kid back to Vietnam? How are you going to feel about that?' So, I think

Murray decided to keep me as long as he could. I never knew that story until Loguey told me years later."

Where is he now? Stuart Irving is now an assistant hockey coach at Merrimack College.

ROUND-ROBIN MEDAL ROUND
GAME ONE
February 5, 1972—8:05 p.m. EST
SWEDEN 5 - USA 1

"When things go wrong as they sometimes will,
And the road you're trudging seems all uphill,
When funds are low and the debts are high,
And you want to smile, but you have to sigh,
When care is pressing you down a bit,
Rest if you must, but don't you quit.

Life is queer with its twists and turns,
As every one of us sometimes learns.
And many a failure turns about
When he might've won, had he stuck it out.
Don't give up though the pace seems slow
You may succeed with another blow.

Often the goal is nearer than
It seems to a faint and faltering man,
Often the struggler has given up
When he might've captured the victor's cup.

And he learned too late when the night slipped down,
How close he was to the golden crown.

Success is failure turned inside out
The silver tint of the clouds of doubt.
And you never can tell how close you are,
It may be near when it seems afar.

So stick to the fight when you're hardest hit.
It's when things seem worse that you mustn't quit."
—"DON'T QUIT" BY AN UNKNOWN AUTHOR,
OFT RECITED BY DICK McGLYNN

Sixteen hours after the U.S. team had expended a tremendous amount of physical and emotional energy in beating Switzerland in their pressure-packed qualifying game, the Americans were back on the ice, lining up to face off against Sweden—one of the tournament's pre-Olympic favorites. Considered by many to be one of the best-skating, most talented, and physical teams in the Olympic tournament, Sweden was well rested, having coasted to a lopsided victory over Yugoslavia early the day before.

Led by Inge Hammarstrom, one of the first Swedish stars to play in the NHL—as well as Lars Nilsson—the Swedes struck quickly as Nilsson scored just 2:32 into the first period. Sweden made it 2-0 nearly four minutes later, when captain Thommy Abrahamsson scored on a power play goal after the U.S.'s Stu Irving was sent off for slashing.

The U.S. fought back. Kevin Ahearn scored his third goal of the young tournament at 8:04, cutting the lead to 2-1 at the end of the first period. In the second period, up-and-down action saw Swedish goaltender Leif Holmquist make 13 saves, while the U.S.'s Mike Curran stopped 13 of 14 shots on goal, beat only by Tord Lundstrom at 7:27 to give the Swedes a 3-1 lead. The up-and-down action of the second period spilled into the third, but the Swedes put the game out of reach when Thommie Bergman scored at 6:12 of the period, and

Hammarstrom added another for Sweden 3:13 later for an impenetrable 5-1 lead.

Two American goals were disallowed on questionable calls earlier in the game—goals that could have changed the game's complexion had they stood. On both, the officials ruled an American player preceded the puck into the Swedish goal crease.

U.S. coach Murray Williamson made no excuses to reporters after the game, stating he thought both goals should have been counted, but added, "They [Sweden] played well enough to win."

The Swedish coach, Canadian-born Bill Harris, after the game also conceded to reporters noting the change in momentum after the disallowed goals could have changed things, "If one had been allowed, and the game was 3-2, it could have changed the game around."

As the Americans trudged into their locker room, they faced the gravity of their defeat. Their spirits were deflated even though they'd just played a tournament favorite much tighter than the score indicated.

"To say we were down would be a little bit of an understatement," remembered Dick McGlynn, "We thought our chance of winning a medal was virtually gone, especially when you lose to one of the co-favorites. There were only three medals, and you had the Russians, the Swedes, the Czechs, who regularly beat the Russians, and there was nothing wrong with the Poles or the Finns. There were great teams everywhere you looked."

As the team got back into the room, McGlynn, who along with Tom Mellor was one of the guys the team could count on to keep things loose, stood up and delivered a rallying cry to his teammates by reciting a poem he had learned from his aunt as a kid—a multi-stanza poem by an unknown author entitled. "Don't Quit."

"Throughout the year, I would get up and recite a stanza like I was done, and they were hoping I was done, but I'd jump back up and continue with the second stanza; and the guys would yell at me to sit down and shut up. Then I'd recite the third stanza, then the fourth, then fifth. They had all heard the poem about 100 times. Eventually, the guys started learning it by rote. We were in the locker room after the Sweden game, and the place was deathly quiet. Most of the guys thought that that was it. We just blew our opportunity. I stood up as the guys were starting to get showered and dressed, and started in with, 'When things go wrong as they sometimes will ...' Everyone kinda stopped and looked at me. I got into the first stanza, and Tommy and Stuey joined in, and then another and another. By the time I got to the end of the poem there were 20 guys screaming, '... So stick to the fight ... you mustn't quit.'"

Czechoslovakia was next.

DICK McGLYNN

Born: July 19, 1948 • Jersey No. 20 • Draft No. 104

"Murray, it's nice to meet you. My name is Dick McGlynn, and I'm going to be one of your players. So where's the locker room?"

"There was a guy standing at the end of the rink with a clipboard looking onto the ice, so I went up to him and asked, 'Where are the locker rooms?'

He looked at me and asked, 'What's your name?'

I said, 'Dick McGlynn.'

He said, 'Okay,' as he looked down his clipboard for my name. There was nothing on there—no Dick McGlynn. 'I'm sorry, your name is not on my list.'

I said, 'Well, what's your name?'

And he said, 'Murray Williamson … I'm coach of the U.S. team.'

I stuck out my right hand and said, 'Murray, it's nice to meet you. My name is Dick McGlynn, and I'm going to be one of your players. So where's the locker room?'

He looked at me with an incredulous look, pointed to the locker room and said, 'That way.'"

ᚳᚫᚦᛞ   ᚳᚫᚦᛞ   ᚳᚫᚦᛞ

Dick McGlynn seemed to be the type of person whom good luck just seemed to follow—and he had enough sense to recognize it. He also was the type of person with enough sense not to squander an opportunity when it presented itself. But it wasn't all luck and opportunity for the 21-year-old from Medford, Massachusetts. He was a hardnosed, blue-collar kid who seized an opportunity and did what anyone else would've done—he ran with it. Or in his case, skated, hit, and talked with it. In hockey parlance, McGlynn had "big balls," and some of the breaks he got were a direct result of having taken a chance, working hard, speaking his mind and then backing it up with action.

McGlynn actually had planned to attend the Naval Flight School after he graduated from Colgate University and had no intention of playing for the Olympic team—or even trying to further his playing career. Drafted by the NHL's St. Louis Blues in 1970, he considered that an interesting option. But during his college days at Colgate, McGlynn had an assistant coach named Brad Houston, who had traveled through Germany and South Africa playing hockey. Houston had set up an opportunity for McGlynn and his roommate to play on a team in a winter league in South Africa with teams from Capetown, Johannesburg, and Port Durbin. McGlynn and his buddy bought their tickets and made their way to the South African consulate in New York City to obtain their visas.

"Although South Africa was considered backwards in many ways, they were very advanced in other ways," said McGlynn. "When we got to the consulate, they told us they had some bad news—they couldn't issue us visas. We found out later that South Africa was thrown out of the Olympic Games, ironically, with the movement spearheaded by Arthur Ashe against their apartheid policies."

McGlynn had originally planned on playing during South Africa's winter time, return home and sign up for the Naval Flight program. He wanted to be a pilot and had passed all the exams. All he had to do was sign on the dotted line to enroll. Ironically, not being able to go to South Africa would afford McGlynn the chance to play in the Olympic Games a year and a half later.

With his original plan foiled, McGlynn opted for Plan B. He gathered up his gear and made his way to the St. Louis Blues training camp in hopes of competing for a job in the minors. After several weeks, only seven rookies were left in camp when he received a call to see the general manager. After meeting with the Blues' general manager, Scotty Bowman, McGlynn was told to call home immediately.

When he called home, his parents told him he had been drafted again. This time Uncle Sam had called his number. With a draft number of 104, McGlynn was not surprised.

"I was pretty sure I would be drafted, so I took the physical at the draft board. In the meantime, I heard about a tryout for the 1971 U.S. National team, the non-Olympic year."

Eastern tryouts for the 1971 U.S. National team took place in Billerica, Massachusetts, at a little place known as the Forum, which served as the college home of the University of Massachusetts-Lowell Chiefs. Those familiar with New England hockey knew it as an intimate sheet of ice where the fans could almost reach out and grab you as you skated. Because of its small dimensions, the action on the ice was played at warp speed. McGlynn decided, after a summer of disappointment in which nothing seemed to go right for him, he was going to try out for the 1971 U.S. National team.

McGlynn started calling around to get information on the tryout. "I called the AHAUS people, the ECAC people, and the responses were almost identical."

"Who are you?" the voice on the other end asked.

"Dick McGlynn."

"Where did you play?"

"Colgate."

"We've never heard of you, and the tryouts are closed."

McGlynn then reasoned, "If you've never seen me play, what's the harm in letting me come out for the day?"

"We've scouted all the people. This is an invitation only, and we've got all the guys we need."

Click.

McGlynn was stonewalled but undeterred. He found out where the tryouts were being held, grabbed his equipment and headed for Billerica. Upon arriving at the rink, he once again had to do some fast talking, this time introducing himself to Coach Murray Williamson, while making his way to the ice for the tryout.

As the tryout progressed, McGlynn soon realized that, other than talking his way onto the ice, he hadn't really done anything to catch Coach Williamson's eye. He figured his best hope of getting some attention was to do something drastic. McGlynn set his sights on a six-foot-five, 240-pound defenseman.

"They had a big defenseman out there during one of our scrimmages. At one point, he was huffing and puffing as he came around the net and looked a little tired. He had his head down a little bit and I started coming at him from center ice. I got around the blue line, and we had a massive collision. I only weighed about 185 pounds at the time, and he definitely took the worst of the hit. They stopped the scrimmage as he was lying on the ice pulling up his drawers trying to get some air in his lungs. I skated over to the bench and sat down."

The next thing McGlynn knew, Williamson glided over to him. With his hands tucked in his jacket pockets, Williamson leaned in casually and asked, "What'd you say your name was?"

"Dick McGlynn."

Williamson reached into his pocket and pulled out a pen and pad of paper and continued, "Where were you born, Dick?"

"Medford, Massachusetts."

"When were you born, Dick?"

"7/19/48."

"Okay," said Williamson as he skated away.

"He didn't say another word," remembers McGlynn. "I turned to my roommate, Tommy, who was sitting next to me and said, 'What do you think he wanted that information for?' Tommy said, 'If you're going to play on the U.S. team, they probably have to make sure you're a U.S. citizen. They're probably going to go to city records and see if they can get your birth certificate.' That was kind of the turning point—that little collision."

From there, McGlynn was invited to Minneapolis, where the four-day tryouts brought guys from everywhere, including Michigan, Minnesota, Massachusetts, and New York. Herb Brooks was there. From being left off the list to getting to the tryout in Minneapolis, McGlynn had already come a long way. But Coach Williamson had decided to cut him, and in the process, he held an exit interview with each player he chose to let go.

He told McGlynn, "Dick, we really liked what we saw in you. We know you didn't play in one of the major programs out there, and we've seen development in you just in the short time, but we're kind of set with our defensive corps."

Despite Coach Williamson's encouraging words during the exit interview, McGlynn quickly turned it into an "enter" interview.

With two strikes against him that summer, McGlynn was not about to accept being cut. He was a crafty, street-smart kid from a working-class neighborhood and one of six children in an Irish-Catholic family whose father placed a premium on hard work, education, and service to your country. McGlynn's father was a World War II veteran who fought under General Patton and knew well the horrors of war. His father also was a guy who was up at 5:30 in the morning working with his father at the family bakery before school, then went home and off to another job before coming home at nine o'clock at night during high school. His father was a guy who went to college and law school at night as well, all while having six kids and the biggest floral business in Medford. Finally, McGlynn's father was a man who became the mayor from very humble beginnings because he outworked everybody.

With all that in mind, the disappointment of his summer to date, McGlynn didn't want strike three for the summer to be getting cut from the U.S. National team. Once again, he had a talk with Williamson.

"How many defensemen are you keeping?" he asked Williamson during the "entry" interview.

Williamson again looked incredulously at the brash youngster and told him he was keeping seven. Once again seizing the opportunity, McGlynn reasoned that created an odd number to scrimmage with so why not let him stick around and fill in during scrimmages. Williamson, surprised by McGlynn's quick reasoning and bold initiative, asked if he had an apartment.

"No," said McGlynn.

"Do you have a roommate?" asked Williamson.

"No."

"A car?"

"No." To top it off, McGlynn added, "And I don't have any money either."

Williamson told him he'd think about it. Once again, the cocksure scrapper was talking his way onto the ice. The next day Williamson called McGlynn and made a deal. McGlynn could stick around if he agreed to pay half the rent on an apartment that would be used by guys who were asked to come in and try out during the domestic schedule. McGlynn agreed and began practicing. He quickly became the seventh defenseman, then sixth, fifth, and ultimately worked his way into the lineup. Like his father, he outworked his teammates and ended up on the team that went to the World Championships in Bern/Geneva, Switzerland.

Making the Olympic team was another matter for McGlynn. Even though he had been a member of the 1971 U.S. National team—which finished dead last at the World Championships—he didn't have the same guarantees that some of his fellow national team teammates enjoyed. Again, like everything else in McGlynn's life at the time, if he could find an angle to exploit, he would. This time, that angle was Lenny Gagnon.

Gagnon was a lifelong resident of Medford who grew up on the same streets as McGlynn. Gagnon ended up a referee at the 1972 Olympic Winter Games who would play an interesting part in the team's pursuit of an Olympic medal.

As a youngster, Gagnon hung around with McGlynn's father and Jack Riley, who went on to coach the gold medal-winning 1960 U.S. Olympic team in Squaw Valley. The young Dick McGlynn learned hockey and lots of life lessons from Gagnon.

With scheduled tryouts for the 1972 Olympic team ready to begin in Minneapolis, Gagnon, who was friendly with Coach Williamson and team manager Hal Trumble, decided to go and watch. After each day, Gagnon would meet with Williamson and Trumble asking them their opinions on prospective players.

Eventually, he always got around to asking, "'What'd you think of McGlynn?'" explained McGlynn more than 30 years later. "They'd say, 'He's tough enough, but we don't know if he can carry the puck.' So Lenny would call and tell me, 'They liked what they saw, but they want to see you carry the puck more.' The next day, all I did was carry the puck. It was as if I was in Murray's head.

"The next day they'd say, 'He did a good job carrying the puck, but what about hitting? We'd like to see him hit some more.' Again, Lenny would call and tell me they wanted to see me hit some more people out there. The next day, I went out there and hit everything that moved. So Murray and Hal would say, 'Hmmm. He can hit. He can carry the puck.'

"Here I am: a college graduate in the service trying out for the Olympic team, and one of my father's grammar-school chums is telling me all I need to know—how they're thinking. I had a direct pipeline of information, and it was unbelievable. I knew what they were looking for, and I was able to give it to them. Lenny was more responsible for me being on the Olympic team than anyone else."

Where is he now? Dick McGlynn now practices law in Medford, Massachusetts.

WALLY OLDS

Born: August 17, 1946 • Jersey No. 3 • Draft No. 149

"I guess my teammates didn't know many other hockey players who went through college with mostly A's."

Coach Murray Williamson described steady defenseman Wally Olds as the "smart one." Olds came from a long line of teachers and educators who stressed a premium on learning and gaining an education. Olds's education came not only in the classroom but also on the ice, where his Olympic experience afforded him the ability to learn more than he ever imagined.

Olds never thought much about the Olympics. The native of the Canadian-border town of Bena, Minnesota, was busy studying computer science and electrical engineering back in the archaic days of two computers filling an entire room and sourcing as much power as one of today's laptops. Though Olds was a solid member of the University of Minnesota hockey team, the Olympics didn't enter his mind until Williamson tabbed the defenseman to attend tryouts in Bemidji.

"There were a lot of guys that came and went that were talented enough to play that he didn't pick," said Olds. "I was fortunate enough to be there."

The young group of overachievers relished the challenge Williamson put forth, and Olds rose to the occasion and earned the respect of his teammates. Paired with Charlie Brown, who was tabbed the "quiet one," Olds and Brown formed a defensive tandem that might best be described as eclectic, but more accurately as dependable and stalwart.

"My defenseman partner and I didn't talk a whole lot, so that made us different I guess," explained Olds. "We didn't feel the need to discuss a lot of things—we just worked. But it wasn't as if we were mute."

Olds's pensive style, teamed with his educational acumen, made it easy for Williamson and the rest of his teammates to categorize him as smart and studious.

"Education was a part of my family and the ability to do well, and I did. I guess my teammates didn't know many other hockey players who went through college with mostly A's."

Ultimately, it didn't matter much to Olds's other teammates. Keeping the puck out of the U.S. nets was his goal, and he and Brown scored high grades in that department. Together, Brown and Olds went through the entire Olympic tournament without ever surrendering an even-strength goal while they were on the ice; which made them a very important part of a team that recognized each other for the sum of their parts and not individual talents.

"The shortest way I put it to people is, we are brothers for life," says Olds. "Thinking more about it, I don't think any one of us played on any team that was any closer or got along any better. I'm sure that made us a little better."

That selfless attitude also created a "one-for-all and all-for-one" approach to a team that remains faceless and undeterred by that distinction after more than three decades.

"We played in the era before there was intense television coverage," explained Olds. "It was in a place in the world before there was truly worldwide television coverage. And then, second place doesn't get that much attention. There were some opportunities to recognize us, but the right people weren't there to think about it. But we, the players, feel like it's kind of a special brotherhood and tradition—and we were glad to have been a part of it."

Olds remains intellectually curious today as he thinks back on his most vivid memory of his Olympic experience. Of course, the hockey stands out. In the end, Olds remembers the interesting differences of culture between Japan and the United States, "like the bath tubs being little square things."

Observing and learning was always part of Olds's life. Williamson's early assessment of the steady Minnesota defenseman holds as true today as it did in 1972. When asked to describe his former defenseman, the old coach paused and quietly extolled, "Ah ... the smart one."

Where is he now? Wally Olds is now a businessman in Marine on St. Croix, Minnesota.

CHARLIE BROWN

Born: October 26, 1947 • Jersey No. 5 • Draft No. 007

"I thought we could win a medal. I was probably naïve in my thinking, but I thought we could."

If hockey-crazed *Peanuts* cartoon creator Charles Schultz had known the 1972 U.S. Olympic hockey team had a player named Charlie Brown on its roster, things might have been different for the fabled comic sad sack by the same name. Instead of Lucy pulling the ball away from him every time he attempted to kick a field goal, the creator might have taken a lesson from the three-sport high school star, college hockey player, and future Olympian who shared his squiggly-hair character's name.

The comic strip Charlie Brown could've discussed what, at the time, it took to reach the pinnacle of amateur athletics and come home with a medal. The cartoon Charlie Brown also would've learned that perseverance and hard work pay off in the end, and trusting your teammates is the greatest aspect of being part of a team.

Charlie Brown grew up in North Minneapolis, Minnesota, with a cartoon strip character's name and athletic ability that eventually took him to Sapporo, Japan, as a member of the 1972 U.S. Olympic hockey team.

"My dad was a speed skater and I had speed skates," explained Brown. "He kept finding me playing hockey in my speed skates, so he asked me what I wanted to do. I told him I wanted to play hockey."

Like most of his teammates—and anyone who has ever laced up skates in the time of open-air ice where a roof was the exception and not the rule for many youngsters—Brown was outdoors playing hockey all the time—all day long. On days when school would "interrupt" his ice time, Brown and his mates would play pick-up games on the ponds after classes.

As he grew up and matured, Brown became a three-sport high school all-star in football, hockey, and baseball and actually fielded more scholarship offers in football. But the wily and tough high-schooler decided he wanted to try to play hockey at the collegiate level. So Brown walked on to the University of Minnesota freshman team, where former Olympian Lou Nanne was the coach. As was the case at that time, collegiate freshmen were not allowed to play varsity athletics.

With playing time scarce during his sophomore season, Brown didn't think he was getting a fair shot; so he left the Division I program at Minnesota and headed north to Bemidji State, a perennial national threat in Division II.

"We got guys who wanted to play hockey and not the ones with big heads, and we won the Nationals the next three years I was there," recalled Brown. "In my junior year, we actually played North Dakota and split with them. That was not a surprise to us, but Minnesota wouldn't play us. We had good teams up there, and it was a good move."

During Brown's junior season, he got a taste of international hockey when he was asked to be a member of the 1970 U.S. National team. Playing games with the national team and then flying back to join his collegiate team, Brown gained valuable experience that served him well when it came time for Olympic tryouts. It also didn't hurt that his national coach, Murray Williamson, was tabbed to guide the '72 Olympic team to Sapporo. But first, there was a matter of answering a draft notice.

By the time Brown was to have reported to Basic Training, Williamson and manager Hal Trumble had a direct pipeline to Washington that enabled them to identify Olympic hopefuls and have their duty assigned to the Olympic team. The players who were tabbed as serious contenders for spots on the 1972 team were set apart so the Pentagon was not surprised when they got a call from Trumble.

Brown took pride in serving his country by representing the United States with inspired dedication and hard work as a member of the U.S. Olympic team.

"That was the other thing," explained Brown. "From the time training camp opened up, we were the USA team—on and off the ice. We were role models out there in public. On and off that ice, we represented the U.S., and we behaved. The pros today say they're not role models. Baloney. We were polite and even moreso because we were representing the United States, and we were proud of that."

For most of the guys on the '72 team, playing on the U.S. Olympic hockey team was not only an honor, but also their dream. Brown was no different in that sentiment.

"In the back of my mind, I thought about someday playing on the Olympic team," said Brown. "To me, playing for the Olympic team was it—and I made it. Everything else was icing on the cake after that. I thought representing the United States was great."

The icing on this cake turned out to be silver and didn't come with as much surprise to Brown as it did to others, "I thought we could win a medal," said Brown. "I was probably naïve, but I thought we could."

Brown was teamed with Wally Olds on defense almost from the beginning. The pair was two of four defensemen Coach Williamson confidently used on a regular shift to kill penalties and add a backbone to the young but talented U.S. squad.

"We fit together unbelievably," remembers the stalwart defenseman. "Playing together, we knew what the other was going to do. We played together as partners and roomed together."

Camaraderie was not an issue with this U.S. team like in previous and future years. Despite the two defensemen both hailing from Minnesota, regional divides did not creep into the game plan for Williamson's Olympic team.

During Brown's time as a member of the U.S. Olympic team, he played in 47 pre-Olympic games and scored five goals while adding 21 assists. When he got to Sapporo, he was shut out on the score sheet, but he and Olds finished the six-game tournament without being on the ice for a goal against the U.S. team during even-strength play.

But Brown and his teammates weren't overly interested in statistics anyway. The only thing they cared about was winning a medal. It didn't matter what color. Looking back today, Brown wonders if the color of their medal has relegated them to a hockey purgatory.

"I don't know about a 'forgotten team,'" said Brown. "It seems like that in a category of all athletes who didn't win. It was as if they didn't pay much attention to you. Winning is everything, it seems. We were the only men's sport to win a medal in those Olympics. That doesn't mean anyone else who participated meant any less. You were playing for the country, and that's what counts."

Looking back, Brown wouldn't change a thing. The experience of a lifetime lifted the one-time high school phenom to the Olympic Games and beyond. Following his playing days, Brown became a physical education, health, and driver's education teacher—and in his spare time, he coached. For the most part of nearly three decades shaping America's youth, Brown enjoyed his tenure as a soccer, hockey, and girls fast-pitch softball coach.

"I did it for 20 years and retired from head coaching. I'm into other things now."

Although Brown has hung up his coach's hat, he hasn't quite hung up his skates. The silver medalist still loves playing the game of his youth once a week and referees 20-25 games a season. His pursuits are modest these days, but the competitiveness that made him an Olympian still burns when he thinks back on the days of his early 20s.

"I went back to training camp [with the California Golden Seals], but I don't know if I lost interest and thought the pro game was something else," remembered Brown. "I had other things. I was married then, and I just had other things. Maybe that's one thing—I could've stuck with that a little longer because all the scouts were pushing to get more American kids."

Then again, maybe Brown knew when to quit. Charlie Brown, the Olympian, most definitely could've taught the comic strip Charlie Brown a thing or two about what it takes to excel—not only on the athletic fields but also on the fields of life.

"I feel proud when I see the Olympics today. I remember it all the time during the Winter Olympics. I remember what we went through, things that happened, and what we did. My most vivid memory is probably the Opening Ceremony representing the United States. You look at how many people are lucky enough to have a skill, develop it, and use it to make a team—not everyone was born with that skill to reach whatever level."

Where is he now? Charlie Brown is now a high school physical education teacher in Eagan, Minnesota.

5

GUT CZECH

GAME TWO
February 7, 1972—2:03 a.m. EST
USA 5 - CZECHOSLOVAKIA 1

"At the time we didn't know it, but that game was for the silver medal, and I had just played the game of my life."

—MIKE "LEFTY" CURRAN

Czechoslovakia, another tournament favorite, was America's second hurdle in the medal round. The game's result came down to two things: the coaching of Murray Williamson in setting the tone and the goaltending of Curran. The U.S. team knew they could beat the Czechs, having defeated them 7-5 and 6-3 in two exhibition games that winter. Williamson pounced upon the opportunity to define the rivalry in another exhibition game—in Tokyo just five days before the

Olympics Opening Ceremony. Sensing that the two teams would meet again in Sapporo, Williamson wanted his team to send a clear message to the Czechs by enforcing a more physical style of play than their Eastern Bloc opponents.

"Coach took us aside and said he wanted us to play as dirty as possible," remembered the then-16-year-old Mark Howe. "It was the most vicious game. He didn't care if we lost, because he reasoned when we play them for real, they'll be looking over their shoulders. That's exactly what happened."

The U.S. did lose the game in Tokyo, 4-1—but if the Czechs thought the U.S. team was going to back down in Sapporo, they were sorely mistaken. The message was sent loud and clear: the U.S. boys were not going to be intimidated.

Even though the U.S. had its share of success against Czechoslovakia, they were still very mindful of the type of team they were facing.

"We knew we could compete with them," said Bruce McIntosh. "They didn't like the way we played the body. I think the Czechs had a better power play than the Russians did, but full strength, I don't think the Czechs were as good as the Russians. So we knew we had to stay out of the penalty box in order to beat them."

But at 3:14 in the first period, defenseman Jim McElmury was penalized for hooking, and Czechoslovakia's Eduard Novak promptly made it 1-0 with a power play goal at 4:32. After trading penalties throughout much of the period—and with goalie Curran making one spectacularly acrobatic save after another in keeping his team in the game—the Americans answered back with a power-play goal of their own.

With two Czechs in the penalty box, Keith "Huffer" Christiansen scored on a loose-puck scramble in front of the net at 16:47 to knot the game at 1-1. The game was tied, but the Czechs clearly dominated the first period, outshooting the U.S. team 19-4.

With the U.S. being badly outplayed and fortunate to be tied, Williamson decided he needed to shake things up between periods.

"We were hanging our heads a little bit. We were tied, but had been outplayed and taken a couple of dumb penalties, so I said to myself, 'Okay, I'm going to have to put on a little act here.' I went into that locker room and went berserk. Here they were playing against this Czech machine, but I told them to forget it."

Their coach's between-periods tantrum worked as the young Americans came out for the second period. For the first half of the period, the Czechs continued dominating the play, but Curran was equal to everything the Czechs shot at him. At 9:41, Ahearn scored his fourth goal of the tournament, putting the U.S. ahead, 2-1.

Three minutes later, the U.S.'s Craig Sarner deflected a McElmury shot from the point past Czech goalie Jiri Holecek to make it 3-1, and suddenly, the U.S. was seemingly in command. After killing off a Christiansen penalty at 16:07, the U.S. once again went on a power play of its own and Frank Sanders blasted a 40-footer past Holecek with 41 seconds left for a 4-1 U.S. lead. Curran continued his spectacular play, making 20 more saves—many of the highlight variety against the Czech's star player, Vaclav Nedomansky, as the U.S. once again was badly outshot in the period, 20-5.

With a 4-1 lead going into the third period, Ron Naslund, who along with Curran was one of the veterans on the team who had played on the U.S. National teams that had taken their lumps a few years before at the hands of the Russians and Czechs, couldn't believe what was happening.

"I was wondering when the roof was going to cave in," said the player affectionately known to his mates as "Daddy Nas."

"We were ahead, 3-1, then 4-1, and I'm thinking, 'Oh my God, we might win this game.' Then we started playing even harder."

At 13:12 of the final period, "Daddy Nas" tipped in the U.S.'s fifth goal to top off a 5-1 win and one of the biggest upsets in U.S. Olympic hockey history at the time. Curran wound up making 51 saves in one of the greatest goaltending performances in U.S. Olympic hockey history. After the game, Curran, a noted chatterbox amongst his teammates who often referred to himself in the third person, was still so focused he was speechless.

"And that wasn't like 'Lefty'," recalled McIntosh. "Because 'Lefty' can talk.'"

The Russian team and coach were thoroughly impressed with the Americans. Despite their star goalie's loss for words after the game, plenty of nonverbal communications between the Americans and Russians occurred the next day. Although neither team could understand the other's respective language, their sentiments came through loud and clear as Tarasov spotted Williamson and ran over to him. The Russian coach dropped to his knees in the snow, bowed to the U.S. coach, then got up and gave him a big bear hug and a kiss on the lips in recognition of America's defeat of the Russians' hated Eastern Bloc rivals.

Perhaps it was the message the U.S. team had delivered to the Czechs in Tokyo—the Czechs were certainly looking over their shoulders every time one of the Americans came near them. Most certainly, it was because of Curran's play. If the international hockey community hadn't taken notice of the Americans up to that point, they surely had their rapt attention now.

"At the time, we didn't know it, but that game was for the silver medal, and I had just played the game of my life," said Curran. "From the second period on, we outplayed them. It was our game. It was so much fun to watch it. I knew the Czechs were right there with the Soviets, and I was thinking, 'We are trashing these guys. We are playing great.' I don't know if they thought it was an aberration, or if they thought the way I thought which was, 'Man, we have just jumped six rungs up the ladder.' But then, of course, a game later. ..."

A collective thought began to permeate the American team's consciousness after beating the Czechs so decisively. As they prepared for their next game—versus the Soviet Union—they told each other, "Hey, we have a chance to do something here."

Born: April 14, 1945 • Jersey No. 30 • Draft No. 231

"I always felt that I had to earn my stripes with that group. It had so much camaraderie. No one ever said anything to make me feel that way. They never made me feel as though I was the 'outside guy.'"

After a stubborn and bitter feud with U.S. Olympic Hockey head coach Murray Williamson, Mike "Lefty" Curran, a 26-year-old teacher and goaltender for the USHL semi-pro Green Bay Bobcats, joined the Olympic squad in mid-January 1972—a little more than three weeks before the team would play its first game at the XIth Olympic Winter Games. Curran was the last piece of Williamson's puzzle, which became the silver medal winning team. Although everything fit together in the end, first some convincing had to occur.

Curran's battle with Williamson dated back to the 1971 World Championships in Bern/Geneva, Switzerland, when the left-handed goaltender decided he couldn't play to his standards following an injury—and that's what he told his coach.

"I hurt my leg pretty bad in the last game we played stateside, and I was on crutches afterward," explained Curran. "We flew out probably three days later, and they decided to keep me over there anyway because of the nature of the injury. It was a bone spur that tore away from the inside of my knee. They brought a third goalie over just in case. I didn't play in any exhibition games. When we opened the tournament, I began to play. I would get some pretty serious shots in my knee with a big needle, and I went out and played. I played the first two games against Sweden and Finland, which we lost. I wasn't happy with the way I was playing. I felt as though I wasn't giving our team a chance to win. My teammates were playing so hard, and you have to have the goaltending.

"It wasn't there for me. I just couldn't perform like I needed to, so I talked to our team doctor and told him, 'This is it.' I wasn't going to play any longer. I wasn't helping the team."

That revelation didn't sit well with Williamson, who felt several others on the team were playing with injuries, so Curran should bury the pain and play as well. Curran didn't see the logic in that scenario, and eventually had a confrontation with Williamson. Curran wanted to return stateside, but Williamson wouldn't allow that to happen, reasoning that it would cost the club far more money to buy the injured goaltender a new ticket. So Curran was forced to stay.

"Murray was mad because he felt that I was going to be his goaltender for that tournament, and I wasn't available. I was mad at him because he didn't support me."

Curran came home from the World Championships and promptly had surgery on his knee to alleviate the problem. He got back on his skates during the summer of 1971 to work a hockey school and told anyone who would listen, including Williamson, that he wasn't interested in playing in next year's Olympic Games. After all, Curran had enough international experience and disappointment to understand the magnitude of what the '72 team would face in February.

"I didn't want to be a part of that. I was going back to Green Bay." Williamson talked to his stubborn goaltender, but they were entrenched in their beliefs about how things happened in Switzerland. "I thought it shouldn't have happened the way it happened in Bern/Geneva. Murray wasn't going to budge on that, so I went on with my life."

Curran went to the Los Angeles Kings training camp in the fall, and Williamson went to Bemidji to train his group of young Americans hungry to make a name for themselves despite everyone's belief—but their own—that they couldn't. Williamson and Curran would cross paths in October when the Olympic team traveled to Green Bay to play an exhibition game. Curran said hello to some of his former teammates but didn't pay too much attention to it afterwards. Curran reasoned that the Olympic team he saw had three goaltenders at the time—Peter Sears, Kim Newman, and Dave Reece.

Williamson was honest with his players—he had Curran in mind to join the team all along. Though the two men were feuding, Williamson knew Curran would probably be in the mix sooner or later.

"As much as I wanted to be an Olympian, I was not going to go until he and I spoke about it," admitted Curran. "We needed to speak about it. Then it was okay. We just agreed to disagree. But until that occurred, it wasn't going to work. Murray made a public statement about it all after the Olympics when he said, 'Lefty and I can only get along for about three weeks.' I liked that."

Williamson also informed Sears, who had played the majority of the pre-Olympic schedule, that the team would probably pick up Curran right before the team traveled to Sapporo and that the lefty would most likely be the starting goaltender.

"At the time, I don't remember Pete and I interacting a lot," said Curran. "I remember him giving me a pat on the back and encouragement. Pete was supportive of me in a quiet way and not in a phony, verbal kind of way. He didn't know me. He was quietly supportive in a beautiful way. It was [the right kind of] support. It actually helped me. I didn't really want to get too involved with Pete at that time. And I don't think Pete felt it was the time for us to start hanging out together either. It was a quiet support. I always admired him for the way he dealt with all of that."

Curran was a veteran of international play, and he knew the odds were long against this U.S. team doing anything more than teams had done in the previous three Olympiads.

He also had no illusions about the magnitude of his position on the '72 team. He was brought in to perform. It wasn't an overwhelming stress, but he certainly felt the burden of responsibility to this group of youngsters who had sacrificed the year preparing for two weeks in February of 1972.

"I was focused on my job, and that was it. In some ways, I probably had more fear in my chest than they had in theirs."

Fear must've been the guiding force when it came time to play the Czechoslovakian Olympic team in Sapporo, because Curran played what some today call, "the greatest game ever played by an American goaltender in the Olympics." At the time, the young Americans didn't know it, but their win versus the medal-favored Czechs turned out to be the silver medal game of the tournament. And Curran, who was "brought in to perform," didn't disappoint. He had the game of his life—maybe of all-time—when he stymied the Czechs on 51-of-52 shots fired his way, but he knew the Soviets loomed as the next opponent.

When the game with the Soviets ended, not one member of the U.S. squad hung his head. They knew going in the Soviets were the best in the world, and a miracle was needed to defeat the Russian juggernaut—a miracle that wouldn't transpire for eight more years.

As time has a way of healing, Curran found new respect for the stubborn coach with whom he locked horns, almost resulting in him missing the Olympics.

"Murray gave a good part of his early life, years when you could be out making a lot of money, developing a U.S. hockey program from as early as 1966, 1967-1973. He was a revolutionary. He did an awful lot for all of us. There was a lot more to Murray than 1972. I'd say he had something to do with 1980, as well as 1972. He was a great American coach and a very significant innovator in developing a USA Hockey program."

Where is he now? Mike Curran, now retired, worked in the trucking business in Maple Grove, Minnesota.

RON NASLUND

Born: February 28, 1944 • Jersey No. 18/22 • Served as a member of Air National Guard—1965-70

"Suffice to say, I didn't sell a hell of a lot of insurance; but that didn't matter."

By October 1971, 27-year-old Ron Naslund had all but retired from hockey. He was a four-time U.S. National team member and had been the last man cut from the 1968 U.S. Olympic hockey team. He had graduated from Denver University in 1965, played international hockey, and was also a player/coach in Lucerne, Switzerland, when he realized he should probably head back home to the United States and find a job. He was selling insurance when the phone rang.

It was the coach of the 1972 U.S. Olympic hockey team, Murray Williamson, who also had coached the 1968 U.S. Olympic hockey team. Williamson's 1972 Olympic team had been playing for nearly eight weeks, and when Naslund answered the phone, he found that his old coach was calling to sell him on giving hockey one last try.

"Come out and try it," Williamson admonished

"I'm too tired and too old," an unimpressed Naslund told Williamson.

But after a couple of more calls, Naslund decided to give it one more shot. "I was the oldest guy on the team. I wasn't that old, but it seemed old then because many of the others were 19 and 20 years old. I was really lucky to make the team."

Naslund grew up in Minneapolis. He used to watch the U.S. National teams, and he always liked the jersey as a kid.

"The first team I ever watched was the 1958 team," remembered Naslund. "I always thought that would be a neat thing to be on the national team."

When he graduated from college, he joined the Air Force in Wyoming. He used to run around Cheyenne, Wyoming, at night.

"I'd run around and do push-ups just to stay in shape," said Naslund.

He came back in 1966 and tried out for the 1966 U.S. National Team. "I couldn't believe that I made the team," admitted Naslund. "We went to Yugoslavia. I was only 22 years old then. It was pretty bleak."

The following year he went over to Vienna with the 1967 U.S. National team. "We had a pretty good team, a lot of good players, and came in fifth."

In the fall and winter of that same year, Naslund played with the 1968 U.S. Olympic team for most of the year before being the last one cut. They ended up coming in sixth at Grenoble, France.

"In 1969, I played on the National team with 'Huffer' Christiansen, Mike Curran, Tim Sheehy, Larry Pleau—he was a great hockey player—and we lost every game. We were 0-10. We lost to the Russians, 17-2."

In 1972, Naslund fit in well enough to affectionately earn the nickname "Daddy Nas," as the graybeard of the peach-faced bunch. When Williamson combined the big winger from Minneapolis with the undersized New England tandem of Robbie Ftorek and Stuart Irving, things clicked.

"I ended up playing with Robbie Ftorek," said Naslund. "He was a marvelous hockey player. I fit in well with him, and my other good buddy, Stuart Irving. There were many skilled guys. I really wasn't one of them, but I just fit in." Naslund fit in well enough to score 17 goals and 20 assists in his 46 games in the pre-Olympic schedule and was a main cog in Williamson's design to shut down their opponents' top lines during the Olympic Games.

How he made it to Sapporo, he still isn't sure. When Williamson called and encouraged him to come out and try one more time, Naslund had conflicting emotions.

"He must've felt I was worth calling, but to this day, I don't know why," said the self-effacing Naslund. "I played for him in 1967, and he cut me in 1968. I couldn't believe that he called me in 1971. I asked, 'Why the hell are you calling me?'"

Not only did Williamson have Naslund in mind, it seemed that he'd created his practice schedules around the only team member with a full-time job.

"I was 27 and needed to get a job," said Naslund. "Most of the other guys were too young or in the Army."

So Naslund sold insurance, trained as an Olympic hockey player, and traveled across the country with the team during its pre-Olympic schedule. With on-ice practices usually around one or two in the afternoon, it literally was "on the job" training for Naslund. His daily routine became regimented.

"I was trying to make some money kind of working for myself in the insurance business," explained Naslund. "I would go to work at about eight in the morning, then go to practice, go home, eat something, go to sleep, then get up the next morning and do it all over. It was a lot of hard work. But it seemed like there was always enough time to do what had to be done. Suffice to say, I didn't sell a hell of a lot of insurance, but that didn't matter."

Despite Williamson's invitation to play, all the time Naslund was pulling double duty between "real life" and his Olympic dream. He never—not even for a minute—thought he was a lock to make the team. Naslund knew from his past experiences with Williamson that nothing was guaranteed—not even for a guy who had known the coach since he was 15 years old.

"I was never sure that I was on the team," admitted Naslund. "All year long, I was playing with Robbie Ftorek and we played very well. There were few teams that ever outplayed us. But I never felt like I was a definite. I was a realist. I sometimes wondered, 'What am I doing out here on the ice against them when I shouldn't even be in the same rink?'

"I was thinking that because that's how good they were. I always thought, 'Am I going to get axed or not?' After a while, I felt as long as I didn't get hurt, I'd be fine—but I never felt that way until January. I just knew that, as long as I kept playing well, I'd be safe. Murray kept bringing in guys. He would bring in guys for about a week, and a lot of them were really good. I'd think, 'Oh shit! I'm outta here.' I don't think there were more than eight or 10 guys out of the whole team that ever felt really safe. There were many good guys floating around. That was always in the back of my mind."

Eventually, Naslund knew he would be accompanying the team to Sapporo because no one told him he wouldn't.

"Basically, I think Murray just told guys who weren't going."

After his 1968 disappointment and his three other national team experiences, Naslund, the insurance salesman, had to take an extended vacation from his day job and tend to the business of representing the United States at the Olympic Winter Games in Sapporo.

Heading to Japan, "Daddy Nas" was the voice of experience, and he knew, as did other U.S. National team veterans Curran, Sheehy, and Christiansen, that winning a medal was going to be a tough order of business for this young group.

At the Opening Ceremony, Naslund and his mates were in awe, but they knew their first game against Switzerland was the key to the tournament. As a former Swiss League player/coach, Naslund warned his young teammates.

"All the guys were thinking, 'It's Switzerland. They can't be that good.' I told them, 'I played there last year, and believe me, these guys are good hockey players—but they're not physical.' They didn't like to get jammed and hacked. We went out and beat the hell out of them. They just quit."

As the tournament progressed, highlighted by the pivotal win against Czechoslovakia, Naslund took especial inventory of how far he and this team had come.

"It was kind of a warm feeling to accomplish something. It was a great feeling to actually win something that's recognized around the world such as an Olympic medal. It was a warm feeling and made me very proud."

More than 30 years later, Naslund still is a realist when it comes to his silver medal-winning experience in 1972.

"In the grand scheme of things in our lives, it was a nice window of fun, happiness, and it was a big deal, but you have to move on," he philosophized. "To tell you the truth, most of my customers don't even know I played hockey.

"One time I was with this guy—he had been a customer for about 10 years—and I was wearing my Olympic ring. He said, 'What's that?' I said, 'Oh, it's my ring from hockey.' He looked at it and said, 'You played

STRIKING SILVER

THE UNTOLD STORY OF AMERICA'S FORGOTTEN HOCKEY TEAM

The Forgotten Team: front row (l-r): Pete Sears, Keith Christiansen, head coach Murray Williamson, manager Hal Trumble, Tim Sheehy, Mike Curran; middle (l-r): Bud Kessel, Bruce McIntosh, Jim McElmury, Larry Bader, Frank Sanders, Ron Naslund, Wally Olds, Charlie Brown, Tim Regan, Dr. George Nagabods; back (l-r): Mark Howe, Craig Sarner, Tom Mellor, Henry Boucha, Dick McGlynn, Kevin Ahearn, Robbie Ftorek, Stu Irving.

Photo appears courtesy of the Murray Williamson collection/USA Hockey.

Twenty-five years later, America's Forgotten Team gathered to remember.

Photo appears courtesy of Mike and Tana Curran.

STRIKING SILVER

THE UNTOLD STORY OF AMERICA'S FORGOTTEN HOCKEY TEAM

Pilgrims' Pride: Members of the U.S. hockey team line up before marching into
the Opening Ceremony of the XIth Olympic Winter Games in Sapporo, Japan.

Photo appears courtesy of Mike and Tana Curran.

Opening Ceremony: The U.S. Olympic team marches into Makomanai Stadium.

Photo appears courtesy of Mike and Tana Curran.

Coach Murray Williamson confers with 1967 U.S. National Team captains and USA Hockey legends Herb Brooks and Bill Masterton.

Photo appears courtesy of the Murray Williamson collection/USA Hockey.

1980 U.S. Olympic coach Herb Brooks sent this note to his friend, former teammate and National and Olympic Team coach Murray Williamson following the "Miracle on Ice" in Lake Placid: "Murray, Your influence as a teammate and coach helped produce this victory—Herb Brooks"

Cartoon appears courtesy of Paul Conrad. Copyright, 1980, Tribune Media Services. Reprinted with permission.

STRIKING SILVER

THE UNTOLD STORY OF AMERICA'S
FORGOTTEN HOCKEY TEAM

Williamson and USSR Olympic hockey coach Anatoly Tarasov engage in hockey détente, with help from a translator, during the 1971 World Championship in Bern/Geneva, Switzerland.

Photo appears courtesy of the Murray Williamson collection/USA Hockey.

Pete Sears served Uncle Sam in 1968 during a tour of duty in Vietnam before making the 1972 Olympic team.

Photo appears courtesy of the Pete and Kay Sears collection.

Stu Irving, shown in front of the net, also saw combat in Vietnam and was pulled from the Mekong Delta to suit up for the U.S. team in Sapporo.

Photo appears courtesy of the Murray Williamson collection/USA Hockey.

New England schoolboy phenom Robbie Ftorek in pre-Olympic action.

Photo appears courtesy of the Murray Williamson collection/USA Hockey.

Tom Mellor and Stu Irving celebrate.

Photo appears courtesy of the Pete and Kay Sears collection.

U.S. goaltender Mike "Lefty" Curran nearly bent over backward to make this save while defenseman Jim McElmury clears Soviet attackers from the front of the net.

Photo appears courtesy of the Murray Williamson collection/USA Hockey.

STRIKING SILVER

THE UNTOLD STORY OF AMERICA'S FORGOTTEN HOCKEY TEAM

Tim Sheehy eyes an open net against Switzerland.

Photo appears courtesy of the Murray Williamson collection/USA Hockey.

Dick McGlynn revels in excitement after he and his mates finished off Poland. He escaped with an American flag souvenir that adorned the team's bench as Mike Curran and Jim McElmury look on.

Photo appears courtesy of the Pete and Kay Sears collection.

Wally Olds, Charlie Brown, and Robbie Ftorek.

Photo appears courtesy of Pete and Kay Sears collection.

Keith Christiansen (8) and Henry Boucha (10) try to connect against legendary USSR goaltender Vladislav Tretiak.
Photo appears courtesy of the Murray Williamson collection/USA Hockey.

Ron "Daddy Nas"
Naslund (22), Kevin
Ahearn, and Craig Sarner.
*Photo appears courtesy of the
Pete and Kay Sears collection.*

STRIKING SILVER

THE UNTOLD STORY OF AMERICA'S FORGOTTEN HOCKEY TEAM

The irony of this telegram from President Richard M. Nixon is not lost. The vast majority of American sports fans had no idea that the U.S. had won the silver in 1972.

Image appears courtesy of Richard McGlynn.

Captain Keith Christiansen accepts the silver medal on behalf of his U.S. teammates.

Photo appears courtesy of the Murray Williamson collection/USA Hockey.

Pete Sears returned to the 1972 Oswego Minor Hockey Association banquet and shared his Olympic experiences with wide-eyed youngsters and their parents including the authors' brother, Kevin.

Photo appears courtesy of the Caraccioli family collection/Floyd Kunzwiler.

in the Olympics? Why didn't you tell me?' I said, 'Why the hell would I tell you that?'"

"Why?" indeed. …

Ron "Daddy Nas" Naslund was selling insurance in the fall of 1971; but by February 1972, he was wearing a silver medal from the XIth Olympic Winter Games.

"I don't think it is something you can live your life on, but it is a bonus."

And that's one bonus that didn't come from selling an insurance policy.

Where is he now? Ron Naslund now works in the insurance business in Minnetonka, Minnesota.

GAME THREE
February 9, 1972—5:03 a.m. EST
USSR 7 - USA 2

"We played as good a game as Team Canada did in their first game of the 'Summit Series.' We were hanging tough. They just beat us."

—U.S. HEAD COACH MURRAY WILLIAMSON

After 47 exhibition games, including five against the Soviet Union, and three games in the Olympic Games, the U.S. reached the point they had been working toward since September in Bemidji. After beating the Czechs, the U.S. had new life, and they were set to take on the mighty Soviet Union. Despite losing to the Russians in each of their five meetings during their pre-Olympic tour, with a 1-1 record in the medal round, the Americans were not going to back down even though they knew the odds of beating them were long.

In Sapporo in 1972, there was no doubt as to who was the best hockey team in the world. This Soviet team, arguably one of the greatest hockey teams of all time, was peppered with some of the greatest international hockey players to ever play, including Valery Kharlamov, Anatoly Firsov, Boris Mikhailov, Vladimir Petrov, Alexander Maltsev and a 19-year-old rookie goaltender, Vladislav Tretiak.

"The Czechs and Swedes were just as talented," said forward Craig Sarner. "But these guys were just so good. They'd skate past us so quick that you would just catch the red. You'd be chasing one guy, and they'd drop it back to the guy behind them, and you'd think, 'What the heck is going on here?' They were just the best. It was like playing against five Michael Jordans making no-look passes like Magic Johnson."

After five exhibition games, a familiar pattern had developed, and the Russians' up-tempo, all-out skating, "shinny hockey" style would quickly produce goals and overwhelm the young Americans. But because of those games, the U.S. team had learned what not to do and adjusted their style of play accordingly for this all-important game. This game started out differently as the U.S. was skating stride for stride with the Soviets for the first half of the first period.

It wasn't until the U.S. team was called for a too-many-men-on-the-ice penalty at 10:46 of the first period that the Russians struck, as Yuri Blinov scored a power-play goal 31 seconds later to give the Russians a 1-0 lead. The Soviets' Kharlamov scored his team's second goal at 15:26 to put his team up 2-0 as the first period ended.

Once again, U.S. goalie "Lefty" Curran was called upon to keep his team in the game by making 19 saves during much of the Russians' first-period onslaught. The Soviets struck quickly in the second period with two goals in a 26-second span as Maltsev made it 3-0 at 4:05, and Vladimir Vikhoulov scored at 4:31 to put the game virtually out of reach.

The Russians made it 5-0 at 8:50, just as Christiansen was returning to the ice after being hauled off for a hooking penalty when the U.S.'s Frank Sanders intercepted a Maltsev pass only to have it redirect off his stick and inadvertently end up in his own goal. Curran continued keeping it as close as he could, with 14 more saves in the second period. Not only was the U.S. team being outscored—the Russians had blasted 69 shots towards Curran, and the U.S. had taken just 28 at Tretiak.

Because part of the tie-breaking system was based on goals-for and goals-against, the Soviets were not about to let up on the Americans as they did at Madison Square Garden. The U.S. finally broke through in the third period, as Sanders made up for his earlier miscue by scoring at the 4:26 mark to make it 5-1. The Russians answered right back less than three minutes later, as Yevgeny Zimine scored to make it 6-1, and Guennady Tsygankov added another at 8:57 of the third period to make it 7-1.

Despite being down, the Americans continued to play the Russians tough as Ahearn scored at 16:01 to round out the scoring. At one point, Robbie Ftorek found himself up against Kharlamov.

"He got a step on me during a power play, and I was in big trouble so I speared him and pulled him back," said Ftorek. "He kinda looked at me like, 'What the hell are you doing? I understand Huffer doing that, but you—you don't play that way.' I could see it in his eyes. I don't know if he understood me or not, but I said, 'I gotta keep you from beating me, and I'll play that way if you get a step on me in an Olympic game.'"

For the third consecutive game, Curran delivered a stellar performance—making 43 saves overall. The final score may have read USSR 7 - USA 2, but the score wasn't completely indicative of the closeness of the game. The U.S. once again had a goal called back and later in the game saw a Russian player block a sure goal as he dove across an open Soviet net to make the save with his head.

Though it was another loss in the medal round, the U.S. took solace in a moral victory as they had played the Russians even from 8:50 of the second period to the conclusion of the game.

"We played as good a game as Team Canada did in their first game of the 'Summit Series,'" said Williamson. "We were hanging tough. They just beat us."

The Americans had played their best game against the Russians, and their confidence was boosted for their final two games against Finland and Poland.

The Americans took a record of 1-2 into their next game of the medal round, but they also took with them the confidence of knowing that, if they play as well as they played in the final period and a half against the Russians, they still had a shot. However, they had to win both of those games if they had any chance at a medal.

Born: May 28, 1955 • Jersey No. 14 • Draft No. Not old enough

"I was sitting in the back seat and can remember thinking, 'Oh shit, if my Mom could see me now she'd have a heart attack.' I had been away from home but nothing like this on my own."

Mark Howe was the ripe old age of 16 when he joined the 1972 U.S. Olympic hockey team just weeks before the team left for Sapporo. Though his mother worried that he would miss too much school, playing for his country at the 1972 Olympic Winter Games taught him more than she or he could have imagined.

"I remember leaving the rink that first day. We were heading down one of the freeways in Minneapolis, and we got off at the wrong exit," said Howe, who following practice that first day was taken under the collective wings of New England teammates and roommates Robbie Ftorek, Stu Irving, and Dick McGlynn. "Dick was driving, and he stopped right in the middle of the exit ramp, put the car in reverse, and started heading back for the freeway. I was sitting in the back seat and can remember thinking, 'Oh shit, if my Mom could see me now, she'd have a heart attack.' I had been away from home but nothing like this on my own."

Howe, who had only just obtained his driver's license a few months before, was an 11th-grade high school student chasing girls and living life without a care when he was plucked from his Junior team in Detroit and asked to try out for the U.S. Olympic team in December 1971. That meant the teenager would have to leave school, go to Minnesota, and try out for a team that would be heading for the Olympic Games in Sapporo in just three weeks.

"I remember my Mom didn't want me to miss too much school and was trying to make sure that, if I went out to Minneapolis, I had a spot on the team," recalls one of the NHL's premier defenseman of his time. "I remember telling her, 'No, I just want to go out there and have a chance.' If I did well, I'd make it. If I didn't, I'd be back. It worked out well."

When Howe arrived in Minneapolis, he went to the rink and was immediately asked how much money he would need to live each week. The 16-year-old, away from home for the first time for any extended period of time, thought $50 could get him through okay. Management gave him $150 for living expenses, and Ftorek, Irving and McGlynn invited him to live with them. Howe was amenable, thanked the trio, and headed to his new home away from home.

He is the son of hockey legend Gordie Howe. In 1972, no shadow cast further than the NHL's "Mr. Hockey," and anyone who played the game knew Mark Howe's hockey pedigree was purebred—that he was just 16 years old didn't matter.

When the U.S. team made its final swing through Detroit before heading to Sapporo, "Mr. Hockey" was there to meet his son's new teammates. When the younger Howe introduced his father to McGlynn, the spirited defenseman could only imagine what the elder Howe had heard from his son. The hockey legend extended his bear claw hand to McGlynn, and said with a pause, "So you're Dick McGlynn ... I want to thank you for taking care of my son Mark."

Howe nearly didn't play on the U.S. Olympic team at all—it turned out to be a twist of fate. In May 1971, Howe was looking forward to playing Junior Hockey in Toronto when he suffered a bad knee injury during a playoff game in Detroit. He was told that he had suffered torn ligaments, but that it would heal okay.

But by the time September rolled around, Howe's knee didn't get better. The doctors had misdiagnosed the problem and told him he would require surgery for torn cartilage. Rather than go to Toronto, Howe decided to stay in Detroit, convalesce, and play another year with his Junior team in the Motor City.

"Had I gone up to Toronto, I don't believe I would've been able to play with the Olympic team because you were considered a pro at the time if you received $10 per week for spending money," explained Howe. "I had the surgery, and my first game back was an exhibition game at the Olympia against the U.S. National team."

Howe's transition to international hockey was made easier because, although he was young, his frame was thick—180 sturdy pounds of muscle and youth. He also could skate. And skating was one of the key components to Coach Williamson's overall design for the 1972 U.S.

team. The fleet-footed Howe quickly realized that his role on the team was to go out, be aggressive, create some energy, and then go to the end of the bench and watch.

"My job was to chip in by banging some bodies, killing the odd penalty, and providing some energy," remembers Howe. "It was so different from the way I had played because I wasn't a banger as a kid. One thing I learned to do very well from my father was to keep my eyes open. I learned a lot. Between our games, Robbie took me to watch the Soviets, Swedes, and Czechs play. The whole thing was just a great, great learning experience."

The Games passed by quickly, and the experience was over almost before it began. But the youngest player to ever play on a U.S. Olympic hockey team soaked it all in—though his memories aren't filled with the games so much as what occurred around him during the Olympic Games. Some of the experience was great, while other parts were taxing on the youngster. Because of his last name, he unwillingly became the face of this lunch bucket brigade—the guy every journalist around the world knew. It was difficult for the youngster to fathom and comprehend. Ftorek helped steer the eventual four-time First-Team NHL All-Star through the rigors that awaited him off the ice. Howe remembers some of the other off-ice activities most about his Olympic experience.

Howe had never been away from home for more than a couple of days. Yet, the next thing he knew, he was in a car on a Minneapolis freeway driven—in reverse—by McGlynn; in Colorado training to get used to altitude; and then sitting in Tokyo with Ftorek as he wrote a letter to his girlfriend at the time.

"I was sitting in the hotel room watching *Bonanza* dubbed in Japanese on television and there was a little Earth tremor," remembers Howe. "The lamps were falling off the table and I said, 'Hell on this, I'm getting outta this room.'"

The youngster went to the five-decker driving range downstairs and spent the 1972 equivalent of seven or eight dollars hitting a bucket of golf balls.

The Olympic Village was another place where the impressionable future NHLer had indelible memories etched. As he made his way through the onslaught of new experiences—new friends and teammates, a new role from scorer to grinder, new coach, and new style of play—Howe also took time to watch and learn. In Gordie Howe, son Mark had the perfect role model to fashion his game and career—especially how to act and play like a professional.

"It was my first experience in a dorm-like situation and we had the four of us in it—two bedrooms with single beds. Every morning, we'd hear this noise at 6:00 a.m., and we'd be thinking, 'What the hell is going on?' We'd look outside and it was the Russian guys in a group playing soccer or running or doing something and we'd all be sound asleep. We just wondered, 'What the hell were they doing?'"

Though Howe's mother was worried her son was missing too much school, "Mrs. Hockey" had no idea the things her son was learning in Japan would carry a lifetime of lessons both professionally and culturally. Howe's memories of the Olympic Village weren't confined just to the dorms; nor was his hockey education in Sapporo limited to how great the Russians were on the ice.

Howe also remembered that the Russians after games would take off their skates and gloves, put their shoes on, and run the two miles back to the Village. He and his teammates would go back to the Village, shower, get cleaned up, and be sitting in the cafeteria. They would start to eat when a foul stench pervaded the air.

Howe remembered thinking, "What the hell is that smell?"

As he and the rest of his teammates soon found out, it was the Russian team.

"They had come in, taken off their gear, sat down, and ate. They didn't get cleaned up, shower, or anything. I remember that as plain and vivid as all hell. Those are the kind of things that stick out to me. It was just amazing to see how they lived and how they trained. It was just so different from anything I'd ever seen before."

The young American had received a first-hand look at just how different it was for the players overseas.

"Nobody was like the Soviets, because you didn't see anybody else running home from the rink as a group," said Howe. "You didn't see anybody else training at six o'clock in the morning. They must have trained six hours on the day of a game. You just didn't see that anywhere else."

Mark Howe took his Olympic experience and launched a 22-year professional career that included four seasons playing with his father and brother, Marty, on the Houston Aeros of the World Hockey Association, where he won back-to-back Avco Cup championships. When the WHA folded and teams were welcomed into the NHL, Howe became a member of the Hartford Whalers for four years and then a stalwart member and 10-year veteran of the Philadelphia Flyers.

In Philadelphia, Howe became one of the National Hockey League's premiere defensemen, helping lead the Flyers to three Stanley Cup Finals and becoming a three-time Norris Trophy runner-up as the league's top defenseman. But it was in Sapporo, Japan, that the seeds of his illustrious professional career were sown.

"The way I looked at it for my career, it was a huge stepping-stone," remembers Howe. "I learned more in the six weeks I was gone than I learned in years and years of going to school. I mean, just about life in general—and just seeing the talent of players from overseas, watching the Soviets play was a whole new level. Coach Williamson pushed me hard. I was a scorer. But when I went to that team, I wasn't. I was the guy who provided energy. I had to fit into a role, and so for me, it was a completely different experience—a tremendous learning experience."

He also learned about generosity amongst teammates. Always known as a good teammate, Howe can look back at his reception to a team just three weeks from heading off to Japan for the Olympics. It was a team that shuffled players in and out of training camp for months on end. It was a team that could have easily resented the teenager as a publicity stunt—"Son of Hockey Legend Plays for U.S."

But they didn't. Nobody showed him any resentment at all.

"Actually, the guys were very nice to me."

Ftorek, who was 19 at the time, was the closest in age. Some of the guys were from Minnesota, and they had their own routines. Some of the others had wives and families. Most of Howe's contact with the guys was at and around the rink. After that, he spent almost all of his time with his three roommates.

"I don't think anyone really lost their spot," remembers Howe. "I think one guy got hurt and couldn't play. All the guys that were there were settled in and ready to play. The best thing that happened to me was living with Stu, Robbie, and Dick. Even though all three of their personalities were so different, those three guys just helped me tremendously. Stuey was pretty quiet, Dick was very outgoing, and Robbie was a down-to-Earth guy. I ended up rooming with Robbie when we went overseas. He definitely helped me out quite a bit."

Even as a wide-eyed teenager, Howe realized the massive accomplishment of this hockey band of brothers, who adopted the 11th grader in the 11th hour. As Howe stood in the back of the pack, silver medal hanging from his neck, it finally struck him that this moment was something to savor.

"I remember looking up at the flag, and that's when I realized what an honor it was to play and represent your country. No matter what I did, I always gave the best I could. Seeing the flag of your country being raised—even though there was one a little higher than ours—was my fondest moment."

When he returned from the Olympics, a harbinger of his future occurred as he sat with his family and friends watching the 1972 Summit Series. As Howe told stories of seeing Valery Kharlamov shake off three cross-checking Czech defenders—while bouncing the puck in the air with his stick and then swatting the disk into the net—he told his father how impressive the Russian players were, and the team of NHL All-Stars would have their hands full.

As Canada jumped out to a quick 2-0 lead in the first three minutes, family members started to mock the youngest Howe saying, "Hell, you're a really good scout, you know a lot."

When the final horn sounded to end Game 1 of that historic series, though, the youngest Howe had the last laugh: Team Russia 7 – Team Canada 3.

Where is he now? Mark Howe is now a consultant and scout for the Detroit Red Wings.

ROBBIE FTOREK

Born: January 2, 1952 • Jersey No. 11 • Draft No. 225

"I had no idea I was at the Olympic tryouts. I was 19 years old. Ice was ice. It was free, so I was on it."

If you grew up in hockey circles in the late 1960s and early 1970s, especially in New England, you remember Robbie Ftorek as a schoolboy hockey phenom from Needham, Massachusetts. Others remember him as a hockey pioneer and one of the few American players who made an inroad in the NHL when nearly everyone who played was Canadian. Ftorek broke in with the Detroit Red Wings, spent time with the Quebec Nordiques, and finished his NHL playing career with the New York Rangers. Along the way, he also played in Phoenix and Cincinnati in the WHA and held head coaching positions with the Los Angeles Kings, New Jersey Devils, and Boston Bruins.

Growing up, Ftorek lived for sports, whether it was hockey, soccer or baseball. But he wasn't the type that was born with a stick and puck in his crib. Oddly enough, Ftorek started out as a figure skater. With the Olympic figure skating coach Maribel Vinson Owen working in Needham with his number one-ranked daughter, Ftorek's skating future may very well have emulated Dick Button more than Bill Cleary.

In 1961, following a tragic plane crash that killed the majority of the figure skating group and team as they returned from a competition in Europe, his aspirations turned to hockey full-time.

"I was about eight years old at the time," remembers Ftorek. "My Dad took me to a Bruins game. After the game, I was taken to the Bruins' locker room, where I was given a stick and met the team. They all signed my stick, cut down another stick to my size, gave me a puck, tapped me on the butt, and said, 'Good luck, kid.' I imagine that evening is when I decided I was going to be a professional hockey player."

During that time, Ftorek's future Olympic path would cross with one of the legends of the gold medal-winning 1960 U.S. Olympic hockey team. Ftorek's father had season tickets to the Bruins with a friend of his. Ftorek was a small player as a man, and even a smaller child, so his dad would sneak him into the game under his coat.

"We had an aisle seat, so I would sit there on the corner," said Ftorek. "The guy in front of me would tell me, 'Tonight, we're going to watch Gordie Howe or whomever.'"

Ftorek would watch the game and the man in front of him would be explaining from the corner of his mouth what was happening on the ice. Between periods, they would talk more about the game. The man talking out of the side of his mouth during those Bruins games turned out to be Bill Cleary.

As a young player, Ftorek never gave the Olympics one thought—even though he remembered watching Cleary and his brother, Bob, win gold in Squaw Valley. The single-mindedness he carries today as a coach was apparent even in his developing years.

"I was focused on whatever game we were playing, whether it was Melrose, or Cohasset, or Worcester—or a soccer game we were playing or a baseball game we were playing," recalls Ftorek. "I'm very much right into the moment and not looking down the road very much. I never even thought about the Olympics. Not even once."

The same could not be said about Ftorek's father. The Ftoreks lived in New Hampshire during the summer, and Robbie enjoyed getting away and spending summer weekends in the Granite State. One day when Ftorek was 19 years old, his father mentioned that he wanted his son to join him. They were going to pick up some ice time over the weekend. Ftorek blindly told his father he had no interest in disrupting the vacation he was currently enjoying. After his father persisted, the son grudgingly relented but had a few questions as they drove south towards Boston.

"What is it?" asked the younger Ftorek.

"It'll be good," replied his Dad vaguely. "These are good players, and you just go out and play. We'll go down to Billerica on Friday, play, and then we'll come back."

"Who's going to be there? Are any of my friends?" Ftorek continued.

"Nope, another group of guys," said his dad.

"Will I know any?" Ftorek asked.

"You'll know some of them. Some of the guys you played against in Cohasset," explained the elder Ftorek.

"Great, the guys from BU," replied younger Ftorek unenthusiastically.

Ftorek and his father arrived at the Forum in Billerica, just north of Boston, and Robbie was sent off hearing his father say, "You're here, you might as well go make the most of it."

When Ftorek finally hit the ice, it became immediately apparent to him that this was no ordinary weekend ice time.

"This isn't a game," Ftorek remembers thinking. "This is a friggin' tryout. This is crazy." When the "ice time" was over, Ftorek showered, changed, got into the car, and took off back to New Hampshire.

"How'd you do?" asked his father.

"I didn't even know those guys, but it was good," said Ftorek.

No sooner had the Ftoreks returned to their "vacation" when the phone rang.

"We're going to skate again tomorrow," said his father.

"What? Where now?" clamored the teenager.

"We're going back down there and playing again," explained his dad.

"Fine, we'll go down," said Ftorek.

Ftorek remembers thinking, "It was free ice, good competition, and I loved to skate."

Only this time, when the Ftoreks returned, people started talking to him, asking him questions. Ftorek had a reporter surprisingly ask him how he thought he was doing.

"What do you mean how am I doing?" Ftorek replied.

"This is tryouts for the Olympics," said the reporter.

"What tryouts for the Olympics?" asked Ftorek.

Ftorek's dad never told him a thing other than to have fun out there.

"I had no idea I was at the Olympic tryouts. I was 19 years old. Ice was ice. It was free so I was on it."

Robbie Ftorek just turned 20 years old when he laced up his skates in Sapporo. In Bemidji during training camp and the exhibition season, Ftorek roomed with fellow New Englanders Stu Irving and Dick McGlynn. When the group bonded as a team, they became brothers. It was a bond that was cemented in pride and competition between the 20 members of the team.

Ftorek became one of the quiet leaders of the team through his pure joy in playing. As many of his teammates soon came to realize following all the practices, workouts, and games, Ftorek was always playing something.

"It was good being with Robbie because he was so active all the time," remembers Stu Irving. "After practice, we'd go have lunch and then head over to the Y or the Decathlon Club, where the Vikings used to train. Robbie, Dickie McGlynn, Tommy Mellor, and I would work out there every day. We'd play racquetball or paddle ball."

Ftorek's leadership was always focused on the team. In his way of thinking, there was no such thing as an individual star—someone who would be responsible for winning or losing. He was, and still is, a team guy. It didn't take long for the 1972 team to gel.

"You made inroads because you had to play with the guy. If you didn't talk to the guy, how could you be the best you could be?"

Ftorek centered the first line along with Irving and 27-year-old insurance salesman Ron "Daddy Nas" Naslund. The trio consisted of the near-Lilliputian Ftorek and Irving, along with Naslund, who filled up his side of the ice with a six-foot-two, 185-pound body that kept opponents honest if they ever thought about taking a run at his smaller, talented linemates. One of the things that separated Ftorek and his linemates—and made them valuable to an always-tinkering coach—was their ability to skate. The three forwards were interchangeable on the ice, crisscrossing, darting in and out while holding onto the puck—a distinctly different style of play than the "dump-and-chase" hockey they grew up playing. Ftorek and Irving especially thrived in this type of play during the pre-Olympic schedule.

As they got closer to the Olympic Games, Coach Williamson asked Ftorek, Irving, and Naslund to become the team's checking line, which meant they would play against the other team's top lines with the job of keeping them off the score sheet. The coach was not concerned with what they did offensively, despite the fact that all three of the linemates were among the top 10 leading scorers on the team during the pre-Olympic exhibition games. Ftorek scored 25 goals and had 72 points, fourth on the team; Naslund netted 17 goals and 37 points, eighth on the team; and Irving scored 20 goals and 36 points, ninth on the team.

"It didn't bother me because whatever he told us to do, we did," said Ftorek.

In mid-December, Ftorek's quiet leadership manifested itself even more when 16-year-old Mark Howe was asked to join the Olympic team just a few weeks before they traveled to Sapporo.

"Mark was in a tough spot," remembers Ftorek.

Ftorek, along with Irving and McGlynn took the teenage Howe under their collective wing and showed him the way. Ftorek grew to learn enough about the level he was playing to insure Howe would not be misled. He knew Howe was gifted with size and was mature enough physically. But Ftorek also knew the off-ice glare of being Gordie Howe's son would be bright. And he knew the teenager would need guidance in that area when they got to Japan. Nobody really understood how tough it was for the son of the man known as "Mr. Hockey." But Ftorek had an idea, and he tried to shelter Howe as best he could. When it came time to fulfill media requests, Ftorek played the role of older brother, PR man and teammate. That type of leadership made Ftorek as integral off the ice as he was on the ice.

The quiet leadership Ftorek possessed made him especially interesting when he decided to speak his mind. It wasn't very often, and to Ftorek's recollection, it only happened once, but it's a good example of what made him so valuable to the team.

"I went out and played the best I could," said Ftorek. "Murray used to tell me what I didn't do right, and I tried to fix it. He told us he wanted us to be a checking line and play against the best lines on the other teams. It was fun and a responsibility in which we took a lot of pride. At one point, there was some talk of changing lines. I was in the cafeteria, and I heard that. So, I left there and walked over to Murray's room. It was very uncharacteristic of me. I knocked on the door and I asked him if we could talk. I told him I heard there might be some lines being changed. He just listened and didn't say much. But I said, 'You gotta do what you gotta do, but I sure as hell hope you don't change our line—because we're a checking line and we've been together all this long while doing what we're supposed to be doing. Now we're going to be changing lines just for changing lines' sake? You can do what you want, but I don't think you should change our line."

Coming from the kid who rarely registered a whisper when it came to questioning authority, Williamson took notice, smirked, and replied, "Okay, it's nice to hear from you." Ftorek, Irving, and Naslund went on to register three goals and four assists during the Olympic tournament while facing off against some of the greatest players of their time and in the tournament—including Russia's Kharlamov, Czechoslovakia's superstar Nedomansky, and Sweden's Hammarstrom.

Admittedly, Ftorek has been a bit of a recluse when it comes to keeping in touch with his 1972 Olympic brethren.

"I read all the e-mails the boys send around," he said. "I don't get overly active in it. I communicate once in a while but very seldom."

Remaining true to the quiet confidence he displayed more than 30 years ago, Ftorek never forgets what it meant to him to don the sweater with "USA" on the front.

"It's a goose-bump thing. Almost every time we went on the ice, we said, 'Come on boys—it's us against them.' It was very personal. It was not only we're better than you on the ice, but we're better than you as a country; and it was very, very important."

What's not so important to the current head coach of the Albany River Rats, but nonetheless confounding, is the 1972 team's place in Olympic hockey history. Like many of his teammates, Ftorek is quick to point out that his 1972 team is most certainly forgotten in the annals of U.S. Olympic hockey.

"If you ask anybody, even hockey people, about Olympic medals, they only know two," said Ftorek. "Even my kids—my players—when they find out that I played on an Olympic team, it's kind of fun because it's always, 'When did you play?' I never say what we did. I always wait to see if anybody asks, and they usually do with, 'So, where'd you finish?' I tell them we won a silver medal. They always say, 'Did you really? No way!' It's always the same reaction from everybody. And that's fine. The guys that were there and the family members know what happened. They are friends, and each and every one of us knows what we did and how we did it."

After a career in which he made a name for himself in the NHL as one of the top American players of his time in a league dominated by Canadians, Ftorek has sipped from the Stanley Cup as a member of the New Jersey Devils organization and guided the Los Angeles Kings and his hometown Boston Bruins as a head coach. But one of the greatest highlights of his career remains being a member of the 1972 U.S. Olympic hockey team.

"We all take a lot of pride in the fact that we're the 'team that no one remembers.' That's a great thing to be able to hang your hat on because we all remember one another."

And they all have a little token that also lets them forever remember they were part of something unforgettable in Japan.

Where is he now? Robbie Ftorek is now head coach of the Albany River Rats in Albany, New York.

TOM MELLOR

Born: January 27, 1950 • Jersey No. 4 • Draft No. 355

"Of all of the times I played hockey, scoring my first NHL goal and all that, there was no bigger thrill than playing for the Olympic team."

In 1971, Boston College defenseman Tom Mellor was like most college students entering their senior years. After some good experiences playing for one of the most prestigious college hockey programs in the East, Mellor began thinking about his future.

For most college students who don't grow up on skates and aren't lucky enough to earn a scholarship, the road to their professional future most likely involves a well-placed internship that, hopefully, will land them a job following graduation. If you're lucky, that internship comes between the junior and senior year.

Tom Mellor was 21 years old in 1971, and his "internship" fell into his lap in the spring of that year. And his mentor was a squatty, internationally savvy, hockey coach from Minnesota who had decided he was going to shake up USA Hockey, try some new techniques, and create a new approach to how Americans would play.

"I actually met Murray Williamson in the spring of 1971," remembers Mellor. The '71 U.S. National team was preparing for the World Championships in Bern/Geneva, when one of the team's defensemen was injured.

"They were short a defenseman who was hurt. I was playing for Boston College completing my junior year, and former BC All-American Tim Sheehy was one of the guys on the national team. I think the coach may have said, 'Who's around?' and Sheehy said, 'You might want to call this guy.' And I got a call from Murray."

The timing worked serendipitously for Mellor, who was sitting out the last game of his junior season after being suspended for fighting, plus BC had been eliminated from the playoff picture. With Mellor not obliged to stay with his Eagle teammates for the last week of the season, he joined the U.S. National team in Montreal.

"We played against the 1971 Montreal Canadiens in the Forum with guys like Guy Lafleur, Yvan Cournoyer, Marcel Dionne, and the place was packed," recalled Mellor. "I played and we beat them that night, and I remember my first time on the ice. I was on the bench for the first period with stars in my eyes. I'm wearing the USA jersey and it's the Montreal Forum. We get a bench penalty, and Murray looks at me and says, 'Okay, you go serve the penalty.' So I hop over the boards, and as I'm skating, I turn back to ask, 'Should I go back on the ice or come back to the bench?' As I turned, I caught an edge, and I fell—here's this guy who just gets on the ice and I fall."

Mellor's eyes were opened wide in his first experience playing international hockey. Up until the 1971 World Championship, Mellor was accustomed to the "old style" North American hockey play of dump-and-chase. Though Bobby Orr was redefining the offensive role of defensemen, that style of play was the exception, not the rule. The experience Mellor gained from the '71 World Championship taught him a valuable lesson in international hockey, and it put him a step closer to his dream of one day competing in the Olympics.

"My first taste of international hockey was against Czechoslovakia," remembered Mellor. "We came out against the Czechs and I'm skating around looking at their white skates, their sticks, the fluffy jerseys. They were wearing belts instead of suspenders, and I'm laughing to myself thinking, 'We are going to kick their asses.' And the rinks are bigger. Well, they dropped the puck, and we never saw it in the first period." Lesson learned.

Mellor had a step up on all but a handful of Olympic dreamers when it came time to try out for the '72 Olympic squad. It was already known that Williamson would serve as head coach of the Olympic team while he coached the '71 National team, and Mellor sponged the intricacies of the international game from a coach he was learning to respect without question or hesitation. Having decided to postpone his senior season at Boston College, Mellor pushed fulltime for a spot on the Olympic team and the fulfillment of his life-long dream.

As a berth on the Olympic team started to come into focus, Mellor constantly thought of his first teacher, his father Don.

"My dad was my hero," said Mellor. "He played on the Boston Olympics in 1941-42, went to war, and was a great hockey player. He had been invited to the Olympic camp in 1948, but he had a job. It was an interesting time. It was very different back then. I remember him telling me he would have a job, and then he'd hop on the train. The train would start up in Boston, and they'd have five players on it. It would stop in Rhode Island, and he and another guy would get on. Then it would stop in New Haven, Connecticut. By the time it reached Madison Square Garden, they would have a team. They would play against the New York Rovers and then go down to Washington and play. He was a telephone man, and he injured his ankle playing hockey and wasn't able to climb the pole for a while. His bosses said to him, 'You either play hockey or work.' So he retired from hockey. But he brought me out when I was about six or seven years old. He'd skate. He'd coach the team. He was my hero."

Mellor had been on a steady climb toward the Olympic Games—whether he knew it right away or not. Williamson would take the BC defenseman under his wing in 1971, but it was years before that other signs were appearing. "I was one of those hockey fans who had pillow cases of the original six teams. I would draw the teams with crayons and plaster them in my room. I went to my first hockey camp when I was 13 years old up in Fennelon Falls, Ontario."

Mellor's father had made the acquaintance of a fellow Cranston, Rhode Island, hockey father who had sent his son to Northwood Prep School in Lake Placid. Mellor's father thought that might be a good route for his 14-year-old son to take to learn more about the game and develop. While the younger Mellor was playing in Lake Placid, he crossed paths with a future '72 teammate who also had visions of Olympic rings in his eyes—Pete Sears.

"At the end of my sophomore year, I was selected to play in what was called a Junior Olympic Tournament, which was held in Lake Placid. There were teams from Chicago, Detroit, Boston, maybe two or three other places. They recruited some players from the northern New York area including Peter Sears, whom I remembered hearing his name. I remember thinking: 'This guy is incredible.' We went to the finals of the tournament and ended up losing to Boston, but he was an amazing goaltender. He was a low-key guy who kept to himself, but man, could he perform. He was an acrobat out there."

The Olympic tryouts were an unexpected destination for Mellor as he traveled through the ranks of minor hockey, high school, prep school, and college. When he finally made his way to Bemidji after being selected to participate in the pre-Olympic schedule, he knew the lessons he learned along the way were about to pay off.

In Williamson, Mellor found a new hockey mentor and the young defensemen used his early hockey experiences, and the people he had met along the way, to his advantage when it came time for training and the pre-Olympic schedule.

"Our training camp was really unbelievable as far as being up early, running," said Mellor. "We were on the ice two or three times a day. There was tennis. There was so much activity. He had us doing exercises taken from the ski teams in Switzerland. Murray brought in a guy, Ron Hall, whom we nicknamed 'Hawaiian Eye.' This was amazing at that time. There wasn't anything about, 'Have your steak and get your rest.' It was get up, get out, and get the blood going."

When the time came to start playing the pre-Olympic schedule, Williamson scheduled the Cleveland Barons as the first two opponents for his young, impressionable squad.

"It was our third time on the ice that day," recalled Mellor. "We had a good work out, another skate in the afternoon, then we played them at night. And we just kicked their asses. Here were these pros, and we were saying, 'Oh man, this is a good club. I think we're going to be overmatched.' We just poured right through them. After, we were saying, 'Wow, this is good stuff. We have a pretty good club here.'"

The fruits of their labor manifested on the nights of September 23-24, as they handily beat the Barons, 5-3 and 6-2, respectively. Williamson's innovative approach was working, and Mellor, along with his teammates, was soaking up every word and idea Williamson was espousing. Months later in Sapporo, Japan, those words, ideas, and actions translated into Olympic silver for the highly underrated U.S. squad.

Mellor's lessons didn't end in the pre-Olympics or even in Sapporo—and it wasn't only Williamson who helped shape the young New Englander.

"I remember after the Czechoslovakia-Russia game was over and going out onto the ice to shake Tarasov's hand. I had my glove on. And he looked at me, he was a big bear of a guy, and took my glove off and threw it to the ground, and he pumped my hand. Even today, if I ever have a glove on, I'm going to take that glove off before I shake hands. It was a lesson that Tarasov taught me."

On the Russian's bus following the medal ceremony, Mellor and Stu Irving both realized how much alike the two cultures were despite their Cold War political contemporaries in Washington and Moscow. As the young Americans sat at the front of the bus with their shiny silver medals draped proudly around their white turtlenecked sweaters, they soaked in a celebration that has never been forgotten.

Mellor also remembered thinking how different the Russians were because they hugged and kissed each other. Different? Maybe. But he realized he had learned lessons from that group of men sitting in the back of the bus singing and celebrating that would resonate and stay with him for the rest of his life.

And just like in school, sometimes you have good teachers who inspire you—Murray Williamson—and bad teachers who don't.

"When I went to play for Detroit after the Olympics, Alex Delvecchio was the coach," said Mellor. "You won't find a bigger slacker in hockey than Alex Delvecchio. When he would coach, we would do a couple of one-on-ones, two-on-twos, three-on-twos, we'd scrimmage, and he would scrimmage with us. At the end of the scrimmage, we'd do a couple of figure eights and then go to the bar. That was the NHL and pro mentality."

For Mellor, graduating to the NHL wasn't even as big a thrill than when he played on the 1972 U.S. Olympic team. The lessons he learned and experiences he had are what resonate in his mind when he looks back on his hockey career.

"The Olympic thing—when I first put that red, white, and blue jersey on—was something really special. It was unbelievable. Of all of the times I played hockey, scoring my first NHL goal and all that, there was no bigger thrill than playing for the Olympic team."

Where is he now? Tom Mellor now works in investments in Boston.

GAME FOUR
February 10, 1972—5:00 a.m. EST
USA 4 - FINLAND 1

"We were prepared for Finland, and we just dominated them. There was no question about it. We just flat-out beat them. They never had a chance. We played very, very well."

—MIKE "LEFTY" CURRAN

If the U.S. win over Czechoslovakia was highlighted by the play of "Lefty" Curran, one could argue that the game against Finland was highlighted by the scoring of Henry Boucha and Craig Sarner—and once again by the goaltending of Curran. Playing with newfound confidence, the U.S. team knew if they won their final two games, they would definitely have a chance of attaining their goal from the beginning—an Olympic medal.

The start of the game saw the Americans take a page from the Russians' playbook. Boucha won the opening face-off and slid it over to Sarner, who streaked down the right side and sent a blistering shot from the top of the face-off circle past Finnish goalie Jorma Voltenen for a 1-0 U.S. lead—just 15 seconds into the game. But the Finns responded with a power-play goal by Lauri Mononen to tie it at 1-1 at 4:35 after Boucha was sent to the penalty box for roughing. Boucha made up for his transgression nine minutes later, when he and Sarner teamed up again to put the Americans up 2-1. This time it was Boucha with the goal on a Sarner assist at 13:35.

Although the U.S. was up 2-1 after the first period, a familiar trend was holding true as the Americans were outshot once again by their opponents. Curran made 12 saves compared to his counterpart's six. As the second period progressed, the U.S. started to put their stamp on this game when Frank Sanders scored at 8:37 of the period to make it 3-1. The game stayed that way until the last minute of play, when Ahearn notched a power-play goal with 22 seconds remaining with assists going to Boucha and Sarner. Curran ended up making 35 saves, and the U.S. players could sense they were on a roll.

"We were prepared for Finland, and we just dominated them," said Curran. "There was no question about it. We just flat-out beat them. They never had a chance. We played very, very well."

The U.S. team had one more game to go after evening their record in the medal round. They started doing the math and knew if they beat Poland, and certain things happened in the other games, they would at least have a chance at a bronze.

Born: June 1, 1951 • Jersey No. 10 • Draft No. 32

"I wanted to play in the National Hockey League at some point, but I really wanted to play for the United States in the Olympics."

Henry Boucha was a "can't-miss" member of the 1972 U.S. Olympic hockey team. As an 18-year-old schoolboy hero from Warroad, Minnesota, Boucha had any one of four options coming off his senior year—in which his team lost the 1969 Minnesota High School hockey state championship in a heartbreaking overtime game.

"I was recruited pretty heavily and signed a letter of intent to the University of Minnesota but changed my mind and went to play Junior Hockey in Canada," remembered Boucha. "I could've played with the Montreal Junior Canadiens. I had a plane ticket lying on my kitchen table, but I ended up going to Winnipeg and playing in Western Canada."

After Coach Murray Williamson saw the talented Minnesota teenager play in Winnipeg, Boucha was presented with his fourth option—an opportunity to try out for the 1970 U.S. National team. Boucha jumped in his car, traveled from Winnipeg to Minneapolis, tried out for the U.S. team, and was notified he had made it. There was no drama, no build-up. The kid was that good, and he proved it. Boucha was headed to Bucharest, Romania, to play for the United States in the 1970 World "B" Championship.

Before he traveled abroad, Boucha had to return to Winnipeg, where he gathered his belongings and passport and took a leave of absence from his team. At the World "B" Championship qualifying tournament in Bucharest, the United States team played Japan, Romania, East Germany, and Poland—winning the tournament. Following the tournament, in the summer of 1970, the young Minnesotan realized he was part of another "can't-miss" scenario.

With draft number 32, Boucha was earmarked as "can't miss" for induction into the United States military. Like many young men who got that call and had their lives turned upside down, Boucha thought his dreams of following in the footsteps of Warroad natives and 1960 U.S. hockey gold medalists, Bill and Roger Christian, were gone forever.

"I called Murray right away."

Williamson, and his manager Hal Trumble, were becoming familiar names to the Pentagon hierarchy, especially when it came to re-assigning U.S. National team and Olympic prospects who were heading to Vietnam. In some cases, it wasn't so easy. For Boucha, Williamson and Trumble were able to stave off the U.S. military—at least for a while.

In August, after placing a call to the Pentagon, Williamson advised Boucha, who was inevitably going to be called to serve, to enlist as a volunteer. And so the hotshot hockey stud from the Gopher State, who was beginning to establish himself as a staple of future national and Olympic teams, was sent to Fort Knox, Kentucky, for boot camp.

"I went to Fort Knox, Kentucky, and went through boot camp. I was out in November back in Minnesota playing a 51-game schedule in preparation for the 1971 World Championships in Switzerland." Boucha, like those that followed and would become his Olympic teammates, was assigned temporary duty to the United States hockey team during his tenure with the '71 National team.

At the end of the unsuccessful World Championships, Boucha's "temporary duty" was reassessed, and Uncle Sam took the talented forward back to his fighting team. Boucha got another draft notice. This time his draft number—two—meant potential money in his pocket as the Detroit Red Wings claimed the young U.S. soldier.

Though he served some time in Germany, Boucha's tour of duty was not complete, so he resumed his temporary duty status and returned to the United States National team. Only this time, Boucha was preparing for a spot on the 1972 Olympic team.

"There was always a nucleus of guys that had been there for the first three years," he explained. "I wanted to wear the red, white, and blue. There was no question about that. Everything kind of just fell into place."

Even Boucha's stint in the Army, in retrospect, kept the young American out of the National Hockey League and gave him the opportunity to live out his dream. From the time Boucha was an 18-year-old kid in Winnipeg with Coach Williamson scouting him as a potential U.S.

National team member, through his time in the United States Army, Boucha seemed destined to fulfill his goal of representing the United States in the Olympic Games. In an ironic twist of fate, Boucha's shocking draft notification in July 1970 disallowed him from turning professional with the Red Wings, thus enabling him to play on the Olympic team.

"To play in the Olympics was one of my goals," recalled Boucha. "It was a dream come true. I probably wouldn't have played in the Olympics if not for the United States Army. That was a blessing. Though I hated being in the Army, it had its moments."

Boucha was a veteran member of the U.S. team, and he fully expected to make the trip to Sapporo in February 1972. The Warroad native didn't leave much doubt in anybody else's minds, either, as he led the team in scoring with 39 goals and 56 assists during the 47-game pre-Olympic schedule. Ironically, the U.S. military policeman also finished the domestic schedule second on the team in penalty minutes with 82.

Towards the end of 1971, Williamson was able to assemble a roster that he thought was the best possible team to compete for a medal in Sapporo.

"Murray, who had looked at a lot of different players over the course of the year and the previous two years, was able to go and pick a team," said Boucha. "We trained hard and did a lot of off-ice and on-ice training. We had the chance to play the Russians five times throughout the year in a series."

When Williamson and his team arrived in Sapporo, there were no illusions as to who was the best team in the tournament. But Boucha and his mates figured they knew that team and its members as well as anybody. Throughout his years of international play, Boucha had laced his skates up nine times against the mighty Russian Bear.

"I knew what they were like," he said. "I just hated playing against them because they moved the puck so well. Some of their smaller players were so damn strong. They could embarrass you. We'd have to go all out, all the time, and we still lost. There was a mutual respect. We had nothing but respect for them."

Playing in the Olympics was a bit overwhelming for Boucha. The realization of his boyhood dream was coming true, yet he wanted to remain focused and not be "happy just to be there." As the American squad progressed through the tournament with a qualifying win over Switzerland, the young team from the U.S. felt like they had a decent shot at making some noise in the tournament.

"We were supposed to play in a [pre-Olympic] tournament in Sweden, and they didn't think we had a strong enough team to compete in their world-class tournament," remembered Boucha. "That really pissed everybody off. That made us work a little harder to get to that level. We wanted to surprise some people and obviously did once we got over to Japan."

Winning three of five games in the medal round was the end result of Williamson's plan for his '72 Olympic squad.

"We knew we could beat the Finns," said Boucha. "The Czechs were on the edge. And Poland? We knew we could beat Poland."

The Russians and Swedes were another story. "The Russians were so good it would've been a miracle for us to beat them," admitted the former NHL star. "The Swedes were a tremendous team. They were so fast on those big rinks, and our loss to them was devastating at the time."

A win over Czechoslovakia propelled the young Americans into serious medal contention when the tournament's final two games were played on Sunday. With Boucha's mates sleeping off a night of celebrating the Sapporo night life following the team's final game on Saturday, Boucha returned to the U.S. dorms bearing good news that the Finns had upset the Swedes early Sunday. Boucha was sent to rouse his groggy teammates from their beds and get them to the field house per Williamson's orders. The American team had just won an Olympic medal with that upset.

"Everybody was stunned," described Boucha. "They were kind of half believing it and half not, but they were getting ready. It was like, 'Really? Really? What was the score? What happened?'"

The only thing left to determine was the color of the souvenir.

Boucha and his teammates had enough experience with the Russians to know they would not let gold slip through their collective hands. Gold meant rubles to the Soviet team, and that meant a better life in the heart of Communism. Boucha had little doubt that he would be wearing a silver medal when the ceremony concluded following the last game of the tournament.

Following the Games, Boucha joined the Red Wings for the final 16 games of the 1971-72 regular season.

"I played in Detroit after the Olympics, and all the guys were talking about playing the Russians," remembered the American rookie. "After skating with Detroit, I thought, 'Wow, these guys aren't that good.' After playing against the Russians and international competition, I thought, 'Shit, these guys are just a bunch of arrogant Canadians. The National Hockey League was a beer and pizza league at that time. I was thinking how arrogant the guys in the NHL are. They were so arrogant thinking, 'We'll kick their ass. They're just amateurs.' I was overwhelmed to see them get their asses kicked in that first game of the Summit Series in Montreal. But they stepped it up and quickly realized the Soviets weren't bad."

Boucha ended his Olympic Games as the third leading scorer on the team with two goals and four assists during the six-game tournament. He went on to play six seasons and 247 games in the National Hockey League, but his Olympic experience stands as his dream come true.

"I wanted to play in the National Hockey League at some point, but I really wanted to play for the United States in the Olympics."

Has the forgotten status of his Olympic team soured his memory of that precious time in his youth? Maybe a little, but the Warroad native remains a "can't miss" character when it comes to describing that time in U.S. Hockey history.

"My most vivid memory was playing in the Olympics and realizing that we *won* the silver," recalls Boucha. "That was the most vivid and shocking thing because nobody believed in us."

And with the "can't-miss" tag adorning every move he made since pee wee hockey, Boucha could've been a prima donna. But he wasn't. He played and spoke with his heart and won the respect and admiration of a fun-loving, hard-working group of forgotten players.

Where is he now? Henry Boucha now works in real estate and is active in Native-American affairs in Warroad, Minnesota.

CRAIG SARNER

Born: June 20, 1949 • Jersey No. 17 • Draft No. 353

"I was very, very proud and it made it very special for me to look over to Frankie and think how far we've come from playing on outdoor rinks in 20 below zero weather and 35 m.p.h. winds in seventh grade."

Since the first time he was old enough to lace up his skates and head out to the ponds near his North St. Paul, Minnesota, home, a five-year-old Craig Sarner knew he wanted to play in the Olympics someday.

"I remember watching the gold medal game in 1960 with Jack McCartan and the Cleary brothers," recalls Sarner. "Those names stuck in the back of my mind, and I remember thinking, 'Wouldn't it be phenomenal to play for your country in the Olympics?' It was every four years and, without a doubt, took precedent over everything else."

Those were the days when kids played on the ponds and started skating at eight o'clock in the morning and didn't stop until 10 o'clock at night. It was an age of innocence when parents let their kids play. Sarner and his buddies would often pack a lunch along with their skates and sticks and spend all day Saturday playing hockey. Every Saturday was the same except for the five weeks or so when the networks would televise a National Hockey League game. On those days, the young Sarner would sit in front of the television and watch the day's greatest players. When the game was over, he and his friends would skate the rest of the day without a worry in the world. When it was time to come home, Sarner's mother would open the back door and let them know with a yell. If the wind was blowing, Sarner and his pals could usually sneak an extra hour of skating, claiming the wind was blowing the other way and they couldn't hear their mothers call.

His dream evolved not only on those ponds but by watching the 1960 U.S. Olympic hockey team, its roster littered with local Minnesota names familiar to all the kids who played hockey, win the gold medal in Squaw Valley.

"Watching the 1960 Olympics certainly sticks out in my mind," said Sarner. "You know when you're six years old, you think, 'Wouldn't that be great?' Was it reality? No. At that time, we were just playing pick-up games in our area. I hadn't even had my first, what you would say, 'real' organized game. It was a dream, and I was just looking forward to playing on the junior high school team, let alone play in the Olympics."

On that junior high team, Sarner developed a friendship with Frank Sanders that began during their days on the pond and continued through high school at North St. Paul High, the University of Minnesota, on to the Olympic Games, and still thrives to this day. Sarner played his high school hockey in a day when the team consisted of nine players: two lines, three defensemen, and one goalie. From that team, six players went on to play college hockey. Three members of Sarner's team played Division I college hockey, and three members went on to play Division III.

"You always thought about playing college hockey, and I used to go with my dad to watch some Gopher hockey [University of Minnesota], which was great," said Sarner. "I always thought it would be fabulous to have that jersey on one day. We were fortunate enough to be in an era where you lived more in the present. If things happened, they happened."

During his senior year in high school, Sarner was heavily recruited and accepted to some of the finest institutions in the country including Harvard, Brown, all of the Ivy League Schools, as well as the University of Minnesota—schools that were simultaneously among the upper echelon of academics and hockey.

"It really came down to Brown and the University of Minnesota," said Sarner. "When you grow up in one place and see that 'M'—to be able to wear the 'M' ... I decided to go to the University."

Since freshmen weren't allowed to play varsity sports, Sarner spent a year practicing and getting into the swing of college life.

Sarner's hockey reality really hit home his next year at Minnesota as a bench-sitting sophomore. He had been one of the nation's top recruits but was having an abominable year. As the season went on, Sarner found himself firmly exiled in coach Glen Sonmor's "dog house." It got so bad for him that Sonmor had him sit in a specific spot on the bench so he could stand with his right foot on the bench and rest his other foot on Sarner's shoulder. His jersey became so imbedded with the stain of his coach's footprint that the team had to buy a new jersey. At that point, any thoughts of going to the Olympics were distant. He was just hoping to retain his scholarship for another year.

Though he struggled his sophomore season, Sarner pulled it together enough to help the Gophers to the WCHA title during his junior season. And in his senior campaign the following year, his team lost the NCAA Hockey National Championship to Boston University. Despite the team's success his senior year, Sarner's dream of one day playing in the Olympics didn't seem any closer to him at the end of the season. He had played the entire season with a cast on his left hand after breaking his wrist in the second game of the season.

"When that happened, I thought, 'Well, this is it. You're going to go on with the season and then get on with the rest of your life when it is over. Either go to grad school or get a job.'"

In fact, Sarner had been put on the Boston Bruins negotiation list after his junior year and removed from it after his senior year.

The dream never fully died, though. Following Sarner's senior season, the unwritten rule among players was that they had to play in the summer. Sarner, not a particular fan of summer games because of the 68-mile roundtrip to the rink, journeyed twice a week to play in either the 7:00 or 9:00 night game. During those games in July 1971, Murray Williamson reached out to the North St. Paul native and asked to meet at the Minneapolis Athletic Club. Williamson wanted Sarner to try out for the Olympic team. During that time, Boston Bruins scout Harry Brown also took notice of Sarner, once again.

Williamson promised Sarner a shot at making the team, and if he made it, the coach was prepared to offer the Minnesota center iceman $150 stipend per week. Meanwhile, Brown also approached Sarner, who had led the summer league in scoring, and told him the Bobby Orr-led Stanley Cup champion Boston Bruins wanted him to come to training camp in the fall. Sarner balked at first, explaining he had already committed to the Olympic team. Brown persevered and told Sarner it would only be for one week and then he could head back to Bemidji for the Olympic training camp.

Sarner was one in a group of about 80 newcomers trying to win a roster spot with the defending Stanley Cup champion "Big Bad Bruins." After one week, Sarner decided to stick to his plan and head back up to Bemidji since he didn't really feel like he had done much during the seven days to distinguish himself with the Bruins. He approached Brown and asked for his plane ticket back to Minnesota. But before he left,

Brown told him Bruins general manager Milt Schmidt wanted to talk with him first.

Schmidt was preparing to sign Sarner to a minor league deal. When Schmidt summoned Sarner to his office he was surprised to learn of Sarner's plan to only be at training camp for a week.

"'We thought you were here to be a pro and we want to sign you,'" Sarner remembered Schmidt saying.

Sarner reiterated his plan from the beginning to the Bruins general manager, "No, I gave my word to Murray that I was coming back [to the Olympic team]. Harry knew this flat out. And that's the way it's going to be."

Schmidt came back to Sarner and said, "Well, we want to sign you. This isn't right you doing this."

Sarner apologized for what he thought at the time was a miscommunication of his plans.

"Looking back, I probably had agreed to that, and maybe I did better than I thought," recalls Sarner. "Anyhow, I came out of the meeting thinking, 'This is good.'"

Not only was it good, it seemed to be a dream come true. After that, Sarner's dream to play in the Olympics was in clearer focus, but he had to take care of the business side of hockey first. Sarner decided to call Williamson and try to leverage the situation by explaining the Bruins' offer.

"I called Murray and told him, 'I went to the Bruins' camp and they want to sign me,'" explained Sarner. "I told him I thought I probably should."

Upon hearing that, Williamson was not pleased.

"He went ballistic," recalled Sarner. "He called me every expletive you can imagine and said, 'You promised me.' I said, 'Murray, I'm going to have to get a little more money to justify my coming back and playing.' Then he started in again. 'You S.O.B … I'll call you back in one hour.'"

Williamson called back an hour later and agreed to give him $250 per week, but warned Sarner, "If you're not at practice on Monday morning, you can stick it up your ass."

By the time the team left for Sapporo, Sarner figured Williamson had his money back and then some due to the fines he levied on the young hotshot.

Sarner arrived in Bemidji along with about 21 other guys who comprised the 1972 U.S. team. Although 20 would ultimately make the team, only 17 players were allowed to dress during the Olympic Games. This made dry-land training, on-ice practices, and scrimmages an all-out affair every day. Though Sarner was mostly assured a spot on the Sapporo roster, Williamson kept all his players on edge—knowing nothing was a sure thing even if the coach had invited the player to tryouts.

Williamson proved to be a thorn in Sarner's side for most of the pre-Olympic schedule, but it wasn't because the coach disliked the talented center. On the contrary. Sarner, who to this day refers to his former coach as Napoleon, also holds his former coach in high esteem.

"Murray was … is unique," said Sarner. "He ran a good practice—very organized—and you always knew what you were trying to do. I think a lot of what Herbie got out of the 1980 team is the same reason why we got a medal—we were in better condition than every other team except the Russians."

Williamson was a Knute Rockne-type motivator who would give his players small goals to achieve but also would push hard enough to let each player know they could give a little more.

"Murray would say one thing that would make you feel great, and at the same time piss you off, because you wanted to be mad at the son of a bitch. He was very good at that."

Through it all, Sarner's childhood dream fueled him all the way to Sapporo. That dream became even more of a reality for Sarner led the team in scoring with 10 points scoring four goals and six assists in the six Olympic games. When it was all over and it came time to receive his silver medal, Sarner thought about his teammates. As the 22-year-old North St. Paul, native stepped on the ice at the medal ceremony, Sarner thought back to the days on the pond with his buddy Frank Sanders, who stood nearby on the same Sapporo ice waiting to receive his silver medal.

"It brought a tear to my eye," said Sarner. "I was very, very proud, and it made it very special for me to look over to Frankie and think how far we've come from playing on outdoor rinks in 20 below zero weather and 35 m.p.h. winds in seventh grade. Even though that was the dream, when you're in junior high skating against that, you never ever really thought that winning an Olympic medal was possible."

Sarner also thought about the future. He knew playing professionally was now a real possibility following his success at the Olympic Games, but those thoughts were dwarfed by what he and his teammates had just accomplished.

"I remember looking around and being excited. At the same time, it was kind of a hollow feeling like, 'This is it. We've gone through a lot with these people, and accomplished a lot, but it will never happen again.' That feeling was something I never got back at any level. I've never felt any hockey moment has ever come close in that sense."

To this day Sarner and his former teammates have a tough time keeping their emotions in check when they speak of their experience more than 30 yeas ago.

"It's unique because, for six games over a period of almost seven months, the closeness you have with the people you played for, and with, you learn a lot about. When you go pro, your first objective of course is to win. But damn it, you want to be up in the NHL where there's no bus rides and everything is a little nicer. So, it's commitment but not a total commitment. It's a job. It's a friggin' job. You still love the game. You still love to play, but it's nothing like being there for six months—to march out there and see the flags going up."

As the teams received their medals and the group of young Americans stood proud realizing what they had accomplished—even if the rest of America had not—Sarner remembered what it was like to be on the second rung of the Olympic podium.

"We had played the Russians six times. By the fifth time, we got so tired of hearing the Russian national anthem! But this was one time when they played their anthem, and we saw the American flag go up that we all realized this was something special."

Where is he now? Craig Sarner now owns a hockey school in Orono, Minnesota.

FRANK SANDERS

Born: March 8, 1949 • Jersey No. 9 • Draft No. 31

"This team was different. You don't have those types of things happen very often in life where you can have people who bonded as well as we did."

Even today, Frank Sanders, the solid defenseman from North St. Paul, Minnesota—and one of the biggest players on the 1972 U.S. Olympic hockey team at six foot two and 225 pounds—still becomes emotional when he thinks about his Olympic teammates and the bond they forged en route to a silver medal at the Olympic Winter Games in Sapporo.

It didn't really sink in until the medal ceremony. After more than six months together as a cohesive unit that lived together, played together, and accomplished something no one other than themselves believed was possible, they were disbanding to live as professional hockey players, lawyers, teachers, coaches, clergy and businessmen. They knew, following the medal ceremony, they might never see each other again.

"These guys were probably the greatest guys you'll ever run into," said Sanders. "We had guys that had some weird characteristics, but nobody was treated badly. We were all treated with respect."

Sanders, like his teammate and childhood friend Craig Sarner, didn't play organized hockey—or skate with a roof over his head, for that matter, until he was in junior high school. That didn't mean Sanders didn't play the game. He skated on the ponds of Minnesota but didn't really learn the rules until he got to high school. From there, he proved to be a quick study in learning the intricacies of the game and went on to become an all-state hockey player at North St. Paul High School and earned a full scholarship to the University of Minnesota in the fall of 1967.

During his college career, Sanders built a reputation as a solid defenseman who was named captain of his team during his senior season. The team's Most Valuable Player led the Gophers to the national championship game, where they lost to Boston University. In 1969, though, the Gophers' top defenseman was drafted into the Army. But as luck would have it, when his draft notice came—during hockey season—a bad skin condition that always seemed to plague him turned out to be his saving grace. At his Army physical, Sanders promptly reported and was turned away because of his skin condition.

Coach Murray Williamson knew that his U.S. Olympic squad needed a big and steady defender like Sanders.

"I just loved the game so much that I didn't worry about the next step," said Sanders. "I figured the next step would fall in line if it was meant to fall in line. I was fortunate because Murray Williamson called me in one day and told me he'd like to have me on the Olympic team after my college coach had recommended a few of us. That's when the dream really hit home. Anybody could try out, but I was asked to come."

Sanders, confident that he would be making the trip to Sapporo, quickly noticed something about this team after reporting to Bemidji for training camp in September. The 22 scruffy-faced kids, who hailed from all parts of the Eastern states, Northern and Southern Minnesota, and Michigan, almost instantly became a team.

"This team was different. You don't have those types of things happen very often in life where you have people who bonded as well as we did."

"I always felt bad for the guys who came in and gave their all and it didn't work out," said Sanders. "Sometimes it may have been the personality or they didn't get along with the coach or they just didn't fit in. There is something about team chemistry that is vitally important to winning. You have to have a good mixture. That's where a coach's job is hard—to make sure you put together the right chemistry. And it's not always the best talent but the best chemistry."

Sanders felt that one component in the team's chemistry was the lack of pressure. Players like Sanders and his Olympic teammates grew up with the targets on their backs as the team to beat. Now, cast in a position as underdogs, Sanders and his mates had a different perspective.

"There we were, nobody expected us to win," he explained. "It was kind of a different feeling for all of us. The pressure was off. We had a blast. You know, we played around out in the snow in Sapporo, and we did all sorts of goofy things. We were a bunch of kids having a blast. That made it special, too."

And, while the Games were unforgettable, he thinks about his teammates mostly these days. Decades after the '72 team won silver in Sapporo, Sanders swallows hard remembering his "brothers," although he isn't shy about expressing himself about his teammates.

"I think about the guys more than the actual games. I think about what they're doing with their lives—their grandkids, how they were involved in sports since then. I do miss them. If you have time to contemplate, you can get pretty emotional over the guys you wish you could be with the whole time."

Contemplation was a part of Sanders's game when he was a world-class athlete. As the world was changing in the 1960s with Vietnam, and in the 1970s with the end of the war and the realization that many innocent lives were lost in Southeast Asia, he was battling an internal struggle of his own. That struggle was spiritual and involved the direction his life would take when his playing days concluded.

As the nation was coming to the end of one of the most tumultuous periods in its history, seemingly spinning out of control at home and abroad, Sanders was playing professional hockey but was contemplating a calling he knew was part of his life even when he was a member of the Olympic team.

"The guys knew I was leaning toward that even when I was playing, because I didn't drink or anything like that," said Sanders. "Craig Sarner, who I grew up with, knew me pretty intimately and knew that I had that desire in my heart."

Following his first year of professional hockey playing for the 1972-73 Minnesota Saints, Sanders came to a decision about his future.
"Athletic-wise, I was fighting internally whether I should continue playing sports or go into the ministry," Sanders admitted. "After one year of playing professionally, I decided to quit and go into the seminary."

After completing his seminary training in 1978, the former Olympic defenseman—who led his defensive teammates in scoring with three goals and one assist during the six-game Olympic tournament—was ordained a minister by the United Pentecostal Church.

As Sanders embarked on his own spiritual journey following his playing days, don't think for a minute that the feisty All-American and Olympic silver medal-winning hockey player lost any fire for his Olympic teammates and the lack of recognition they've received through the years.

"I get irritated a little bit. For us to go on foreign soil and play as well as we did and win a silver medal, I thought that would garner some more appreciation from the hockey world. It is a little frustrating to have accomplished something that I consider very great with a bunch of kids—just like the '80 Olympic team. I don't let it kill me or bother me to the extent it throws my life off, but I wish that someone would recognize the success the team had."

With Sanders, the conversation always revolves around his teammates and the bond this team created with each other. For those who never played on a team, it's hard to describe.

"You have to understand the game. To get to where we were was phenomenal. Yet, people will not recognize that because it's second place."

And winning, especially in the United States, is everything.

Sanders describes the emotional bond he shares for his teammates, the Olympic experience, the tremendous sense of accomplishment, his disdain for the way current Olympic teams are selected, and the pride he feels when people ask him about his silver medal. He is a deep thinker. Pensive and honest, his memories of the Sapporo Olympics take him back, intersecting with his current occupation.

"There's a great spiritual aspect to the Olympic experience," reflects Sanders. "If everyone were truthful, they'd say the same thing. There's something about those times and being with those guys that were very spiritual moments for me."

Sanders is open about emoting his feelings about America's obsession with winning. Sanders is also smart enough to know that had his teammates defeated the Russians and won gold, it would be the '72 team that would be celebrated. Instead, Sanders and his brothers of 1972 are relegated to near obscurity in the hockey world including, until recently, this country's governing body—USA Hockey.

"I look back at the Games with pride at accomplishing what we accomplished," reflects Sanders. "I can say that we did something that not too many people ever had a chance to do—win a silver medal—win a medal of any kind at the Olympic Games. You just have to be very thankful that you had that opportunity and were able to accomplish that."

That accomplishment is the foundation on which Sanders lives his ministry today. He, as anyone who has achieved something as extraordinary as representing your country in the Olympic Games and winning a medal, is befuddled as to why no one remembers this accomplishment. But that confusion aids his calling and helps him serve and inspire the young people of his native St. Paul, Minnesota. Being an underdog and being forgotten has given Sanders a perspective from his Olympic experience he otherwise may not have been afforded.

"It's not necessarily about winning the medal, because if we still had the same team we had and didn't win the medal, I'd still be very proud. The medal just adds that much to it. It is just a tremendous group of guys."

That's what it all comes back to with Frank Sanders—Team and Brotherhood. In this case, the 1972 United States Olympic hockey team, his hockey brethren that set out to accomplish something—and did.

Where is he now? Frank Sanders is now a Pentecostal minister in Oakdale, Minnesota.

6

NEW MATH

GAME FIVE
February 12, 1972—5:34 a.m. EST
USA 6 - POLAND 1

"My feelings were torn between playing and not playing and supporting the team. It was hard watching. Of course, I wanted to be in there. But I told him, if you think it's better for the team, I'll sit this one out, too."

—LARRY BADER

The U.S. was set to play its final game on the second-to-last day of the Olympics. Their record in the medal round was 2-2, and they started figuring out exactly what needed to happen for them to be in the hunt for a medal. They knew they couldn't control the other games yet to be played, but one thing was certain—they had to beat Poland in their final game to have any chance at a medal.

Williamson had it figured out the night before. He had promised to play everyone, but with the team on a roll and having a chance at a medal if they won, he approached some of the guys who hadn't yet seen action in the Olympics including back-up goalie Pete Sears, defenseman Bruce McIntosh, and forward Larry Bader. Sears knew he could be called into action at any moment, but with Curran playing as he was, only an injury would get him into the game. McIntosh had injured his shoulder, and though he was mentally ready, physically he just wasn't there. So Sears, McIntosh, and Bader—to a man—each put their egos aside for the good of the team and told Williamson to maintain his current lineup.

"Murray came to me and said, 'Larry, you should play. I should put you in. But you've been off the ice now for two and a half weeks. Do I throw you in there so you have the opportunity to play when, if we win this game, we have an opportunity to win a medal? I'll leave it up to you. I'm going to ask you what you want to do,'" remembers Bader.

Down from an 18-skater roster to 15, the team couldn't afford the luxury of a fourth line that could suit up and sit the bench until their shift was called. Once you suited up, you played. Although the decision was tough, each player knew that one couldn't go without playing for two and a half weeks and then be thrown onto the ice.

"My feelings were torn between playing and not playing and supporting the team," admitted Bader. "It was hard watching. Of course, I wanted to be in there. But I told him, 'If you think it's better for the team, I'll sit this one out, too.' Once the realization that we could win a medal meant I didn't play, I was okay with it. Some might've said, 'I'd rather not win a medal and play,' but I didn't feel that way."

It was that example of selflessness that epitomized this team.

Though they respected the Poles, the young Americans would not be denied. Once again, they came out like gangbusters, as Tim Sheehy scored a goal that put the U.S. up 1-0 at the 0:57 mark of the opening period. The Poles held their own throughout much of the period, but then Sarner scored at 14:41 to put the U.S. up 2-0.

The U.S. pumped in two more goals in the second period as Boucha, at 6:08, and Irving, at 14:53, each potted one, and the U.S. was in full swing with a 4-0 lead at the end of the period. The Poles closed the gap to 4-1 with a goal by Taduesz Obloj at 2:40 of the third period. But the U.S. responded with two goals in a 28-second span as Sarner netted his second of the game—and fourth of the tournament at 11:05—and Sheehy scored his second of the game and fourth of the tournament at 11:33 for a 6-1 U.S. lead. By this time, the U.S. was in full command, but the referees decided to make the game a little bit more interesting.

"We had a Canadian official and a German official who hated us—absolutely hated us," explained Williamson. "I used to see all these coaches try to intimidate the officials, so I jumped on the ship and tried doing the same. And they hated me. They called a penalty shot, and it gave us a good look at the character of 'Lefty.'"

Poland's Feliks Goralczyk swept down to the left of Curran, who came out to cut down the angle, and forced him to miss wide. But the referee said that Curran had left the crease too soon and awarded him a second shot.

"So their guy comes down again, and Lefty stones him again," remembers the U.S. coach. "'Lefty' skates over to the bench and says with a devilish grin, 'Coach, let's give 'em another try.' He was cocky as hell."

As the horn sounded to end the game, the U.S. players poured onto the ice to congratulate each other on the 6-1 win and the completion of a well-played Olympic tournament. With a 3-2 record in the medal round, the U.S. team was now squarely in the mix for what had seemed improbable just days before—a medal. The members of the U.S. team knew that, depending on what happened the next day between Finland and Sweden and Czechoslovakia and the Soviet Union, they could end up with a silver medal, a bronze medal, or nothing but their pride.

CRBD   CRBD   CRBD

Many of the guys on the team had been through the embarrassment of the 1971 World Championship tournament, so they made a pledge not to go out partying or drinking until after they finished their schedule. Following their final game, the U.S. boys decided to experience the Olympics in another way—that night they had a very good time experiencing the nightlife that Sapporo had to offer.

"I can remember walking into a club, and the Beatles were upstairs playing," recalls ringleader Dick McGlynn. "We couldn't believe it. The Beatles were at the Olympic games. This was the coolest thing ever. We walked upstairs, and it was four Japanese guys singing phonetically. They were absolutely reproducing the Beatles sound. We thought it was the Beatles. We partied and partied, met people, and then we saw Murray there."

With their coach and several other athletes from all over the world also enjoying the end of their long and winding Olympic roads, McGlynn, Tommy Mellor, and Sarner decided to have a little fun at the expense of the man who had been controlling their lives for the past year. One of the other athletes there was the beautiful, blonde U.S. Olympic figure skater, Jo Jo Starbuck.

McGlynn went over to Starbuck and introduced himself.

"I said, 'I'm with the hockey team, and we're out partying because we just finished our schedule and want to have a little fun,'" said McGlynn. "Would you do me a great favor? See that guy over there? He's the coach of our hockey team. Would you go over there and ask him to dance?' She said, 'Sure.' Obviously, she knew we had been partying, and she was a pretty good kid. So she goes over to Murray and says, 'Hi, I'm Jo Jo Starbuck.' Everyone knew who she was because she was one of the greatest skaters of the time and a great-looking girl—'Wanna come out and dance?'

"Of course, Murray put down his drink and got up with his chest all puffed out. He always fancied himself a debonair man. We were off to the side howling, laughing. He was out there doing the Monkey, and it was so funny. He was beaming—*beaming*. Finally, Murray comes over to us, and says, 'I still got it.' We howled with laughter. We were always trying to get the edge on him by doing stuff like that."

The following day, a few stragglers from the night before, including Mellor, Irving, Ftorek, McIntosh, and Boucha, woke up early and decided to join Williamson at the first game—Finland versus Sweden. All along, when analyzing all the possible permutations and medal options, they were convinced that Finland was not going to beat Sweden. They were thinking that they would have to count on the Soviet Union to take care of business against the Czechs. That was no guarantee, either—but as Williamson had pointed out at breakfast to the group, there was no love lost between the Finns and the Swedes, nor the Czechs and the Russians.

LARRY BADER

Born: September 12, 1949 • Jersey No. 21 • Draft No. 270

"I sat there trying to take in as much as I could, because I knew I wanted to remember it from a perspective of deep down wanting to play, but on the other hand, knowing the team was doing pretty well."

He was on the outside looking in. He was an aberration. A Midwest kid from Southern Minnesota traveled East and found himself at one of the most prestigious universities in the country—University of Pennsylvania—trying to keep himself from harm's way as the campus around him was exploding with anti-Vietnam venom. By his reckoning, he was the last one chosen to be a member of the 1972 United States Olympic hockey team.

Larry Bader was one of the top high school hockey players in the state of Minnesota but had no scholarship offers when it came time to choose a college to continue his education and hockey career.

"I made the first team all-state, but the University of Minnesota didn't choose me to have a scholarship. I needed a full ride to go to college because I didn't have a lot of money. Because the University of Minnesota didn't take me, I went to the University of Pennsylvania and did okay."

Bader, indeed, did okay. By his senior year, the native of Minnetonka, Minnesota, was the Ivy League school's vice president and one of the team's top scoring forwards. Though he never expressed it outwardly, he always wondered why his home-state university never offered him a scholarship to play. And, as a 22-year-old Ivy Leaguer from a non-traditional hockey school in the East fighting for a spot on the 1972 Olympic team, he was constantly proving himself.

"Five or six guys that were on the team, and at times as many as eight or nine guys were from the University of Minnesota. I identified with those guys from Minnesota. I always wanted to show them I was as good as they were and could play with them. I had a personal feeling that I wanted to play as well and be a part of that group."

Wanting to be part of that group proved elusive for Bader. As a "bubble" player—someone who wasn't sure he would be around for the next practice or game because he might be cut from the team—friendships were hard to establish because most players didn't want to get too close to someone and then have that person be cut from the team. It may have been a psychologically-ignorant attitude, but that was the reality of the situation.

"Some of the guys on our team were going to make it all the way. They had their cliques. I identified with some of the players that were more empathetic to me. Some of those players with whom I mostly identified were Ron Naslund, Wally Olds, Charlie Brown, and a couple of the guys that didn't make the team. That's what happens on any team. You begin to identify with what level you are on the team. One other player I identified with, who was one of the stars of the team, was Henry Boucha. He was a friend to everybody—a good guy."

Recognizing his situation, the burly six-foot-two left-winger made the most of each opportunity but always knew the reality of his Olympic plight.

"I think I was on the bubble for the whole season. I was there the whole season with a revolving door of people coming in and out throughout the season. Some of the people that came in you knew were going to stay, like when 'Lefty' Curran came in late in the season. Others came and were there for a while and just left. I thought I was going to be the last one to leave. It was kind of down to me and two other guys. I thought I would be cut that last weekend. Mark Howe got on the plane when we were in Ann Arbor, and we didn't know. It was like, 'Okay, he's not getting on the plane to go with us to go out to the Broadmoor for our last week of practice if he's not going to be on the team.' So we didn't know who was going to be let go. But I made it."

Interestingly, though he was a bubble player throughout the entire season, Bader not only contributed six goals and 12 assists as an occasional linemate of Robbie Ftorek and Stu Irving in 37 games played; he also tapped into emotions that made his Olympic experience vastly different from the majority of the group.

"I watched the games and had the experience watching from the bench or stands. I sat there trying to take in as much as I could because I knew I wanted to remember it from a perspective of deep down wanting to play, but on the other hand, knowing the team was doing pretty well."

Bader dutifully watched as his Olympic teammates defeated the Swiss, lost to Sweden, stunningly upset and dominated the Czech team 5-1, then set their sights on the heavily favored Russians.

"I just thought it was all over when we got beat by the Russians."

With a 4-1 win over Finland in the tournament's waning days, Bader thought he might get a chance to suit up in the team's final game against Poland on the next-to-last day of the tournament.

"It wasn't pointed out to me that we actually had a chance to win a medal until some of the guys started figuring it out: 'If this happens, then this. If that happens, then that.' Of course, Murray had it figured out."

Williamson did have it figured out and sought out Bader before the final day of competition. "Murray came to me with one game left. We were playing one of the lesser teams—Poland—and I thought for sure now that we had gone through the giants that I'd get into that game."

But true to the team, Bader accepted his role and watched the final game as well. Bader's experience was watching—watching other players, watching other teams—and wondering how he could fit in. Because he didn't play, Bader worked out extra on game days, working out in addition to what his teammates were doing before the game that day. He would get up in the snowy mornings, put on his running shoes, and run 10-15 times around the block to keep his legs going in case he was called into action that night. That was something the other guys on the team didn't do.

"Probably the biggest thing that I picked up on was at the cafeteria. There was this big wheel that had a pie with areas of food. In one section would be North American, in another section would be Eastern European, in another Western European foods. You would sit in the area that you were from or had food that was a part of your diet. When we were going to play a team, they would eat about the same time we would. We would look over and see the Russians eating. I watched them eat noodles and yogurt and drink water. We sat down and would have a 12-16 ounce steak and baked potato. We couldn't have done it worse four hours before a game. We used to talk about how poor that team must really be if they could only afford to eat noodles, so they got used to it and ate them here when they could be eating steak. They were way advanced to us in terms of nutrition. On off-days, we could go over there and eat whatever we wanted and as much as we wanted. But that was kind of interesting to see how the Russians ate and prepared for the game—and how wrong we did it."

At the conclusion of the hockey tournament, Bader continued to observe and learn. Following the Russians' gold medal-winning day, Bader found himself in a room with some of Red Army's most talented and renowned players of all-time.

"I stayed up until about four o'clock in the morning in the Russian rooms with Kharlamov, and Tretiak was in and out eating caviar and drinking vodka. They had won the gold medal. The next morning, we were getting on the plane and heading out. I somehow hooked up with a couple of their players and ended up being in their room. I congratulated them on winning the gold, and they said, 'You did better than us. You beating the Czechs was a better deal than us winning the gold. We were supposed to win the gold. You weren't supposed to win the silver.'"

In the end, as Bader reminisces about his Olympic experience, his tales are not filled with glorious feats on the ice in Sapporo. The cerebral Ivy Leaguer from Minnesota has a simpler view on what motivated him toward Olympic silver.

"The guys kind of identified with me as being one of them, but I just didn't play with them. There was always this alumni feeling that I never had. I had that internal feeling that I wanted to do well in game recognition for myself. I didn't do it for money because we weren't paid money. I didn't do it to stay out of the Vietnam War because I had a very, very, very high draft number. I did it to show the people that I knew, the small group of people I knew that, even though I went to school back East, I was as good as them. It just came down to that. I wasn't as good as them as it turned out. They were a little bit better, but there was a very fine line between being 20th versus 10th on a team. That's what drove me. Every wind sprint, I tried to win. Every time the puck went into the corner, I tried to take it away from Sanders or Sarner."

It was harder for Bader to watch. As with any world-class athlete, he didn't want to sit, stand or pace during any game in which his teammates are playing. Unlike today's athletes, Bader is a special breed who found joy in the experience of being an Olympian.

"I think back about what might have been if it had been me who went home instead of Timmy Cutter. It's a unique situation to be the bubble player on a U.S. national team."

It's also unique to have a silver medal in a frame with an Olympic jersey in the den of your house.

Where is he now? Larry Bader is now an independent businessman in Fairbault, Minnesota.

BRUCE McINTOSH

Born: March 17, 1949 • Jersey No. 7 • Draft No. 33

"I was a good player, but I was no superstar. I thought, 'Gosh, I'll give this a try. It sounds like fun.'"

"Our team, because of the fact that nobody paid much attention to us, has remained very close through the years," says Bruce McIntosh, the native from Edina, Minnesota. McIntosh was one of a handful of players on the 1972 U.S. Olympic hockey team who signed a contract with coach Murray Williamson stating he would not leave the program to pursue a professional career.

McIntosh was a gifted player from Minnesota who made a name for himself in the hockey-rich community of Edina, where he starred on the reputed high school hockey team, and then as a scholarship player at the University of Minnesota. Success on the ice followed the center-turned-defenseman during his college days as the Golden Gophers made it all the way to the NCAA national championship game during his senior season in 1971. Despite a loss to Boston University, McIntosh went home to Minnesota satisfied with his team, college hockey career, and education.

"I was put on the Detroit Red Wings negotiation list," explained McIntosh. "Detroit sent me a letter at the end of my senior year at the University saying that they anticipated me going to training camp in Port Huron that next fall. They didn't offer me a contract. They just said they'd send me an airline ticket to get me out there and put me up in a hotel for the 10 days of camp."

The era was different back then—there was no such thing as an entry draft and only 12 teams comprising the National Hockey League. McIntosh wasn't sure he wanted to do that because he had his degree and some different opportunities in front of him.

One day in June, the 22-year-old McIntosh received a call from fellow Edina resident and 1972 U.S. Olympic coach Murray Williamson. Williamson invited McIntosh out to lunch and laid out a scenario for the youngster to think about and get back to him with an answer.

"Murray said, 'We're going to form a nucleus of players that we're going to have an agreement with—at least 12 players—where they won't turn pro at least until after the Olympics.' We actually signed contracts that said, 'If you are selected to play on the Olympic team, you will not turn professional until after the Olympics.' He didn't want to waste all of his time and efforts putting a team together. I understood that completely."

McIntosh was second team All-America, second team All-WCHA, a member of the NCAA All-Tournament team, and he understood the opportunity Williamson was presenting.

"I was a good player, but I was no superstar. I thought, 'Gosh, I'll give this a try. It sounds like fun.'" So he signed the contract.

Only after decades of reminiscing and reunions did McIntosh realize how much fun it really was. Despite the days and months of grueling hard work—plus the sacrifice of leaving his family and friends behind in order to create a squad that was designed to peak for two weeks in the winter of 1972—McIntosh realized he had become a member of a "new family."

"The part I remember most was just hanging out with the guys—all these other guys from the East like McGlynn, Tommy Mellor, Stu Irving," said McIntosh. "I know guys that played in 1968, 1976, 1984—they don't see each other any more. They don't talk to each other unless it's some odd occasion. But for me, I get the urge four or five times a year to call Dickie McGlynn; call Tommy Mellor to catch up with those guys. When I built my golf course in Minnesota, a big article was written in the local Minneapolis paper. Ron Naslund emailed the article to all of my teammates. I hadn't heard from Robbie Ftorek in 10 years—he had been coaching and playing. He had been unable to attend any of our reunions because he was so busy. He had just been named coach of the Bruins, and he called me up and said, 'Mac, it's Robbie.'

"It was like we hadn't missed a day. He said, 'We're both living our dream.' I said, 'You're right, Robbie.' That's the kind of guys we had on our team. They really care about the other guys," reiterated McIntosh with a catch in his voice more than 30 years later.

The team's love for one another is testimony to what guided Williamson as he set out to change USA Hockey's planned trajectory since its historic gold medal in 1960. When training camp in Bemidji broke, there were guys that didn't fit in or weren't quite good enough to make the team.

"Murray had a lot of different combinations," remembered McIntosh. "He had wingers playing with defensemen and defensemen up on the forward line. He was really searching for chemistry. And, if there was anything that our team had, it was good chemistry."

Despite the team's wide range of backgrounds and players from all types of families and histories, the 1972 team really ended up a very close-knit group—exactly what Williamson had in mind.

The team camaraderie carried over in McIntosh's case when they arrived in Sapporo. A bad shoulder separation during the domestic schedule put McIntosh on the shelf for six weeks of the tour.

"I healed up and was playing pretty well when we got over to Sapporo. After playing a couple of games in Tokyo, I tweaked my shoulder again," he said. "I was hurting pretty good. Murray and I sat down, and we talked. I said, 'Look, I'm not going to jeopardize what the team has going here, so you use me however you want to use me.' I didn't play a whole hell of a lot over there."

That attitude was instilled in every single man who suited up for the 1972 U.S. Olympic hockey team. Even when the team was preparing for the medal ceremony, sacrifice was the order of the day when the big defenseman arrived to the rink wearing a different color of turtleneck than his teammates since the one that he was issued before the Olympics was two sizes too small.

"I was wearing a different turtleneck than everybody else, and our manager Hal Trumble said, 'You can't wear that turtleneck.' So he traded with me because he wasn't going on the ice."

Nobody knows the depths in which men will endure when a common goal is within reach. McIntosh was one cog in a wheel of undistinguished Americans who played for each other in search of gold and struck silver in the land of the rising sun.

Where is he now? Bruce McIntosh now owns a golf course in 50 Lakes, Minnesota.

PETE SEARS

Born: March 14, 1947 • Jersey No. 1 • Vietnam War Veteran— served 1968-69

"I really had to make a decision because I was married and had a young daughter. It meant I was going to have to travel out there without a job, without hardly any money to speak of— it was a question of is this something that I could really afford to do?"

Pete Sears was 24 years old in the Buffalo Sabres training camp when he had to make the decision of his life.

After spending two years playing hockey and studying at Oswego State University, a tour of duty in Vietnam carrying a .60-caliber machine gun through the jungle; returning to college, where he earned All-America honors; a bout with malaria; and driving halfway across the country and back with his wife and baby pursuing an opportunity to be seen by the 1972 Olympic coach during summer league hockey in Minneapolis, it came down to answering one question from Coach Murray Williamson.

"Murray asked me if I was still interested in playing with the Olympic team."

Sears was a native of the cozy, Adirondack winter chalet village made forever memorable in 1980—Lake Placid—where Olympic dreams were interwoven in the fabric of the population since 1932.

"Growing up in Lake Placid, you would talk with people who had lived through that. And there were a lot of people that lived in the community that had participated in the Olympics—not in hockey but in other sports. There was always something in the papers and conversation around town about this guy and what he did. That just helped me build up an interest, probably more than a lot of the kids there."

Sears's small-town roots served him well when it came to playing sports at Lake Placid High.

"Our school was extremely small—only 65 in my senior class. Almost all the same guys played baseball, hockey and football together, so we knew each other extremely well. I was fortunate in hockey that I got to play regularly as a freshman goalie. I got to play in every game all the way up through high school."

The success Sears had experienced in high school attracted interest from North Country neighbor Clarkson University in Potsdam, New York. The young goaltender wanted to continue his playing career but had no interest in attending prep school, as suggested by the Clarkson coaches, for one more year of seasoning.

"I had a couple of friends who had come down to Oswego State where they had just started a program in the mid-'60s, and they were very high on the program. They convinced me to come down there and talk to the coach, George Crowe. I went down to talk to him, watched a few games, talked with some of the players, and really liked the place. That's what convinced me. I ended up at Oswego State and played two years there."

In 1967, Sears made another bold decision that ultimately would affect his future Olympic dream. Sears, 19, left Oswego to try out for the 1968 U.S. Olympic hockey team. Sears loaded up his gear and headed for the open tryout being held in Massachusetts.

"It's not like it is today," Sears explained. "Anybody who wanted to try out would show up, and they would put you through their paces for about three or four days."

Following the first day of tryouts, Williamson came over to talk to Sears and told him the team was basically picked, but he was using the tryouts to see as many players as he could for the future. Having no formal scouting bureau, Williamson used the open tryouts to "discover" players who might otherwise have been overlooked because of lack of exposure.

Sears continued through the four days of tryouts, and Williamson again approached the goalie. "We don't really have a place for you now, but I'd really like for you to play at a higher level. What would your feelings be about possibly going out and playing in Green Bay, Wisconsin?"

With the encouragement of Williamson, Sears figured he was being given an opportunity to try to live his dream someday—playing on an Olympic hockey team. Following the Olympic tryout, Sears went home to Lake Placid and decided to pack his car and head to Green Bay.

"I headed out to Green Bay all by myself, got myself a job. Actually, the guy who owned the team in Green Bay owned a chain of grocery stores, so I got a job working in a grocery store, practiced every night, and on the weekends, we played games every Friday and Saturday. I did that for about three or four months until I got my notice that I was being drafted into the Army."

In December 1967, Sears once again returned to Lake Placid, this time to ready himself for induction into the United States Army. After eight weeks of Basic Training and eight more of Advanced Training, he received his orders—he'd be shipped to frontline Vietnam for the next year.

Having served his country on the battlefield, Sears again set his sights on trying to resume a hockey career at Oswego State and hoped he would have another shot at an Olympic tryout for the 1972 U.S. team. Despite being off skates for nearly two years while serving in the Army, Sears contacted the new hockey coach at Oswego State, Herb Hammond, and told him he'd like to once again come out for the team. After receiving a very enthusiastic letter encouraging him to come out, Sears re-enrolled in September 1969.

"When I got back to Oswego, I came down with some kind of sickness," he explained. "I was extremely sick with a temperature of 105 degrees. Nobody could figure out what it was in the college infirmary. They sent me to Oswego Hospital, and they couldn't figure out what it was. Finally, my father and my wife, Kay, said we couldn't go on any longer with this, and they sent me down to the VA (Veterans Administration) Hospital in Syracuse. Within two days, they knew exactly what I had—malaria. They knew exactly how to treat it, and within a couple of weeks, they had it under control. I was able to get out of the hospital and get back to school. I started my classes even though I was a couple of weeks late."

With that auspicious re-start, Sears finished his last two years at Oswego, played hockey, and was named the school's first-ever All-American.

"Our team had a fair amount of success," explained Sears. "We had some good hockey players. It was a little bit different back then because our team wasn't officially a Division II school until my senior year. Other than that, we pretty much played an open schedule. We played a lot of

Division I teams, a lot of Canadian teams. It was good for me because I played against a lot of good competition. It really helped me build my skills back up again after having been off the ice for so long."

Having graduated from Oswego in 1971, Sears once again focused on attaining his Olympic dream. He again wrote Williamson to express his interest in being considered for the 1972 Olympic team. Williamson wrote the now-Vietnam veteran and told him it had been a while, but he was willing to give the goalie a chance if Sears was willing to come out to Minnesota and play in a premier summer league featuring the best Division I players in the West and other potential Olympic hopefuls. Again, Sears had to make another major life decision.

"I really had to make a decision because I was married and had a young daughter. It meant I was going to have to travel out there without a job, without hardly any money to speak of—it was a question of, 'Is this something that I could really afford to do?' With the encouragement of my wife, we headed out there. When I got there, I went to the unemployment office and told them I was a veteran. They got me a job working in a factory during the day. At night, I was playing hockey in a summer league."

Sears played all summer long and had limited contact with the low-key Olympic coach throughout his stay.

"The Olympic coach stopped by to see me a few times after I played to let me know he was watching, but I don't think I talked to him more than twice."

The summer came to an end, and Sears didn't know where he stood with Williamson so he headed back East to the Buffalo Sabres training camp after receiving a letter expressing interest in having the goalie come to tryout camp.

"Since I hadn't heard anything from the Olympic coach, I knew I had to do something," remembered Sears. "So my wife and I headed back East. She went back to Lake Placid with our daughter, and I headed to camp with the Buffalo Sabres in St. Catherine's, Ontario."

The Sabres, coached by the legendary Punch Imlach, featured Rick Martin and Gilbert Perreault, who were only in their second years. Sears started skating on the ice every day with Buffalo and was there for a week when he got a call from his wife. She told him Murray Williamson called her and wanted to know where he was.

A confused Sears asked his wife, "'What do you mean?' She said, 'Well, he called and was rather upset. He said that he brought you out to Minneapolis for the summer to watch you play and all of a sudden you were gone.' So she gave me his number, and I called him up and he gave me a little bit of hell. He said, 'What the heck ya doin'?' I told him I hadn't heard from him and I had the chance to go to camp with Buffalo so that's where I am."

Williamson asked Sears if he was still interested in playing with the Olympic team. Sears was emphatic with his reply and the coach told him about the next tryout in Minneapolis coming up in about three or four days. Williamson wanted Sears at that tryout.

"I hung up the phone and went to talk with Punch Imlach and told him my story," said Sears. "He said, 'Pete, I would never want to talk you out of something like that. I would encourage you to do that. I wouldn't be able to promise you anything here with the Sabres anyway. I would encourage you to do that if you think you have a chance to make it.'"

Once again, Sears packed up from Buffalo, hopped in his car and drove out to Minneapolis all by himself. Again, his wife Kay and daughter Ranee were home in Lake Placid.

Following the tryout in Minneapolis, Sears went to Bemidji and established himself as a "first on the ice, last off the ice" type of player. Figuring that was his best chance at making the team, Sears decided he would not be out-worked for a position on the team. In December 1971, the team was in Dartmouth, New Hampshire, preparing for the night's game with a morning practice when Williamson took Sears aside and told him he would be traveling to Japan in February with the team. After 30-plus games—in which Sears had played the majority—and nearly six weeks before the Olympic Games, the introverted Vietnam veteran and All-America college goaltender from Lake Placid was named to the Olympic team.

"I called my family and told them, and I don't think they could believe it," recalled Sears. "A lot of people probably thought I was just chasing a dream that really couldn't happen. It really was just a tremendous weight off my shoulders. Everyone would say, 'You must have really enjoyed the Olympic experience?' It was really hard to enjoy anything because it was such a mentally draining type of thing working out every day and not knowing what was going to happen."

Having played half of the pre-Olympic schedule as the No. 1 goaltender on the team, Sears was confronted again by Williamson several weeks before the team was to travel to Sapporo.

"Murray said, 'We're going to pick up Mike Curran a couple of weeks before we head out, and he's going to be our starting goalie. You gonna have a problem with that?' I said, 'Hell no!' Just being told I was going to be on the team was all I ever really wanted."

And Sears meant it.

"I was just happier than hell to be a member of the team. I just did my job and tried to stay out of everybody's way."

The way Sears saw the situation, he was just fortunate to have gone through Vietnam and come back with the ability to continue his hockey career and aspire toward his Olympic dream.

"To me, the Vietnam thing, the hockey part of it, the Olympic part of it, is one in the same thing. You're representing your country. You're willing to do anything you can for your country. In the Army, it's give your life. In hockey, it's represent your country even though you know you may not play but you want to be a part of it. In a way they're kind of the same thing—you're going out busting your butt every day in Vietnam. You're going out there and busting your butt every day in hockey. You develop friendships in the Army with guys you want to depend on you, and you depend on them for your life. In hockey, you want to be able to depend on your teammates to support you when you play well or if you're not playing so well. To me, they kind of went together."

Where is he now? Peter Sears, now retired, taught middle school in Oswego, New York.

TIM REGAN

Born: December 28, 1949 • Jersey No. 24 • Draft No. 128

"I was just a kid from nowhere. I was able to take part in something that an awful lot of kids only dream about, and that's all that they are able to do—dream. For me it happened."

Tim Regan made a habit of coming up big when it mattered most and capitalizing on opportunities presented to him. Regan did it as a schoolboy goaltender in Cranston, Rhode Island, and later as a 21-year-old on the nationally prominent Boston University clubs of the early 1970s, where he earned an Olympic chance, and then as a young pro out of college for the Buffalo Sabres.

Regan was asked to try out for the 1972 U.S. Olympic hockey team in August 1971. The would-be senior goaltender at BU was coming off a NCAA Championship season when he decided that leaving school to pursue an Olympic dream might not be in his best interest.

"I did not have a family," explained Regan. "I did not have a mother or father. I didn't do it because I thought if I left school I wouldn't be able to maintain my scholarship, and that I'd probably never go back to school. So I opted to not try out."

As Regan settled into his final season as the Terriers' backstop, the Olympic Games in Sapporo were far from his mind. Not until November, during a flu epidemic on the Boston College campus, would Regan have the opportunity to capitalize on a career break, which ultimately carved out his hockey destiny.

The Olympic Committee had organized an Olympic night at the Boston Garden where figure skater Janet Lynn skated, pairs figure skaters also took the ice, and the evening culminated with the U.S. Olympic hockey team playing an exhibition game against the Boston College Eagles. A week before the "Olympic Garden Party" was to occur, several members of the BC team got the flu, requiring them to spend time in the school's infirmary. Boston College called the Olympic team and informed them the Eagles probably wouldn't make a fair representation for the evening, and then suggested that they call NCAA champion and Commonwealth Avenue nemesis Boston University. BU coach Jack Kelley informed his group at practice of the development, and the Terriers were thrilled at the opportunity to challenge the impending U.S. Olympic team.

The night ended with a 4-4 tie as Regan sparkled in the nets for the Terriers. The next morning Regan's dormitory phone rang. It was Olympic coach Murray Williamson.

"He congratulated me on the game and asked me if I wanted to join the team," recalled the flabbergasted Regan. "I was shocked. I was 21 years old, and I told him I'd have to check with the University and my uncle, who was the Superintendent of the Rhode Island State Police."

Williamson informed him there was actually someone already at the State police barracks in North Scituate talking to his uncle.

"I thought to myself, 'Boy, these guys are really serious.'"

After receiving blessings from his uncle and his school, Regan wanted a guarantee that, if he joined the team, he would go to Sapporo. Williamson obliged, and Regan joined the team one day after Christmas.

"I was just a kid from nowhere," said Regan. "I was able to take part in something that an awful lot of kids only dream about, and that's all that they are able to do—dream. For me, it happened."

Regan's introduction to international play was as swift as his ascent onto the Olympic team. He arrived in Colorado Springs, went directly to the Broadmoor Hotel, and then to the hockey rink to prepare for the upcoming World Cup Tournament with Russia and Czechoslovakia. As Regan was sitting in the stands watching a team practice, a man approached the peach-faced college student.

"Are you Tim Regan?"

"Yes, I am."

"I'm Murray Williamson, coach of the Olympic team." Williamson continued by asking, "What do you think of these guys?"

"Who are these guys? They look like a beer league team," Regan answered.

"That's the Russian hockey team," Williamson informed him.

"That's the Russian hockey team? Geez, they don't look like much to me," said Regan.

"Well, we're actually playing them—we're playing them tonight, and you're starting in goal," Williamson responded.

"I went down to the dressing room, laid out my equipment, and then went to my room at the hotel for a nap. While we're playing them later that night, about 10 minutes into the game, the score was 6-0 Russians, and they were moving the puck like I'd never seen in college hockey. Tommy Mellor, who I grew up with, comes up to me during a face-off, leans in and says, 'How ya doing?'

"I looked at Tommy and said what Butch said to Sundance, 'Who the fuck are these guys?' He started laughing. We finished the first period, and we're getting beat like 8-0. Murray comes up to me in the locker room, and says, 'What do you think of these guys now?' 'You know, they're not that bad,' I said. Everybody started laughing. We got beat 13-3."

Regan was a plucky competitor who played eight games before the team headed to Sapporo. Although he was promised a trip to Sapporo, he was not guaranteed playing time when the team arrived in Japan. In fact, when it came time for Coach Williamson to name his goaltending tandem for the Games, Mike Curran was named the starting goaltender and Pete Sears garnered back-up duties—relegating Regan to sitting in his civilian clothes and watching from the stands.

"I was a little disappointed in not playing in the Olympics, but Mike Curran was playing great. He was a great guy, and that's the way it was."

In fact, Regan left Sapporo before the Games were completed because of a deal that his college coach, Jack Kelley, made with Williamson. Kelley agreed to relinquish Regan—but only under the condition that his goaltender return to Boston if he wasn't playing. Plus, BU needed him to tend their nets in case of an injury to their back-up goalie Dan Brady. Williamson received a call reporting that Brady had twisted his knee—Kelley needed his senior back in the Terrier lineup if he wasn't going to see action in Sapporo.

"I got a call from Murray, and he told me Jack Kelley had called," remembered Regan. "Dan Brady got hurt, and I'd have to go back. So I packed my bags and got on a plane in Sapporo to Tokyo to San Francisco to Boston."

Although Regan missed the rest of the Olympic tournament, he felt it was his duty to uphold the deal made between his college and the Olympic program.

"I missed not staying with the Olympic team to be honest with you," admitted Regan. "We won the silver medal, and Robbie Ftorek brought back my silver medal. He brought it over to BU, and said, 'Hey, you're part of the program, you're part of the team, and this is yours.'"

Although the moment was anticlimactic, Regan had perspective.

"I went back to BU, made it to the National Championship Tournament, and was named the Most Valuable Player in the National Tournament. I kind of got it all."

Shortly after his college career ended, having won two NCAA championships and a silver medal during his time at Boston University, Regan's hockey future would have another moment that earned him respect and an opportunity to continue his hockey career.

"I was with Buffalo, and it was either in an exhibition game or at the very beginning of the season that we played the Philadelphia Flyers," remembered Regan.

"I wasn't playing, and it was during the height of the Flyers as the Broad Street Bullies. There was about two minutes left in the game, and Gil Perreault was cross-checked by Dave Schultz, who was their tough guy at the time. All of a sudden, it became a bench-clearing brawl. So I jumped off the bench and saw Bernie Parent skating down the center of the ice towards the brawl. I grabbed him at about center ice and said, 'Mr. Parent, sir, I'm really sorry, but I have to grab somebody. I just graduated from college.'

"He said to me in broken English, 'You pull me. I pull you. You pull me. I pull you.' We were going at pretend fighting pretty good when one of their defensemen, Ed Van Impe, grabs me by the scruff of the neck to protect his goalie, Parent, who had just won the Vezina Trophy the year before. Parent said something to him in French, and Van Impe let go of me. Parent grabbed me again, and continued saying, 'You pull me. I pull you.' It all broke up, and I skated over to our bench re-adjusting my jersey and shoulder pads. The guys thought I had balls as big as all outdoors for taking on Parent. I gained instant credibility. I never did tell any of them what we were saying to each other."

Regan played for three more years in the Sabres organization, mostly in the American Hockey League. Throughout his career, he had found himself in the right place at the right time. Fate and the hockey gods seemed to have had a way of shining brightly on the Rhode Island native, and he was fortunate enough and smart enough to capitalize on his opportunities.

Where is he now? Tim Regan now works in the lumber business in Cranston, Rhode Island.

February 13, 1972—7:04 p.m. EST
FINLAND 4 - SWEDEN 3

"Henry, don't bullshit me, because I'm gonna knock you through the window if you're telling me something that's not true."

—DICK MCGLYNN

The first game ended up being a seesaw battle as the Finns jumped out to a quick 1-0 lead behind Heikki Jaern's goal at 2:48 of the first period. The Swedes tied the game, then quickly took a 2-1 lead with goals late in the period by Tord Lundstrom and Bjorn Palmquist. The second period once again saw the Finns charging as Juhani Tamminen scored to tie the game at 2-2 just 35 seconds into the period. It stayed that way until 16:32, when Sweden's Palmquist scored his second of the game to give his team a 3-2 lead after two periods. But the Finns fought back in the third period as Matti Keinonen scored at 12:43 to knot the game at 3-3. Two minutes and 15 seconds later, the Finns scored the go-ahead goal on a power play as Lauri Mononen put his team up for good, 4-3, completing the scoring for what turned out to be another of the tournament's most improbable upsets. With just about five minutes left in the game, the attending U.S. players and their coach couldn't believe what they were seeing.

"It was unbelievable that it was going to happen," said Mellor. "We were going to get a medal, and we could get a silver medal if what should happen, happens in the next game—Russia beating Czechoslovakia."

The game ended, and the unexpected had happened, the Finns knocked off the Swedes, 4-3. The U.S. had won a medal. Now it was up to the Czechs and the Soviets to determine the color—silver or bronze.

Williamson and the others who were at the Finland-Sweden game rushed back to the Olympic Village to round up the rest of the team and tell them the good news that they had won a medal.

"A lot of us were still sleeping and into my room—I was rooming with Mark Howe, Stuey, and Robbie Ftorek—comes Henry Boucha," remembers McGlynn. "He said, 'Dickie, the Finns just upset the Swedes! Murray said to wear your wine-colored pants and your white turtlenecks with the Olympic logo on them and get down to rink for the Czech-Russia game. We're in the hunt for a silver medal.'"

Amidst a team of practical jokers, McGlynn wasn't sure if Boucha was kidding or not.

"I said, 'Henry, don't bullshit me, because I'm gonna knock you through the window if you're telling me something that's not true,'" continued McGlynn. "He said, 'Dick, I'm telling you—the Finns upset the Swedes. I swear.' So, we were running around yelling while getting our clothes together in order to get down to the rink."

Because they were assured of a medal, they all needed to wear the same uniform for the medal ceremony, which would take place immediately following the Czechoslovakia-Russia game. As the players were running around getting ready to go to the game, some of the players started to worry about the unthinkable—a Czechoslovakian win over the Russians. Their goal from Day One was to win a medal, and they had done that—if the Russians just did what they're supposed to do, the U.S. players naturally wanted the now almost-tangible silver medal.

As the players were making their way to the rink, they spoke about the possible scenario of a Czech win. McGlynn turned to his New England buddy, Mellor, and said, "Tommy, don't worry."

But Mellor was unconvinced saying, "But if the Czechs win. ..."

McGlynn cut him off before he could finish adding, "Tommy, that is never going to happen."

Still not totally convinced by his buddy, Mellor asked, "How do you know?"

McGlynn replied, "Because Lenny Gagnon is refereeing the game, and that will never happen."

Gagnon, who just over a year earlier had been the one whispering in Williamson's ear about McGlynn during the Olympic tryouts, was the childhood friend of McGlynn's father, and he was well aware of what a Russian win meant to the United States. As an experienced international referee, he was well versed in how the Europeans liked to referee as well. He was going to make sure that the ice was on an even plain for the two teams during the gold medal game.

KEITH "HUFFER" CHRISTIANSEN

Born: July 14, 1944 • Jersey No. 8 • Draft No. Deferred

"I was told as captain I got to go up on the podium and accept the medal for the team. I was just the lucky guy, that's all."

In any photograph you examine or any eight-millimeter movies you may have seen of Keith "Huffer" Christiansen standing on the second podium to accept a silver medal on behalf of his United States teammates during the medal ceremony of the 1972 Olympic ice hockey competition, you may think he's alone. That couldn't have been further from the truth.

"I was told as captain I got to go up on the podium and accept the medal for the team. I was just the lucky guy, that's all."

In fact, "old-timer" Christiansen at 27 years old, was one of a handful of veterans on a team that averaged 22 years old and had been one of Coach Murray Williamson's first picks when it came time to build a nucleus for his Olympic team. On that fateful Sunday in February, Christiansen was far from being alone on that medal podium. Not only was a piece of every one of his teammates with him, he also carried thoughts of his wife and kids, who sacrificed time away from their husband and father so he could pursue a career that he thought would lead him to the National Hockey League.

"I was one of the older guys on the team, and I was about ready to hang it up except for that '71 team that made a pretty good effort. Then with the '72 team, I knew that I was going to be there. It was a great effort— a lot of blood, sweat, and tears. I was married. I had a family. It was hard on my wife, and I had a son and daughter. It was hard on the whole family, but thank goodness, they were behind me. They knew at the time it was a big dream of mine, and it became a reality."

For the Canadian-born-and-raised Christiansen, his dream centered around playing in the National Hockey League one day. It wasn't until he transferred across the border to International Falls High School and became an American citizen that an Olympic dream ever crossed his mind. A full four-year hockey scholarship to the University of Minnesota-Duluth followed Christiansen's high school years, and the snowball effect of success took hold in Duluth.

"I was pretty lucky. I was All-America and MVP of the WCHA (Western Collegiate Hockey Association) and had a pretty good career. From there, I played on two U.S. National teams, and that's where it really started. I played for Murray, and he was the coach in 1970 and '71, so I guess I was one of the few that had a spot on the '72 team even before the tryouts. There were a few of us who had international experience— myself, Tim Sheehy, Henry Boucha, and Jim McElmury. We were all young guys that came through the '71 team that Murray coached. So he knew most of us."

As one of the veterans, Christiansen also had the honor and distinction of wearing the venerable and time-honored "C" on the left breast of his jersey, which already puffed with pride from having U-S-A stitched across the chest. With the "C" also came responsibility that made him stand out amongst his teammates and coach—especially when it came time to help make a peace offering between his coach and Mike Curran.

That moment of leadership, while it may have caused conflict on some teams, was a testimony to the level of confidence Christiansen had in himself—and the level of trust Williamson and the rest of his teammates had placed in the former All-American from Minnesota-Duluth. Christiansen knew Williamson was steadfast to sticking with and implementing his plan, program and style.

"We played a little bit more of a European style than previous teams. Murray was a real student of the game."

And if Christiansen's coach and teammates supported him unequivocally, the same can be said about his family as well.

"They were always behind me. My wife was one of my biggest supporters. We had to move to different cities with two kids. She was home with the kids while I was running around all over the country playing hockey. Without her support and the way she did it, it never would've happened in my situation. There is no two ways about that. She's just as proud of it as I am."

Still outspoken, Christiansen opined about the state of Olympic hockey and is disgusted. "What we did and what the '80 Miracle team did will never be duplicated because they [the Olympics] sold out to the NHL. I honestly don't care to watch Olympic hockey anymore. Those guys don't care as much about playing for an Olympic team as we did. Going back to amateurs in Olympic hockey would probably be more exciting and probably more people would care about it."

To this day, Christiansen has not forgotten the roles played by all of his teammates, coaches, administrators, and family when the conversation arises about his Olympic experience. Though one thing the '72 captain does find disparaging when discussing their unthinkable success in Sapporo is the fact this team has been forgotten.

"We flew mostly under the radar. I don't think most people knew what was going on and where we were. I had a friend who was a ski jumper and was aware of what we were doing but, generally, nobody really knew that we were going to get a medal. It's a little frustrating because sometimes the hockey people forget us, too. We were the only team to win a medal outside the United States since 1956. So, we're pretty proud of that."

Steadfast and true, Christiansen still stands up for his 1972 Olympic brethren—just as he did in Sapporo over three decades ago—and just as true today as it was then, Christiansen knows he's not alone.

Christiansen was inducted into the USA Hockey Hall of Fame along with Murray Williamson in November 2005.

Where is he now? Keith Christensen is now a car salesman in Duluth, Minnesota.

JIM McELMURY

Born: January 1, 1946 • Jersey No. 2 • Draft No. 236

"Us small college guys took heat for being small town, but they accepted us as being a part of that team."

When you hail from a place known as Little Canada, Minnesota (population 9,971), it might not be too much of a stretch to think there are three things that could immediately cross the minds of people who know nothing about it.

- The place is named "Little" for a reason, if you blink, you'll miss it.
- This Little place is little, but it's a great place to grow up and think of big dreams to accomplish.
- Little Canada, Minnesota might not be so little after all, just 15 minutes from Minneapolis-St. Paul.

Even though the name is Little Canada, it fostered big dreams for 1972 U.S. Olympian Jim McElmury. In fact, McElmury never bothered to worry about little, big, or in-between when it came to hockey. When it came time to decide where he would go to college, McElmury looked 225 miles north of Little Canada to the Ojibwe Tribe region and opted for the little-known college—except in hockey circles—whose name means "a lake with crossing waters"—Bemidji State.

While playing at Bemidji for coach Bob Peters, McElmury took his first small steps toward an unbeknownst berth on the 1972 U.S. Olympic team.

"I started with Murray and some of the guys in 1970 on the U.S. National team," explained McElmury. "Murray knew my college coach, so to have him as the coach of the Olympic team helped me at least to open the door and have a chance. There were three of us from Bemidji State that year, including Charlie Brown and Bryan Grand."

McElmury and Brown were seniors on the '71 National team. "The next year worked out great because we were done with our senior year and done with college," said McElmury. "It was just a natural progression from there. The Olympics were next. They were trying to keep a core bunch of guys together, and we both ended up staying and playing with the team that year. For me, it went from 1970 to 1971 to 1972, so it worked out great."

Joining the "small-town guys" from Minnesota was Pete Sears, who came from the Olympic hamlet in the North Country of New York State—Lake Placid—and was an All-America goaltender at Oswego State. McElmury, Brown, and Sears were aberrations when it came to big-time college hockey programs.

"Us small college guys took heat for being small town, but they accepted us as being a part of that team," recalled McElmury. "There was no animosity just because some guys went to a different school."

As long as you could play, and McElmury could—17 goals and 14 assists during the 47-game pre-Olympic schedule—where you hailed from didn't matter. With guys coming in and out of the system throughout the course of the schedule, it was imperative to worry most about your own job and not worry about the other guy and where he might have attended school.

McElmury's college roots served him well when it came time for training camp for the 1972 Olympic team, which took place on the Bemidji campus. McElmury couldn't have been happier about this little development.

"For me, having gone to school there, it was great that Bemidji was one of the sites for training in the fall. That took a little pressure off because I was around a place that I had been around before. I felt pretty good about it, though. There were other defensemen and forwards coming in, but having played two years before helped in terms of Murray seeing what you could and couldn't do."

Training at Bemidji was difficult. USA Hockey had never set up a program like this before, and Williamson ushered in an entirely new way of thinking about the Olympics and training after having visited Russia's coach Anatoly Tarasov in the summer. In years past, guys would meet in New York, fly to wherever the World Championships or Olympics were held, and play. Some guys barely knew each other and had virtually no ice time together as a team. That changed in Bemidji.

"In years past, the U.S. sent a team, but as far as doing anything as a team practicing and training-wise beforehand, they didn't really do anything until they got over to where they were playing," explained McElmury. "Murray brought everyone together. His feeling was in order to be successful this is what had to be done."

In Bemidji, the members of the '72 team knew they were going to have to do things differently if they stood a chance of competing in Sapporo.

"We were going to have to be in a little bit better shape than other teams," thought McElmury. "We were going to have to be better prepared, both mentally and physically. Having that extra off-ice training that no one ever took the time to do before gave us a better outlook and more confidence."

McElmury is quick to point out that Williamson's little idea to have his group train, eat, play, and live together paid big dividends not only for the '72 team but beyond.

"Everybody talks about how much the '80 team did with the training and extra schedule, but we did that in '72. There was never any credit given for that or the schedule that we put together back then, which was a model for '80 and the off-ice training that they did."

And when McElmury thinks back on the days when he stepped onto the biggest stage of the athletic landscape during the winter of 1972, his most vivid memory was the Opening Ceremony and walking into the stadium with a group of athletes from around the world.

"Going through the initial ceremony was really something," reflects McElmury. "There was a lot of snow, and they had all these snow sculptures around. The snow sculptures were unbelievable—how big they were and what it took to make those things. The whole city was decorated. When I see the Olympics now, it's automatic that I think back on what we were wearing and all the memories."

The native of Little Canada still marvels at the idea of what he and his teammates accomplished in February 1972. Not many people outside the hockey world had ever heard of the little town in Minnesota he called home, let alone the small school in the northern part of the state—Bemidji State—that produced two Olympians.

Ultimately, McElmury realized big dreams were built from taking small steps. Before it was over, he was standing on the second step of the podium in an Olympic ceremony that produced one of the biggest and most lasting memories of his life.

Where is he now? Jim McElmury now runs a sporting goods business in Cottage Grove, Minnesota.

HAL TRUMBLE

MANAGER

1970 U.S. National Team (Bucharest, Romania)
1971 U.S. National Team (Bern/Geneva, Switzerland)
1972 U.S. Olympic Team (Sapporo, Japan)

"They were an excellent team that represented the country well."

When the last chapter of history is written about the silver medal-winning 1972 U.S. Olympic hockey team, it would be an unfortunate mistake if team manager Hal Trumble's name was not included as an integral member of that team. After all it was Trumble, along with Williamson, who spearheaded the efforts to retrieve players such as Stu Irving, Dick McGlynn, Henry Boucha, and others from military duty at home and abroad in order for them to serve their country at the Winter Olympics.

Trumble is the first to admit his job was mainly administrative: arranging travel and accommodations, making sure the U.S. team was aware of all the rules they had to comply with from the different alphabet organizations of any Olympic Games—IOC, IIHF, USOC—and anything else that helped Williamson stay focused on the business of how to win hockey games.

And win they did.

Trumble is quick to point out not one of the 20 players that comprised this "Forgotten Team" gave them a hard time. "They were an excellent team that represented the country well."

Where is he now? Hal Trumble, a former USA Hockey Executive Director, is now retired and living in San Clemente, California.

DR. GEORGE NAGABODS

TEAM PHYSICIAN

1967 National Team (Vienna, Austria)
1968 U.S. Olympic Team (Grenoble, France)
1970 U.S. National Team (Bucharest, Romania)
1971 U.S. National Team (Bern/Geneva, Switzerland)
1972 U.S. Olympic Team (Sapporo, Japan)
1976 U.S. Olympic Team (Innsbruck, Austria)
1980 U.S. Olympic Team (Lake Placid, New York)

Dr. George "Doc Nags" Nagabods's athletic resume places him at some of the United States' most interesting, exciting, and unforgettable Olympic Winter Games ever. The Olympic career of the Edina, Minnesota, resident originally from Riga, Latvia, spanned from the seedling year of 1968, when Murray Williamson was trying to transform the way the United States approached the game, through the silver medal-winning year of 1972, a miracle in 1980, ending more than two decades later.

In all, Nagabods's longstanding medical career with USA Hockey began in 1967 and ended in 1990 after serving 23 years for 15 U.S. men's and women's National teams and four men's Olympic teams. In addition to his work with the National and Olympic teams, Nagabods looked after players on five U.S. National junior teams, two Canada Cup squads, the first-ever U.S. Women's National team in 1990, 1988 U.S. Select-17 team, and members of the 1989 Spengler Cup.

Besides more than two decades with Team USA, Nagabods served as team physician for the University of Minnesota men's ice hockey team from 1958 until 1992. During that time, the Golden Gophers hoisted the NCAA Championship trophy three times. And to top it off, Nagabods's hockey career encompassed a stint as team physician for the National Hockey League's Minnesota North Stars as well, from 1984-92.

Where is he now? George Nagobods is now retired and lives in Edina, Minnesota.

FRANCIS "BUD" KESSEL

Equipment Manager

1972 U.S. Olympic Team (Sapporo, Japan)
1980 U.S. Olympic Team (Lake Placid, New York)
1984 U.S. Olympic Team (Sarajevo, Yugoslavia)

The late Bud Kessel's career culminated in 1980 as equipment manager for the gold medal-winning U.S. Olympic hockey team, but prior to that, he also served in the same capacity for the silver medal-winning 1972 U.S. Olympic hockey team and the 1984 U.S. Olympic hockey team. Affectionately known as "Buddy the Owl," Kessel spent more than three decades attending to this sometimes-thankless trade.

A native of New York City, Kessel began his career with the New York Rovers of the U.S. Hockey League before moving on to work with Fred Shero as equipment manager of the St. Paul Saints of the Central Hockey League. Following the 1972 Olympics, Kessel became the first equipment manager of the NHL's Atlanta Flames. He then moved to Colorado, where he worked for the St. Louis Blues' farm team, the Denver Spurs, and then returned to the Gopher State and the Minnesota Fighting Saints of the World Hockey Association (WHA). When the Fighting Saints folded, he became the equipment manager for Herb Brooks's University of Minnesota teams of the 1970s.

Besides serving as equipment manager for three U.S. Olympic hockey teams, Kessel also served in the same capacity for several U.S. National teams.

Where is he now? Francis "Bud" Kessel passed away in June 1998 at the age of 70.

GOLD MEDAL GAME
February 13, 1972—10:33 p.m. EST
USSR 5 - CZECHOSLOVAKIA 2

"They were skating around in warm-ups giving us the 'wink, wink' and raising their hands, like saying, 'Don't worry, we're not going to let the Czechs beat us here. We're going to take care of everything for you.'"

—JIM MCELMURY

Dressed in their white turtleneck sweaters and cabernet pants—despite their collegial relationship with the Soviet players—the U.S. team was in the stands doing the unimaginable: rooting for the Russians. Because the tie-breaking system also was based on head-to-head competition, if the Czechs lost, they would be tied with the U.S. with a 3-2 record. Since the U.S. beat the Czechs in their medal-round game, if the Russians won, it was silver for the U.S.—if the Czechs pulled the upset, it was bronze.

"The Russians obviously saw us and knew we would all be there," remembers defenseman Jim McElmury. "It seemed like the Russians wanted us to finish higher than the Czechs anyway. There was no question about that in their minds."

Most of the U.S. players thought, much as the previous game with Sweden being a heavy favorite over Finland, there was no way the Russians were going to lose this game. They were playing for the gold and weren't about to leave their "A" game back at the Olympic Village, especially playing against their hated rivals. Either way, the U.S. squad had accomplished their goal of winning a medal—but since they had the chance, silver would make it even better.

The Russians struck first when Blinov scored at 5:25 of the first period to give the USSR a 1-0 lead. Nearly eight minutes later, Mikhailov made it 2-0 for the Russians despite the Czechs forcing much of the play in the first period. In the second period, Firsov—one of the greatest Russian players in their history playing in his last game—made it 3-0 at the 2:05 mark. With each Russian goal, the Americans celebrated in the stands as if they were on the ice and had just scored as the realization of winning a silver medal was coming to fruition.

The Russians made it 4-0 as Yevgeny Mishakov scored at 13:41, but the Czechs got one back before the period ended when Vladimir Martinec scored at 18:41 to make it 4-1. Despite the score, the Czechs played tough and actually outshot the Soviets through two periods, 20-19. When the third period started, the once-comfortable four-goal lead had been cut in half as the Czech's Josef Cerny scored to make it 4-2 at 4:44. But five minutes later, the Russians' Mishakov scored his second of the game at 9:50 to give the USSR an insurmountable 5-2 lead. As the clock wound down, the Americans in the stands were growing more excited, and the Czechs on the ice were growing more frustrated.

As the game moved into the later stages of the third period, the tough, chippy game between the two rivals quickly evolved into one of the most violent games the U.S. players had ever witnessed with vicious stick work from both sides. The Americans saw things they'd never seen in a hockey game before or since. Most knew all about the intense hatred the teams harbored toward each other, but they had never seen anything like this first-hand. As time wound down, the Czechs were on a power play as Mishakov was sent off for spearing in the last minute of play. With frustrations boiling over, the Czech's star player, Nedomansky, turned towards the Russian bench 20 feet away and fired the puck straight at them.

"We couldn't believe what we had just seen," said U.S. forward Ron Naslund. "He just turned around and zinged one right at the bench. It just missed one guy's head. If it had hit anybody in the face, it would have killed them."

When the game ended, the U.S. contingency of players, coaches, and officials couldn't believe what had transpired. They were hugging each other and crying as they prepared to go onto the ice for the medal ceremony. The months of hard work had paid off, and they had accomplished their goal. They had finished second in the Olympics to one of the greatest hockey teams ever assembled.

They had won the silver medal.

CR80   CR80   CR80

Overall records (in parenthesis) and standings for the 1972 Olympic Winter Games hockey tournament.

Team	W-L-T	Goals for	Goals against	Points
USSR (4-0-1)	4-0-1	33	13	9
USA (4-2-0)	3-2-0	18	15	6
CZECHOSLOVAKIA (4-2-0)	3-2-0	26	13	6
SWEDEN (3-2-1)	2-2-1	17	13	5
FINLAND (3-3-0)	2-3-0	14	24	4
POLAND (1-5-0)	0-5-0	9	39	0

7

*W*INNING
*S*ILVER

"We all put our white sweaters on, went down on the ice and lined up. IOC President Avery Brundage came around with the medals, and I was thinking, 'This is unbelievable. A schmuck like me from Minneapolis is getting this thing.' He put it around my neck. It was just a wonderful feeling."

—RON NASLUND

As the Czechoslovakia-Russia game wound down with the Russians well in command on their way to a 5-2 win and third-consecutive Olympic gold medal; a realization hit the American players—they were going to win a silver medal.

Like a bunch of 10-year-old kids, they hugged giddily, slapped each other on the back, and cried as they came together from where they were watching in different parts of the rink. All they knew was that they were taking home an Olympic medal—an unexpected feat that no one could've imagined or dreamed of but them. They were

189

going to be able to go home and proudly show all of their family and friends an Olympic medal. That it was silver didn't matter—it could've been bronze or gold and not made any difference. They had done it. They had won a medal.

"That was the goal that we had talked about all year," said Bruce McIntosh. "We're going to the Olympic Games to win a medal. We want to bring something back. At times that didn't look like that was going to be at all possible. Right up to the last day, it didn't look that promising. Then all of a sudden, we went from nothing to a silver medal. We were on Cloud Nine, and there was no coming down for a couple of days."

CRSD   CRSD   CRSD

When the time came for the team to go onto the ice and line up to receive their medals, many of the players couldn't help but remember where they'd come from—all of the people who had helped fuel their dreams, their teammates, and what it meant to be playing for their country in the Olympics. The improbability of it all overwhelmed them with joy.

"We were overwhelmed," said Henry Boucha, who also had thoughts of the Christian brothers, Bill and Roger, who were from Warroad, Minnesota, and had played on the 1960 U.S. gold medal team. "It was just overwhelming to go out there and receive a medal. Everybody had tears in their eyes in celebration. It was just disbelief that we finished second in the world. Winning the silver medal was just amazing. There were so many thoughts racing through my mind. It was just so hard to imagine standing on that podium, winning that silver medal, and remembering how proud I was."

Mike "Lefty" Curran's thoughts were of how far U.S. hockey had come since his days on the 1969 U.S. National team, when they were embarrassed in the World Championship in Stockholm, Sweden, losing every game. At 26 years old, he was the second-oldest player on the team and one of the "gray beards."

"I was thinking we'd go over there [Sapporo] and try and survive," he said. "But I don't think those kids thought that. I told every one of those guys that I went over there hoping that we could come out of there with our pride intact, and instead, we came out of there with a silver medal. It was really rather overwhelming."

Though many of the players were thinking about the past, some were very much in the moment, thinking about the 20 guys they had lived with, fought with, and played with for the past six and a half months.

"I was looking at all the guys with the white sweaters on with medals around their necks," said Robbie Ftorek. "And I was looking up at the flag as it went up and being a little disappointed that ours wasn't going to the top. It was pretty emotional."

Ron Naslund, the oldest player on the team and a veteran of past U.S. National teams, remembered as they got their medals, "We all put our white sweaters on, went down on the ice and lined up. IOC president Avery Brundage came around with the medals, and I was thinking, 'This is unbelievable. A schmuck like me from Minneapolis is getting this thing.'

"He put it around my neck. It was just a wonderful feeling. I was so happy. I was so happy for everybody else. I was happy for the young guys. They were running around. I remember Dickie McGlynn running around, saying, 'I wouldn't sell this thing for $100,000 right now.' I can still remember hearing him say that. Everybody was just very happy and excited."

Others like Craig Sarner and Frank Sanders, who had grown up together, thought not only of the improbability of what this team had accomplished, but also of the improbability of the two of them experiencing it together.

Because Keith "Huffer" Christiansen was the team captain, he was chosen to accept the silver medal for his teammates and stand on the podium.

"One guy on the team got to do that, and I was the guy," said Christiansen. "I was chosen. I was extremely proud of that, and it's something that I'll remember for the rest of my life. I was just so high. We were hoping for a medal, but to stand up on that Olympic podium to accept a medal for your team, it was just unbelievable."

Others couldn't help but think about what it meant to be representing their country. "I have never looked at the American flag quite the same way since I played on this team," said McGlynn. "I have never heard the national anthem where I don't get goose bumps. You know, it affects your whole life. It affects how you think about the country. It is impossible to describe the feeling. But when they raised the flags, and we were all standing there with our medals draped around our necks in those white turtlenecks, all of us were focused on the U.S. flag. When they started to play the Soviet national anthem, we were all humming the U.S. national anthem and watching our flag. We weren't focused on their flag at all. It was unbelievable. And we all talked about that afterwards. It was an emotional experience—tears were running down our cheeks. That one moment is the one that changed my life watching that flag go up the pole. And every time I see the flag and hear the national anthem, it reminds me of that single moment—the greatest athletic moment of my life."

Yet, with all the joy of the moment also came the disappointment of not having the medal ceremony broadcast home to the United States. After pulling off what, at that time, was one of the greatest upsets in U.S. Olympic hockey history, NBC had decided to pull the plug on its coverage of the day immediately following the Czechoslovakia-Russia game. While the American players were preparing to go out onto the ice for the medal ceremony, they saw the red light of the camera and realized that finally the folks back home were going to get to see what they had accomplished—even if it was only the medal ceremony.

"As the officials were rolling out the red carpet, preparing the three podiums for the captains—1-2-3—the red light goes off, and they pull the plugs out and start putting the cameras away," recalls McGlynn. "I was thinking, 'You gotta be shittin' me! That's not possible.' We had just pulled off the upset of the tournament, and they turn the cameras off. I couldn't believe it. I asked Dr. Nagabods to take my camera and take movies of the medal presentation."

There also was disappointment and sadness amongst the team after the medal ceremony because it was over. After nearly seven months, this team of 20 young men that had grown so close was all going to be going their separate ways within days. Some were going to the NHL, some to the WHA, others to semi-pro teams, and others back to school. It didn't seem to sink in until after the medal ceremony—that the warm feeling of accomplishment would soon just turn into lasting memories.

"I don't think we felt it following the Poland game as much as we felt it at the medal ceremony—when we knew this was the last time we were going to be together," remembers Sanders. "After being together for so long, it was a highly emotional time. You're saying, 'Where do I go from here? What's going to happen now?' But, you know, going through your mind when you're sitting there over 10,000 miles from home waiting to be crowned with a medal—first of all, you're overwhelmed with appreciation that you ever had a chance to be in this position. Second, you think of the luck sometimes it takes, along with the hard work that puts you in a position to receive that.

"And then you realize that you probably won't see these guys very often anymore."

8

1960 TO 1972 TO 1980

"When you see that other people before you have done it, and that it can be done, it's a big, big boost to believing you can do it also. I really believe we did set a tone for a lot of athletes."

—ROBBIE FTOREK

The words "on whose shoulders we stand" have been uttered in presidential inaugural addresses, on days of remembrance, and inspirational sermons to put in historical perspective those who came before us.

For the United States Olympic hockey program, the 1972 Olympic team and its coach helped bridge a generation of players from 1960 to 1980 and beyond, creating dreams, breeding success, and ultimately helping to forge a whole new system for how the United States competed and succeeded in international hockey.

Bill and Bob Cleary, Bill and Roger Christian, and Jack McCartan are but a few of the names of the players who helped inspire the next generation of U.S. hockey players when they won the gold medal in Squaw Valley in 1960. For several of the future Olympians who played on the 1972 team, the black and white television images of the U.S. defeating the Soviet Union, Czechoslovakia, and Canada brought some of the first thoughts of playing for the red, white, and blue in the Olympics.

"I was probably 15 years old when we won it in Squaw Valley," remembered goalie Mike "Lefty" Curran. "I was watching this thing happen, the whole game, and I see Jack McCartan playing his role as a goaltender. I was in ninth grade. I had an art class where we were doing some work with paper, and I made an Olympic goalie out of papier-mâché. I thought about how wonderful it would be to represent my country—and to hope to be a goalie for my country and do some of what Jack McCartan did. My dream started then— absolutely."

McCartan's performance in '60 had a similar impact on the '72 team's other goalie as well.

"It definitely had an impact on me," said Pete Sears. "Because I was interested in the Olympics myself, I remember watching several of the U.S. games on television. They showed the whole games of our U.S. team playing there. I remember watching the gold medal game and Jack McCartan playing.

"When Jack McCartan finished, he was selected by the New York Rangers and played a few games for them. I was such a huge Rangers fan that I listened to every game on the radio. I could pick up New York City on my radio in Lake Placid, and I listened at night to every game. I remember the first game he ever played—it was a 2-2 tie. He played a few more games, and they sent him down to the minors to play."

Dick McGlynn also watched those games on television, but he was influenced more personally when he attended the Cleary Brothers Hockey School when he was 12 years old.

"I used to go over to the Brighton Skating Club and watch the Clearys skate," recalled McGlynn. "They had their USA hockey jerseys turned inside-out, but you could see it said USA across the chest. I thought that might be a neat thing to do."

Another strongly influenced member of the '72 team was Warroad, Minnesota native Henry Boucha, as the lore of the Christian brothers and their success in the hockey rink was legendary to all the aspiring kids.

"We had a great opportunity because the Christian brothers are from Warroad," explained Boucha. "Growing up watching the Christian brothers and some of these other great players really gave me the incentive to carry on with my hockey career."

CʒEꝹ   CʒEꝹ   CʒEꝹ

Although the success of the '60 squad might have sparked the dreams of many future hockey players, including the '72 team, the dozen years in between were far from gold, silver, or bronze for USA Hockey. As international hockey shifted into a new style of play, the Russians, Czechs, Swedes, and Finns were becoming the dominant forces. Lack of success in the 1964 and 1968 Winter Olympics—as well as poor showings in other international hockey world championships—proved that the U.S. would have to adapt to the new styles and training methods in order to succeed in the future. The days of informal team selections, when players were told to meet in New York to fly out together without very little practice together (if at all), were gone.

A turning point occurred as USA Hockey chose its team for the 1968 Olympic Games. Under Murray Williamson, a new style of American play was emerging—one that incorporated training methods and a system of play that was foreign at the time, but ultimately would revolutionize American hockey.

With players like Herb Brooks and Lou Nanne leading the team, Williamson introduced a system that included a grueling, but very successful three-month, 35-game domestic and international pre-Olympic schedule against Central professional and International leagues, as well as a pre-Olympic tournament in Grenoble, France. That approach to the Olympic Games would be repeated and strengthened until it bore silver, and then gold in years to follow.

"In '68 we had a great team," remembered Williamson. "We came out of the shoot real good and beat the Czechs, but we finished in sixth out of 10 teams. But we learned many lessons. The seeds for what happened in 1980 were sown that year and in '72. We had a great domestic schedule, team unity with character and chemistry, but we were still inexperienced in international competition."

As Williamson coached the 1970 and 1971 U.S. National teams, he continued to consider preparation for the 1972 Winter Olympics. Not only did he continue with a system of playing a tougher domestic schedule with a core group of players, he also was studying the game and how the Russians and other Europeans were changing the way it was being played. By the time the 1972 U.S. Olympic team was paring down for Sapporo, Brooks, a stalwart of U.S. Olympic and National teams since 1960, who had been playing with the team all along, decided to call it quits in December 1971.

CRBD   CRBD   CRBD

As a student of the game, Williamson continued thinking about trying to build a team that had a better chance of surviving and competing against an international juggernaut like the Soviet Union. He understood that North American hockey, specifically American hockey, had to change, and he knew it was going to take something out of the ordinary to get USA Hockey to the next level—a medal. Because of that, Williamson was drawn to studying the Russian system and how they, along with other European teams, trained.

Williamson's philosophy for American hockey continued to change as he began building the 1971 U.S. National team. With eyes squarely fixed on the 1972 Winter Olympics, the coach was making a conscious effort to build the team around youth. The program was set in motion by picking a team early that was young and had speed and character, then to train it hard and put it under heavy fire with a tough schedule—a formula that would breed the future of American hockey.

Out of his friendship with Russian coach Anatoly Tarasov, which evolved during the 1971 World Championships in Switzerland, came an invitation to observe the Soviet team practice in person.

Williamson gathered all the new training techniques that he learned there, including dry-land training methods, and incorporated them with his ideas of de-emphasizing the dump-and-chase style of American hockey. The new system focused on puck movement, using players as interchangeable parts, and playing lines in tandem with defensive pairings (in units of five instead of units of three).

CRØD   CRØD   CRØD

Subtly, Williamson integrated his new system and philosophy as the '72 team trained in Bemidji. As the players acquiesced and began to understand the unique training regimen and system, their confidence grew stronger, and their outlook improved.

"It was like, 'Hey, we're doing the same thing they are. We're running, and this big Hawaiian guy is putting us through it in the morning," said defenseman Jim McElmury. "Then we're going on the ice, and we're doing what major European teams are doing to be successful.'"

As Williamson and his '72 team embraced the principles of international hockey and its new training regimen, dividends paid off for USA Hockey in Sapporo and, eventually, eight years later in Lake Placid.

"What Murray and Herb did was study the Russians very carefully and adopted what Tarasov was doing at that time as far as conditioning," reiterated forward Kevin Ahearn. "Robbie Ftorck was probably the closest guy to a Russian that we've ever had because of his soccer ability with his feet. He was deceptively quick. He wasn't fast, but he really played with his head up all the time and had tremendous hand-eye coordination, which was so obvious with the Russians."

CRØD   CRØD   CRØD

The dividends of 1972 weren't just lined in silver that later became gold in 1980. A new breed of American hockey players was emerging, and they were entering the National Hockey League, which previously could boast only a handful of Americans amongst its ranks. Hockey was a Canadian sport, and Canadians dominated the NHL.

As 16-year-old Mark Howe and 20-year-olds Robbie Ftorek and Henry Boucha watched Team Russia, arguably the greatest hockey team of all time, send virtually the same squad that had captured gold just months earlier to face Team Canada, the young men knew in their hearts and minds that they could play in the NHL. Team Canada's best, led by Phil Esposito, Pete and Frank Mahovlich, Ken Dryden, Gilbert Perreault, Yvan Cournoyer, Stan Mikita, Bobby Clarke, and Paul Henderson were no match for the Soviet juggernaut in Game 1 of the historic Summit Series.

"The Olympic silver was one thing," said Curran, "but I think some of the guys like Robbie, Mark, and some of the other younger guys on the team, when the Soviet Union stepped onto the Forum ice in Montreal, Canada, and beat them, 7-3, they sat there and said to themselves, 'I can play in the NHL, too.'

"And they did. They all did it, Boucha, Ftorek, Howe, and some others. I think that cemented it in their minds. That's what gave them all the confidence in the world to go on and become great hockey players—not just great American hockey players, but great hockey players."

Williamson's band of overachieving brothers not only served to validate a new brand of American hockey, but also a new breed of player and a newfound confidence for those yet to come.

"When you see that other people before you have done it, and that it can be done, it's a big, big boost to believing you can do it also," explained Ftorek. "I really believe we did set a tone for a lot of athletes."

CʒꙬ   CʒꙬ   CʒꙬ

For over a decade, Herb Brooks had been involved in the Olympic and amateur programs of USA Hockey. Like his old friend, teammate, and coach Murray Williamson, Brooks also was a student of the game. International hockey became his love, and he spent a lot of time in that game. When Brooks began his coaching career, it only stood to reason that he would take parts of what he learned and apply them in his own coaching philosophy. Most certainly one of those people he learned from was Williamson.

"A good coach learns from every coach he had," explained Craig Sarner, who was one of Brooks's first players when he was the assistant coach at the University of Minnesota during his senior year in 1971. "I'm sure Herb took some from Murray because he spent a lot of years with him. I'm also sure he probably took some that Murray didn't do—but that's how you grow as a coach."

Upon Williamson's return home from the Olympics, Brooks was in his formative years as a young head coach of the University of Minnesota and his fascination with international play was piqued even further by his friend and Minnesota neighbor.

Years later when the time came to select a coach for the 1980 Olympic hockey team, Brooks was chosen. With the knowledge from his playing days and studying of the international game, Brooks was about to expand on what he had learned and let the world know the United States was going to continue changing its approach to the game.

"If Herb Brooks wasn't strong enough to really make that change, we never would've seen that miracle in 1980 take place," said defenseman Frank Sanders, another of Brooks's first players from the 1971 University of Minnesota team. "He really did quite a bit of changing on how they played the game and how they attacked the game. However, if the Russians would've played 10 more games, they probably would've won 10 times. Fate plays a big part in some of this. Sometimes things are just meant to happen."

CRNO   CRNO   CRNO

The 1980 Russian Olympic hockey team, though older, still had many of the same players from the team that had won gold in 1972—including Tretiak, Maltsev, Mikhailov and Kharlamov. Heading into the first medal-round game, they had won four consecutive Olympic gold medals and had amassed an Olympic record of 33-3-2 since the

1960 Games. As in years past, they were the favorites, and all the experts believed the USSR would win its fifth straight gold medal.

Twenty years after wide-eyed youngsters Curran, Sears, McGlynn, Mellor, Sarner and others watched the 1960 Olympic hockey team capture gold in Squaw Valley on television, they were watching again as their friend, teammate, and former player led a new generation of U.S. hockey players in Lake Placid.

February 22, 1980, became a night where millions of Americans in general—and several in particular—knew exactly where they were and what they were doing around 5:30 p.m. EST.

"I took a towel with me to my room to watch the Russian game," recalled Curran. "I took a towel and a bottle of wine to watch with my wife. As we sat down she said, 'What's the towel for?' I said, 'Because I'm gonna cry watching these guys beat the Soviet Union—not just compete with them.' And that's just what they did."

Similar emotions flooded others as they watched and listened.

"I remember I had my jersey on, and I'm sitting in my kitchen listening to the game," remembered Mellor. "I had tears in my eyes. Then I watched the game, and tears were rolling down my face. It was one of the most emotional moments of my life—watching the United States beat the Russians. We had so much respect for those Russian guys. The 1980 team was the greatest thing ever. I was so proud of those guys. I said to myself, 'Herbie did it.'"

9

A MEDAL FOR MURRAY

"No other note, no other letter, no other commendation in the past 30-plus years has touched me more than the note I received back in January 2002."

—MURRAY WILLIAMSON

After revolutionizing USA Hockey as the Olympic and National teams head coach in the late 1960s-early 1970s, Murray Williamson was enjoying his retirement when he received a package at his home in Eden Prairie, Minnesota, in 2002.

The package's postmark and return address clearly identified the sender as a member of his 1972 U.S. Olympic silver medal-winning team—30 years after they had traveled halfway around the globe to stun the hockey world.

The team had been forgotten almost before it had a chance to be remembered by most people in 1972—and 30 years weren't going to reveal any surprises or adulation from anybody who wasn't a part of that team. Yet, this package intrigued and excited Williamson.

A letter dated January 16, 2002, accompanied the package. Three pages long, it was filled with memories created 30 years before, as well as a sentiment invoked since Williamson's squad stood on the ice in Sapporo in their white turtleneck sweaters and wine-colored pants as they accepted their silver medal amidst no fanfare or television cameras recording the history that was written during the two-week tournament.

Dear Murray,

For 30 years now, I have carried the honor of being an Olympic silver medalist. It's nice to know I'll carry that honor forever. Not a week goes by without some reminder. And, of course, every four years the memories come back with more focus. I've never been prouder of anything in my life.

However, there has been something that's always bothered me. You were the reason that this whole wonderful experience culminated on a medal stand in Sapporo. Yet, when the winners were getting medals draped around their necks, you were an anonymous face in the crowd watching from a distance. As each year passes, I continue to be haunted by this.

As Williamson pored through the letter, memories of Ahearn, Bader, Boucha, Brown, Christiansen, Curran, Ftorek, Howe, Irving, McElmury, McGlynn, McIntosh, Mellor, Naslund, Olds, Regan, Sanders, Sarner, Sheehy, and Sears flooded his mind. How had life treated his boys from 30 years ago?

Today, however, is a very happy, fulfilling day for me because, today, Murray, I'm fixing this problem. I've enjoyed this medal for 29 years and 337 days! It's been to school functions, family picnics, and parties. My dad has shown it to his friends, kids have worn it, touched it, and enjoyed it. It had originally been framed and hung on the wall, but that wasn't right. The medal is meant to be touched, held, and adored. Its place today is the right-hand side of my sock drawer.

The hockey innovator and Cold War peacemaker on skates was rendered speechless as he digested the words.

"No other note, no other letter, no other commendation in the past 30-plus years has touched me more than the note I received back in January 2002," Williamson reminisced.

Murray—I want you to have it now. More than any one of us, you deserve it. They will never take my name off this team as a silver medalist. But now, I want you to enjoy the symbol.

Today—my void is gone ... this makes me feel so good, Coach. As Olympic time approaches—it's especially nice to just keep it on your desk and enjoy it. All I can say today is ... Thanks, Coach. ... You're the best!

When he finished reading the letter, he looked further into the package and found a navy blue velvet box, which contained one of the 20 silver medals handed out on February 13, 1972, in Sapporo. Because the International Olympic Committee didn't give medals to coaches as such, there were only 20 medals for the 20 members of the team, and Williamson did not receive one. That is until one of his "boys," who represented the feeling in the hearts of his 19 brothers, decided the coach should have a token to enjoy from that day more than 30 years ago.

Several months later, at the team's 30th reunion party in Naples, Florida, members of the 1972 team presented Williamson with a near-exact replica of the medal that the team received in Sapporo, after painstakingly having one made for their coach. Only Williamson and one member of this historic "Forgotten Team" share an untold secret that, along with each other, will never ever be forgotten.

APPENDIX

FINAL STATISTICS

SCORING

	ALL GAMES						WINTER OLYMPICS					
	GP	G	A	Pts.	PEN	PIM	GP	G	A	Pts.	PEN	PIM
Henry Boucha	53	39	56	95	30	82	6	2	4	6	3	6
Tim Sheehy	41	37	42	79	17	51	6	4	1	5	0	0
Keith Christiansen	53	21	52	73	30	91	6	1	2	3	3	6
Robbie Ftorek	51	25	47	72	18	36	6	0	2	2	0	0
Craig Sarner	53	27	34	61	5	21	6	4	6	10	0	0
Kevin Ahearn	50	32	26	58	21	61	6	6	3	9	0	0
Tom Mellor	52	19	31	50	28	68	6	0	0	0	2	4
Ron Naslund	46	17	20	37	9	18	6	1	1	2	1	2
Stuart Irving	52	50	16	36	25	64	6	2	1	3	3	6
Jim McElmury	53	17	14	31	19	38	6	0	1	1	3	6
Charlie Brown	49	5	21	26	19	44	6	0	0	0	4	8
Wally Olds	44	12	13	25	1	?	6	0	0	0	0	0
Larry Bader	37	6	12	18	3	6	-	-	-	-	-	-
Frank Sanders	47	5	11	16	27	68	6	3	1	4	1	2
Bruce McIntosh	36	5	10	15	7	17	-			-	-	-
Dick McGlynn	50	1	14	15	20	43	6	0	0	0	1	2
Mark Howe	11	3	1	4	0	0	6	0	0	0	0	0
Pete Sears	27	0	1	1	1	2	-	-	-	-	-	-
Mike Curran	11	0	0	0	2	7	6	0	0	0	0	0
Tim Regan	10	0	0	0	0	0	-	-	-	-	-	-
Others	-	17	18	35	16	38	-	-	-	-	-	-
TOTALS:	*53*	*308*	*439*	*747*	*298*	*757*	*6*	*23*	*22*	*45*	*21*	*42*

Hat Tricks: Sheehy 10/30/71 vs. Waterloo (3 goals); 12/17/71 vs. RPI (4 goals)
Ftorek 12/20/71 vs. Detroit (3 goals)
Naslund 10/23/71 vs. Green Bay (3 goals)
Boucha 12/11/71 vs. Syracuse (3 goals)

GOALTENDING

	ALL GAMES					WINTER OLYMPICS				
	GP	Saves	GA	SO	GA Avg.	GP	Saves	GA	SO	GA Avg.
Mike Curran	10.33	334	35	0	3.39	6	209	18	0	3.00
Pete Sears	22.60	641	77	1	3.41	-	-	-	-	-
Tim Regan	8.00	270	50	0	3.41	-	-	-	-	-
Others	12.07	341	45	0	3.73					
TOTALS:	*53*	*1,586*	*207*	*1*	*3.91*	*6*	*209*	*18*	*0*	*3.00*

DOMESTIC AND PRE-OLYMPICS SCHEDULE

Record: 33 wins, 11 losses, 3 ties

September 23	U.S. 5 vs. Cleveland 3
September 24	U.S. 6 vs. Cleveland 2
September 26	U.S. 10 vs. Junior Stars 0*
September 30	U.S. 5 vs. Omaha 2
October 1	U.S. 4 vs. Omaha 4
October 3	U.S. 9 vs. Junior Stars 0*
October 7	Denver (CPHL) 6 vs. U.S. 5
October 12	Denver (CPHL) 6 vs. U.S. 2
October 23	U.S. 10 vs. Green Bay 2
October 29	U.S. 10 vs. Waterloo 2
October 30	U.S. 15 vs. Waterloo 1
November 5	U.S. 8 vs. North Dakota 1
November 6	U.S. 5 vs. Minnesota-Duluth 1
November 7	U.S. 6 vs. North Dakota 2
November 12	U.S. 3 vs. University of Calgary 1
November 13	U.S. 7 vs. University of Alberta 6
November 17	U.S. 8 vs. Kansas City (CPHL) 4
November 19	U.S. 5 vs. Braintree 3
November 22	U.S. 4 vs. Boston University 4
November 23	U.S. 6 vs. Dartmouth College 4
November 26	Denver University 5 vs. U.S. 2
November 27	Denver University 6 vs. U.S. 4
December 1	U.S. 5 vs. Bemidji State College 3
December 2	U.S. 5 vs. Lakehead University 5
December 3	U.S. 10 vs. Bemidji State College 1
December 7	U.S. 8 vs. University of Minnesota 0
December 11	U.S. 12 vs. Syracuse 6
December 12	U.S. 10 vs. Long Island All-Stars 1

December 13	U.S. 8 vs. Princeton University 3
December 16	U.S. 3 vs. Brown University 2
December 17	U.S. 11 vs. Rochester Polytechnic Institute 5
December 19	U.S. 5 vs. Harvard University 2
December 20	U.S. 6 vs. Detroit Jr. Red Wings/Port Huron 1
December 22	Kansas City (CPHL) 7 vs. U.S. 4
December 27	Russia 13 vs. U.S. 3
December 28	U.S. 7 vs. Czechoslovakia 5
December 30	Russia 7 vs. U.S. 3
January 1	Russia 11 vs. U.S. 1
January 2	U.S. 6 vs. Czechoslovakia 3
January 4	Russia 9 vs. U.S. 3
January 6	Russia 11 vs. U.S. 4
January 9	U.S. 6 vs. Warroad Lakers 3
January 12	U.S. 7 vs. University of Minnesota 4
January 15	U.S. 9 vs. Saginaw Stars 1
January 18	Fort Worth (CPHL) 5 vs. U.S. 3
February 18	U.S. 9 vs. Las Vegas Outlaws 5**
February 19	U.S. 9 vs. Las Vegas Outlaws 2**

*not included in individual statistics
** exhibition games following return from Sapporo – stats not included

PRE-OLYMPIC WINTER GAMES – TOKYO, JAPAN
| January 28 | U.S. 7 vs. Poland 5 |
| January 29 | Czechoslovakia 4 vs. U.S. 1 |

1972 OLYMPIC WINTER GAMES – SAPPORO, JAPAN
February 4	U.S. 5 vs. Switzerland 3 (Qualifying Game)
February 5	Sweden 5 vs. U.S. 1
February 7	U.S. 5 vs. Czechoslovakia 1
February 9	Russia 7 vs. U.S. 2
February 10	U.S. 4 vs. Finland 1
February 12	U.S. 6 vs. Poland 1

Statistics and game results compiled courtesy of www.murraywilliamson.org

*The official score sheets from the United States'
hockey tournament at the 1972 Olympic Winter Games
in Sapporo, Japan, appear in chronological order.*

アイスホッケー ヨセン コウシキ キロク
ICE HOCKEY ELIMINATION OFFICIAL RESULTS
HOCKEY SUR GLACE RESULTATS DE OFFICIELS ELIMINATOIRE

SAPPORO , 1972 - 2 - 4 , 14:04 - 16:05

U.S.A.   5 : SWITZERLAND   3 (2- 1 1- 1 2- 1)

	U.S.A.	(USA)	POSITION		SWITZERLAND	(SUI)	
30	MICHAEL	CURRAN	G.K	1	GERARD	RIGOLET	
1	PETER	SEARS		22	ALFIO	MOLINA	
5	CHARLES	BROWN	L.D	11	MARCEL	SGUALDO	
4	THOMAS	MELLOR		5	CHARLES	HENZEN	
9	FRANK	SANDERS					
2	JAMES	MCELMURY	(A)	R.D	4	GASTON	FURRER	(A)
20	RICHARD	MCGLYNN		2	RENE	HUGUENIN	(C)
3	WALTER	OLDS		3	PETER	AESCHLIMANN	
16	KEVIN	AHEARN	(A)	L.W	6	RENE	BERRA	
19	STUART	IRVING		8	JACQUES	POUSAZ	
23	MARK	HOWE		12	HEINZ	JENNI	
				17	HANS	KELLER	(A)
10	HENRY	BOUCHA	C.F	10	MICHEL	TURLER	
8	KEITH	CHRISTIANSEN	(C)	16	PAUL	PROBST	
11	ROBBIE	FTOREK		19	GERARD	DUBI	
18	RONALD	NASLUND	R.W	9	FRANCIS	REINHARD	
17	CRAIG	SARNER		7	TONY	NEININGER	
15	TIMOTHY	SHEEHY		13	GUY	DUBOIS	

REFEREE 01 BAADER   (GER)   02 BATA   (TCH)

(C) : CAPTAIN
(A) : ALTERNATE CAPTAIN

** 1ST PERIOD **

GAME TIME   SCORE --- NAT ---- NAME ------------ ASSISTED --------- PENALTY ------- MIN

		(USA) - (SUI)						
G	02:48	1	-	0	USA	16 AHEARN	17 SARNER	
							10 BOUCHA	
G	04:34	2	-	0	USA	15 SHEEHY	8 CHRISTIANSEN	
P	12:51				USA	9 SANDERS		TRIPPING	2
G	13:45	2	-	1	SUI	11 SGUALDO	4 FURRER	
		2	-	1				

```
                        アイスホッケー ヨセン コウシキ キロク
                        ICE HOCKEY ELIMINATION OFFICIAL RESULTS
                        HOCKEY SUR GLACE RESULTATS DE OFFICIELS ELIMINATOIRE

** 2ND  PERIOD **

GAME TIME - SCORE --- NAT ---- NAME -------------- ASSISTED --------- PENALTY ------- MIN

           (USA) - (SUI)
G  01:59  3   -   1   USA   16 AHEARN
P  03:21              SUI    4 FURRER                              TRIPPING           2
G  19:22  3   -   2   SUI    5 HENZEN        10 TURLER

          3   -   2


** 3RD  PERIOD **

GAME TIME - SCORE --- NAT ---- NAME -------------- ASSISTED --------- PENALTY ------- MIN

           (USA) - (SUI)
G  01:03  3   -   3   SUI    9 REINHARD     10 TURLER
G  02:12  4   -   3   USA   15 SHEEHY        9 SANDERS
P  07:21              USA    5 BROWN                               ELBOWING           2
P  07:21              SUI    4 FURRER                              BOARDING           2
P  08:52              USA    4 MELLOR                              HOOKING            2
G  17:19  5   -   3   USA   19 IRVING

          5   -   3


PENALTIES --    1ST 2ND 3RD  TOTAL  TIME   --- SHOTS ON GOAL---        1ST 2ND 3RD TOTAL
         USA     1   0   2     3      6                          USA    32  45  22   99
         SUI     0   1   1     2      4                          SUI     9  10   6   25

                                            --GOALKEEPER SAVE --
                                                     30 USA    6   5   4   ·15
                                                      1 SUI   15  25  14   54

ATOMOSPHERIC CONDITIONS

     HUMIDITY                61  %
     ICE TEMPERATURE      -  5.6°  C
     ICE THICKNESS           4  CM
```

N. Suzuki

'72.2.4   16:33

アイスホッケー ケッショウ コウシキ キロク
ICE HOCKEY FINAL OFFICIAL RESULTS
HOCKEY SUR GLACE RESULTATS DE OFFICIELS FINAL

SAPPORO , 1972 - 2 - 5 , 10:05 - 12:12

--- GROUP A ---

                    SWEDEN   5 : U.S.A.   1   (2- 1 1- 0 2- 0)

        SWEDEN   (SWE)   POSITION   U.S.A.   (USA)

    1 LEIF   HOLMQVIST   G.K   30 MICHAEL   CURRAN
    2 CHRISTER ABRAHAMSSON   1 PETER   SEARS

    4 STIG   OSTLING   L.D   5 CHARLES   BROWN
    7 LARS-ERIK SJOBERG   (A)   4 THOMAS   MELLOR
    9 KENNETH EKMAN   9 FRANK   SANDERS

    3 THOMMIE BERGMAN   R.D   2 JAMES   MCELMURY   (A)
    5 BERT-OLA NORDLANDER (C)   20 RICHARD   MCGLYNN
    6 THOMMY   ABRAHAMSSON   3 WALTON   OLDS

   12 STIG-G   JOHANSSON   L.W   16 KEVIN   AHEARN
   18 BJORN   PALMQVIST   (A)   19 STUART   IRVING
   23 HANS   LINDBERG   23 MARK   HOWE

   11 TORD   LUNDSTROM   C.F   10 HENRY   BOUCHA
   17 MATS   LINDH   8 KEITH   CHRISTIANSEN (A)
   21 HAKAN   PETTERSSON   11 ROBBIE   FTOREK

   10 HAKAN   WICKBERG   R.W   22 RONALD   NASLUND
   15 LARS-G   NILSSON   17 CRAIG   SARNER
   19 INGE   HAMMARSTROM   15 TIMOTHY   SHEEHY   (C)

   REFEREE 12 VIITALA   (FIN)   13 WYCISK   (POL)

   (C) : CAPTAIN
   (A) : ALTERNATE CAPTAIN

** 1ST PERIOD **

GAME TIME - SCORE --- NAT ---- NAME --------------- ASSISTED -------- PENALTY ------- MIN

          (SWE) - (USA)
G 02:32 1 - 0   SWE   15 NILSSON
P 05:02   USA   19 IRVING   SLASHING   2
G 06:28 2 - 0   SWE   6 ABRAHAMSSON   18 PALMQVIST
G 08:04 2 - 1   USA   16 AHEARN   17 SARNER
P 12:27   USA   10 BOUCHA   INTERFERENCE   2

          2 - 1

アイスホッケー ケッショウ コウシキ キロク
ICE HOCKEY FINAL OFFICIAL RESULTS
HOCKEY SUR GLACE RESULTATS DE OFFICIELS FINAL

** 2ND PERIOD **

GAME TIME - SCORE --- NAT ---- NAME ---------------- ASSISTED ---------- PENALTY ------- MIN

```
        (SWE) - (USA)
G  07:27  3   -   1    SWE   11 LUNDSTROM

          3   -   1
```

** 3RD PERIOD **

GAME TIME - SCORE --- NAT ---- NAME -------------- ASSISTED ---------- PENALTY ------- MIN

```
        (SWE) - (USA)
G  06:12  4   -   1    SWE    3 BERGMAN        5 NORDLANDER
G  09:25  5   -   1    SWE   19 HAMMARSTROM

          5   -   1
```

PENALTIES	1ST	2ND	3RD	TOTAL	TIME
SWE	0	0	0	0	0
USA	2	0	0	2	4

-- SHOTS ON GOAL--	1ST	2ND	3RD	TOTAL
SWE	28	21	21	70
USA	13	21	16	50

--GOALKEEPER SAVE --	1ST	2ND	3RD	TOTAL
1 SWE	5	11	8	24
30 USA	13	13	11	37

ATOMOSPHERIC CONDITIONS

```
    HUMIDITY            58  %
    ICE TEMPERATURE    - 5.5° C
    ICE THICKNESS        4  CM
```

'72.2.5 12:26

アイスホッケー ケッショウ コウシキ キロク
ICE HOCKEY FINAL OFFICIAL RESULTS
HOCKEY SUR GLACE RESULTATS DE OFFICIELS FINAL

SAPPORO , 1972 - 2 - 7 , 16:03 - 18:10

-- GROUP A --

                    CZECHOSLOVAKIA 1 : U.S.A.   5   (1- 1 0- 3 0- 1)

          CZECHOSLOVAKIA (TCH)   POSITION   U.S.A.   (USA)

    1 VLADIMFR DZURILA   G.K   30 MICHAEL   CURRAN
    2 JIRI   HOLECEK   1 PETER   SEARS

    7 FRANTISEK POSPISIL   L.D   2 JAMES   MCELMURY   (A)
    9 KAREL   VOHRALIK   4 THOMAS   MELLOR
                                                         9 FRANK   SANDERS

    3 JOSEF   HORESOVSKY   (A)   R.D   5 CHARLES   BROWN
    4 OLDRICH   MACHAC   20 RICHARD   MCGLYNN
   19 VLADIMIR BEDNAR   3 WALTER   OLDS
    6 RUDOLF   TAJCNAR

   15 JOSEF   CERNY   (C)   L.W   16 KEVIN   AHEARN
   20 JIRI   HOLIK   (A)   19 STUART   IRVING
   12 BOHUSLAV STASTNY   23 MARK   HOWE

   11 RICHARD   FARDA   C.F   10 HENRY   BOUCHA   (A)
   21 IVAN   HLINKA   8 KEITH   CHRISTIANSEN   (C)
   14 VACLAV   NEDOMANSKY   11 ROBBIE   FTOREK

    8 JIRI   KOCHTA   R.W   22 RONALD   NASLUND
   10 VLADIMIR MARTINEC   17 CRAIG   SARNER
   18 EDUARD   NOVAK   .   15 TIMOTHY   SHEEHY

    REFEREE   03 EHRENSPERGER   (SUI)   09 NADIN   (CAN)

    (C) : CAPTAIN
    (A) : ALTERNATE CAPTAIN

** 1ST PERIOD **

GAME TIME - SCORE --- NAT ---- NAME ------------ ASSISTED -------- PENALTY ------- ! 1

           (TCH) - (USA)
    P 03:14   USA   2 MCELMURY   HOOKING   2
    G 04:32   1 - 0   TCH 10 NOVAK   7 POSPISIL
    P 08:27   USA   2 MCELMURY   INTERFERENCE   2
    P 09:33   TCH   7 POSPISIL   INTERFERENCE   2
    P 10:00   USA   8 CHRISTIANSEN   HIGH STICK   2
    P 10:00   TCH 21 HLINKA   HIGH STICK   2
    P 15:09   TCH   9 VOHRALIK   CROSS CHECKING   2
    P 15:37   TCH   6 TAJCNAR   INTERFERENCE   2

           1 - 0

```
                    アイスホッケー クッショウ コウシキ キロク
                    ICE HOCKEY FINAL OFFICIAL RESULTS
                    HOCKEY SUR GLACE RESULTATS DE OFFICIELS FINAL


** 1ST  PERIOD **

GAME TIME - SCORE --- NAT ---- NAME ------------- ASSISTED -- ------- PENALTY ------- MIN
          (TCH) - (USA)
G  16:47  1  -  1    USA    8 CHRISTIANSEN
P  19:38             USA   10 BOUCHA                              EXCLUSIVE ROUGH-      2
                                                                  NESS

          1   -   1


** 2ND  PERIOD **

GAME TIME - SCORE --- NAT ---- NAME ------------- ASSISTED -------- PENALTY ------- MIN
          (TCH) - (USA)
P  05:07             USA    5 BROWN                               TRIPPING             2
G  09:41  1  -  2    USA   16 AHEARN         17 SARNER
G  12:40  1  -  3    USA   17 SARNER          2 MCELMURY
P  16:07             USA    8 CHRISTIANSEN                        SLASHING             2
P  18:14             TCH    6 TAJCNAR                             HIGH STICK           2
G  19:19  1  -  4    USA    9 SANDERS         8 CHRISTIANSEN

          1   -   4


** 3RD  PERIOD **

GAME TIME - SCORE --- NAT ---- NAME ------------- ASSISTED -------- PENALTY ------- MIN
          (TCH) - (USA)
P  05:16             USA   19 IRVING                              HOOKING              2
P  08:28             USA   22 NASLUND                             CROSS CHECKING       2
P  09:22             TCH   12 STASTNY                             HOOKING              2
G  13:12  1  -  5    USA   22 NASLUND

          1   -   5


- PENALTIES --     1ST 2ND 3RD  TOTAL   TIME     -- SHOTS ON GOAL--         1ST 2ND 3RD TOTAL
              TCH   4   1   1     6      12                          TCH    24  32  25   81
              USA   4   2   2     8      16                          USA     9  11  13   33

                                                 --GOALKEEPER SAVE --
                                                               2 TCH    4   5   -    9
                                                               1 TCH    -   -   9    9
                                                              30 USA   19  20  12   51

ATMOSPHERIC CONDITIONS

       HUMIDITY              35  %
       ICE TEMPERATURE     - 5.0° C
       ICE THICKNESS         4  CM
```

内村英樹

```
                                              '72.2.7  18:49
```

アイスホッケー ケッショウ コウシキ キロク
ICE HOCKEY FINAL OFFICIAL RESULTS
HOCKEY SUR GLACE RESULTATS DE OFFICIELS FINAL

SAPPORO , 1972 - 2 - 9 , 19:03 - 21 06

--- GROUP A ---

                    U.S.S.R.   7 : U.S.A.   2   (2- 0 3- 0 2- 2)

        U.S.S.R.   (URS)   POSITION   U.S.A.   (USA)

   20 VLADISLAV TRETIAK   G.K   30 MICHAEL CURRAN
    1 ALEXANDRE PACHKOV   1 PETER   SEARS

    2 VITALII   DAVYDOV   (A)   L.D   5 CHARLES BROWN
    3 VLADIMIR LOUTCHENKO   19 STUART   IRVING
    5 ALEXANDRE RAGOULINE   4 THOMAS   MELLOR
    6 IGOR   ROMICHEVSKII   9 FRANK   SANDERS

    4 VICTOR   KOUZKINE   (C)   R.D   2 JAMES   MCELMURY   (A)
    7 GUENNADII TSYGANKOV   20 RICHARD MCGLYNN
                                          3 WALTER   OLDS

   17 VALERII   KHARLAMOV   L.W   16 KEVIN   AHEARN
    9 YURII   BLINOV   23 MARK   HOWE
   14 EVGUENII ZIMINE

   18 VLADIMIR PETROV   C.F   10 HENRY   BOUCHA
   11 ANATOLII FIRSSOV   (A)   8 KEITH   CHRISTIANSEN   (A)
   10 ALEXANDRE MALTSEV   11 ROBBIE   FTOREK

   12 EVGUENII MICHAKOV   R.W   22 RONALD   NASLUND
   18 VLADIMIR VIKOULOV   17 CRAIG   SARNER
   15 ALEXANDRE IAKOUCHEV   15 TIMOTHY SHEEHY   (C)

   REFEREE 12 VIITALA   (FIN)   01 BAADER   (GER)

   (C) : CAPTAIN
   (A) : ALTERNATE CAPTAIN

** 1ST PERIOD **

GAME TIME -- SCORE --- NAT ---- NAME -------------- ASSISTED --------- PENALTY ------- MIN

        (URS) - (USA)
 P 10:46   USA   20 MCGLYNN   MEMBER OVER   2
 G 11:17 1 - 0 URS   9 BLINOV
 G 15:26 2 - 0 URS   17 KHARLAMOV   18 VIKOULOV

          2 - 0

```
                       アイスホッケー ケッショウ コウシキ キロク
                       ICE HOCKEY FINAL OFFICIAL RESULTS
                       HOCKEY SUR GLACE RESULTATS DE OFFICIELS FINAL


  ** 2ND  PERIOD **

  GAME TIME - SCORE --- NAT ---- NAME -------------- ASSISTED ---------- PENALTY ------- MIN

              (URS) - (USA)
   G  04:05  3  -  0   URS   10 MALTSEV        15 IAKOUCHEV
   G  04:31  4  -  0   URS   18 VIKOULOV       17 KHARLAMOV
                                              11 FIRSSOV
   P  06:49           USA    8 CHRISTIANSEN                     HOOKING              2
   G  08:50  5  -  0   URS   10 MALTSEV
   P  15:40           USA    5 BROWN                            HOLDING              2
   P  17:54           URS   15 IAKOUCHEV                        HOOKING              2

              5  -  0


  ** 3RD  PERIOD **

  GAME TIME - SCORE --- NAT ---- NAME -------------- ASSISTED ---------- PENALTY ------- MIN

              (URS) - (USA)
   G  04:26  5  -  1   USA    9 SANDERS        15 SHEEHY
   G  07:08  6  -  1   URS   14 ZIMINE         16 PETROV
                                               9 BLINOV
   G  08:57  7  -  1   URS    7 TSYGANKOV      17 KHARLAMOV
                                              18 VIKOULOV
   G  16:01  7  -  2   USA   16 AHEARN         22 NASLUND
   P  16:50            URS   15 IAKOUCHEV                        HOOKING              2
   P  19:36            USA    5 BROWN                            HOLDING              2

              7  -  2
```

```
 - PENALTIES --       1ST 2ND 3RD  TOTAL  TIME    -- SHOTS ON GOAL --            1ST 2ND 3RD TOTAL
              URS      0   1   1     2      4                             URS    40  29  22   91
              USA      1   2   1     4      8                             USA    16  12  20   48

                                                   --GOALKEEPER SAVE --
                                                              20 URS     8   7  10   25
                                                              30 USA    19  14  10   43

 ATOMUSPHERIC CONDITIONS

        HUMIDITY              58  %
        ICE TEMPERATURE     - 5.5° C
        ICE THICKNESS         4  CM
```

菊田陽三.

'72.2.9 21:27

アイスホッケー ケッショウ コウシキ キロク
ICE HOCKEY FINAL OFFICIAL RESULTS
HOCKEY SUR GLACE RESULTATS DE OFFICIELS FINAL

SAPPORO , 1972 - 2 - 10 , 19:00 - 21:00

-- GROUP A ---

                    FINLAND   1 : U.S.A.   4   (1- 2 0- 1 0- 1)

        FINLAND   (FIN)   POSITION   U.S.A.   (USA)

    1   JORMA   VALTONEN   G.K   30 MICHAEL   CURRAN
   20   STIG   WETZELL   1 PETER   SEARS

    2   ILPO   KOSKELA   L.D   2 JAMES   MCELMURY   (A)
    3   SEPPO   LINDSTROEM   (A)   4 THOMAS   MELLOR
    5   HEIKKI   RIIHIRANTA   9 FRANK   SANDERS
    6   HEIKKI   JAERN

    7   PEKKA   MARJAMAEKI   R.D   5 CHARLES   BROWN
                                                    20 RICHARD   MCGLYNN
                                                     3 WALTER   OLDS

   18   LAURI   MONONEN   L.W   16 KEVIN   AHEARN
                                                    19 STUART   IRVING
                                                    23 MARK   HOWE

    9   VELI-P.   KETOLA   C.F   10 HENRY   BOUCHA   (A)
   12   MATTI   MURTO   (A)   8 KEITH   CHRISTIANSEN   (C)
   17   SEPPO   REPO   11 ROBBIE   FTOREK

   10   MATTI   KEINONEN   R.W   22 RONALD   NASLUND
   11   HARRI   LINNONMAA   17 CRAIG   SARNER
   13   JUHANI   TAMMINEN   16 TIMOTHY   SHEEHY
   14   LASSE   OKSANEN   (C)
   16   ESA   PELTONEN
   19   TIMO   TURUNEN

    REFEREE   05 HANQVIST   (SWE)   09 NADIN   (CAN)

    (C) : CAPTAIN
    (A) : ALTERNATE CAPTAIN

** 1ST PERIOD **

GAME TIME - SCORE --- NAT --- NAME ------------ ASSISTED -------- PENALTY ------- MIN

         (FIN) - (USA)
G 00:15 0 - 1   USA   17 SARNER   10 BOUCHA
P 04:23   USA   10 BOUCHA   EXCLUSIVE ROUGH-   2
                                                           NESS
G 04:35 1 - 1   FIN   18 MONONEN   3 LINDSTROEM
G 13:35 1 - 2   USA   10 BOUCHA   17 SARNER

          1 - 2

アイスホッケー クッショウ コウシキ キロク
ICE HOCKEY FINAL OFFICIAL RESULTS
HOCKEY SUR GLACE RESULTATS DE OFFICIELS FINAL

** 1ST PERIOD **

GAME TIME - SCORE --- NAT ---- NAME ------------ ASSISTED -------- PENALTY ------- MIN

(FIN) - (USA)

P 19:18　　　　　FIN　3 LINDSTROEM　　　　　　　TRIPPING　　　　2

1 - 2

** 2ND PERIOD **

GAME TIME - SCORE --- NAT ---- NAME ------------ ASSISTED -------- PENALTY ------- MIN

(FIN) - (USA)

P 05:03	USA	2 MCELMURY		HIGH STICK	2
P 05:03	FIN	16 PELTONEN		HIGH STICK	2
G 08:37 1 - 3	USA	9 SANDERS	11 FTOREK		
P 18:29	USA	4 MELLOR		CROSS CHECKING	2

1 - 3

** 3RD PERIOD **

GAME TIME - SCORE --- NAT ---- NAME ------------ ASSISTED -------- PENALTY ------- MIN

(FIN) - (USA)

P 18:44	FIN	17 REPO		TRIPPING	2
G 19:38 1 - 4	USA	16 AHEARN	10 BOUCHA		
			17 SARNER		

1 - 4

-- PENALTIES --

	1ST	2ND	3RD	TOTAL	TIME
FIN	1	1	1	3	6
USA	1	2	0	3	6

-- SHOTS ON GOAL --

	1ST	2ND	3RD	TOTAL
FIN	26	22	27	75
USA	14	18	24	56

-- GOALKEEPER SAVE --

		1ST	2ND	3RD	TOTAL
1	FIN	6	12	15	33
30	USA	12	9	14	35

ATOMOSPHERIC CONDITIONS

HUMIDITY　　　　　35 %
ICE TEMPERATURE　- 5.0° C
ICE THICKNESS　　　4 CM

T.ONODERA

'72.2.10 21:15

アイスホッケー ケッショウ コウシキ キロク
ICE HOCKEY FINAL OFFICIAL RESULTS
HOCKEY SUR GLACE RESULTATS DE OFFICIELS FINAL

SAPPORO , 1972 - 2 - 12 , 19:34 - 21:27

-- GROUP A --

                          POLAND   1 : U.S.A.   6   (0- 2 0- 2 1- 2)

        POLAND   (POL)   POSITION   U.S.A.   (USA)

    1 ANDRZEJ   TKACZ   G.K   30 MICHAEL   CURRAN
   20 WALERY   KOSYL   1 PETER   SEARS

    2 LUDWIK   CZACHOWSKI   (C)   L.D   2 JAMES   MCELMURY   (A)
   11 STANISLAW FRYZLEWICZ   (A)   4 THOMAS   MELLOR
   15 JERZY   POTZ   9 FRANK   SANDERS

    4 ROBERT   GORALCZYK   (A)   R.D   5 CHARLES   BROWN
   12 ADAM   KOPCZYNSKI   20 RICHARD   MCGLYNN
    5 ANDRZEJ   SZCZEPANIEC   3 WALTER   OLDS

    3 FELIKS   GORALCZYK   L.W   16 KEVIN   AHEARN   (A)
    7 TADEUSZ   KACIK   19 STUART   IRVING
                                                   23 MARK   HOWE

   10 KRZYSZTOF B-BIALYNICKI   C.F   10 HENRY   BOUCHA
    6 JOZEF   SLOWAKIEWICZ   8 KEITH   CHRISTIANSEN
   18 LESZEK   TOKARZ   11 ROBBIE   FTOREK
   14 WIESLAW   TOKARZ

   17 JOZEF   BATKIEWICZ   R.W   22 RONALD   NASLUND
    9 TADEUSZ   OBLOJ   17 CRAIG   SARNER
    8 WALENTY   ZIETARA   15 TIMOTHY   SHEEHY   (C)

    REFFREE 09 NADIN   (CAN)   01 BAADER   (GER)

   (C) : CAPTAIN
   (A) : ALTERNATE CAPTAIN

** 1ST PERIOD **

GAME TIME - SCORE --- NAT ---- NAME ------------- ASSISTED --------- PENALTY ------- MIN

        (POL) - (USA)
G 00:57 0 - 1   USA   15 SHEEHY   11 FTOREK
                                           19 IRVING
G 14:41 0 - 2   USA   17 SARNER   10 BOUCHA
                                           16 AHEARN
P 17:10   USA   19 IRVING   SLASHING   2

          0 - 2

アイスホッケー ケッショウ コウシキ キロク
ICE HOCKEY FINAL OFFICIAL RESULTS
HOCKEY SUR GLACE RESULTATS DE OFFICIELS FINAL

** 2ND PERIOD **

GAME TIME - SCORE --- NAT ---- NAME ------------ ASSISTED -------- PENALTY ------- MIN

```
        (POL) - (USA)
G  06:08  0  -  3   USA   10 BOUCHA        16 AHEARN
                                           17 SARNER
G  14:53  0  -  4   USA   19 IRVING

          0  -  4
```

** 3RD PERIOD **

GAME TIME - SCORE --- NAT ---- NAME ------------ ASSISTED -------- PENALTY ------- MIN

```
        (POL) - (USA)
G  02:40  1  -  4   POL    9 OBLOJ
P  03:50            USA   20 MCGLYNN                    HOLDING         2
P  06:08            POL   12 KOPCZYNSKI                 MEMBER OVER     2
G  11:05  1  -  5   USA   17 SARNER       16 AHEARN
G  11:33  1  -  6   USA   15 SHEEHY

          1  -  6
```

```
PENALTIES --    1ST 2ND 3RD  TOTAL  TIME    -- SHOTS ON GOAL--       1ST 2ND 3RD TOTAL
          POL    0   0   1     1      2                         POL   12  22  20   54
          USA    1   0   1     2      4                         USA   20  21  17   58

                                              --GOALKEEPER SAVE --
                                                        20 POL   10   8   5   23
                                                        30 USA    6  13   9   28
```

ATOMOSPHERIC CONDITIONS

```
    HUMIDITY              50  %
    ICE TEMPERATURE     - 5.5° C
    ICE THICKNESS         4  CM
```

小平喜作

'72.2.12 21:44

アイスホッケー ケッショウ コウシキ キロク
ICE HOCKEY FINAL OFFICIAL RESULTS
HOCKEY SUR GLACE RESULTATS DE OFFICIELS FINAL

SAPPORO ｖ 1972 - 2 - 13 ｖ 09:04 - 11:13

-- GROUP A --

SWEDEN   3 : FINLAND   4   (2- 1 1- 1 0- 2)

	SWEDEN	(SWE)	POSITION		FINLAND	(FIN)	
1	LEIF	HOLMQVIST	G.K	1	JORMA	VALTONEN	
2	CHRISTER	ABRAHAMSSON		20	STIG	WETZELL	
4	STIG	OSTLING	L.D	2	ILPO	KOSKELA	
6	THOMMY	ABRAHAMSSON		3	SEPPO	LINDSTROEM	(A)
9	KENNETH	EKMAN		5	HEIKKI	RIIHIRANTA	
				6	HEIKKI	JAERN	
3	THOMMIE	BERGMAN	R.D	7	PEKKA	MARJAMAEKI	
5	BERT-OLA	NORDLANDER	(C)				
7	LARS-ERIK	SJOBERG	(A)				
12	STIG-G	JOHANSSON	L.W	8	JORMA	VEHMANEN	
18	BJORN	PALMQVIST		18	LAURI	MONONEN	
23	HANS	LINDBERG					
11	TORD	LUNDSTROM	(A) C.F	9	VELI-P.	KETOLA	(A)
17	MATS	LINDH		12	MATTI	MURTO	
21	HAKAN	PETTERSSON		17	SEPPO	REPO	
10	HAKAN	WICKBERG	R.W	10	MATTI	KEINONEN	
15	LARS-G	NILSSON		13	JUHANI	TAMMINEN	
19	INGE	HAMMARSTROM		14	LASSE	OKSANEN	(C)
				16	ESA	PELTONEN	
				19	TIMO	TURUNEN	

REFEREE 03 EHRENSPERGER   (SUI)   09 NADIN   (CAN)

(C) : CAPTAIN
(A) : ALTERNATE CAPTAIN

** 1ST PERIOD **

GAME TIME - SCORE --- NAT ---- NAME ------------ ASSISTED ----------- PENALTY   MIN

			(SWE) - (FIN)					
G	02:48	0	-	1	FIN	6 JAERN	9 KETOLA		
P	05:02				SWE	3 BERGMAN		INTERFERENCE	2
P	16:24				FIN	17 REPO		ELBOWING	2
G	17:13	1	-	1	SWE	11 LUNDSTROM	10 WICKBERG		
G	17:51	2	-	1	SWE	18 PALMQVIST			
P	18:06				SWE	23 LINDBERG		HOOKING	2

                    2 - 1

アイスホッケー ケッショウ コウシキ キロク
ICE HOCKEY FINAL OFFICIAL RESULTS
HOCKEY SUR GLACE RESULTATS DE OFFICIELS FINAL

** 2ND PERIOD **

GAME TIME - SCORE --- NAT ---- NAME ------------- ASSISTED --------- PENALTY ------- MIN

```
        (SWE) - (FIN)
G  00:35  2  -  2   FIN   13 TAMMINEN
P  13:52            FIN    9 KETOLA                      EXCLUSIVE ROUGH-        5
                                                         NESS
P  13:52            SWE    1 HOLMQVIST                   DISPUTING OUTSIDE       2
                                                         CREASE
G  16:32  3  -  2   SWE   18 PALMQVIST
P  19:21            FIN   14 OKSANEN                      HOOKING                2
P  19:21            SWE   21 PETTERSSON                   HIGH STICK             2

          3  -  2
```

** 3RD PERIOD **

GAME TIME - SCORE --- NAT ---- NAME ------------- ASSISTED --------- PENALTY ------- MIN

```
        (SWE) - (FIN)
P  06:31            FIN    6 JAERN                        HOOKING                2
G  12:43  3  -  3   FIN   10 KEINONEN      9 KETOLA
P  14:32            SWE   12 JOHANSSON                     ELBOWING              2
G  14:58  3  -  4   FIN   18 MONONEN

          3  -  4
```

```
- PENALTIES --      1ST 2ND 3RD  TOTAL   TIME     --- SHOTS ON GOAL--        1ST 2ND 3RD TOTAL
             SWE     2   2   1     5       10                           SWE  10  19  15   44
             FIN     1   2   1     4       11                           FIN  18  14  21   53

                                                   --GOALKEEPER SAVE --
                                                                        1 SWE  10   7  10   27
                                                                        1 FIN   5  14   6   25
```

ATOMOSPHERIC CONDITIONS

```
        HUMIDITY              54  %
        ICE TEMPERATURE     - 5.5°  C
        ICE THICKNESS         4  CM
```

内村英樹

'72.2.13 11:41

```
          アイスホッケー ケッショウ コウシキ キロク
          ICE HOCKEY FINAL OFFICIAL RESULTS
          HOCKEY SUR GLACE RESULTATS DE OFFICIELS FINAL


          SAPPORO , 1972 - 2 - 13 , 12:33 - 14:40

-- GROUP  A --

                    U.S.S.R.        5 ·  CZECHOSLOVAKIA  2   ( 2- 0  2- 1  1- 1 )


        U.S.S.R.         (URS)        POSITION        CZECHOSLOVAKIA  (TCH)

    20  VLADISLAV TRETIAK              G.K       1  VLADIMER  DZURILA
     1  ALEXANDRE PACHKOV                         2  JIRI      HOLECEK

     2  VITALII   DAVYDOV     (A)      L.D       7  FRANTISEK POSPISIL
     3  VLADIMIR  LOUTCHENKO                      9  KAREL     VOHRALIK
     5  ALEXANDRE RAGOULINE
     6  IGOR      ROMICHEVSKII

     4  VICTOR    KOUZKINE     (C)      R.D       3  JOSEF     HORESOVSKY      (A)
     7  GUENNADII TSYGANKOV                       4  OLDRICH   MACHAC
                                                 19  VLADIMIR  BEDNAR
                                                  6  RUDOLF    TAJCNAR

    17  VALERII   KHARLAMOV              L.W      15  JOSEF     CERNY           (C)
     9  YURII     BLINOV                          20  JIRI      HOLIK           (A)
                                                 12  BOHUSLAV  STASTNY

    16  VLADIMIR  PETROV                 C.F      11  RICHARD   FARDA
    11  ANATOLII  FIRSSOV     (A)                 21  IVAN      HLINKA
    10  ALEXANDRE MALTSEV                         14  VACLAV    NEDOMANSKY
    12  EVGUENII  MICHAKOV                         5  JAROSLAV  HOLIK

    13  BORIS     MIKHAILOV              R.W       8  JIRI      KOCHTA
    18  VLADIMIR  VIKOULOV                        10  VLADIMIR  MARTINEC
    15  ALEXANDRE IAKOUCHEV


     REFEREE  01 BAADER       (GER)    04 GAGNON           (USA)

    (C) : CAPTAIN
    (A) : ALTERNATE CAPTAIN


 ** 1ST  PERIOD **

 GAME TIME - SCORE --- NAT ---- NAME ------------- ASSISTED --------- PENALTY ------- MIN

           (URS) - (TCH)
 G  05:25  1  -  0   URS    9 BLINOV        16 PETROV
 G  13:12  2  -  0   URS   13 MIKHAILOV      9 BLINOV
 P  19:53            URS    2 DAVYDOV                      TRIPPING           2

           2  -  0
```

アイスホッケー ケッショウ コウシキ キロク
ICE HOCKEY FINAL OFFICIAL RESULTS
HOCKEY SUR GLACE RESULTATS DE OFFICIELS FINAL

** 2ND PERIOD **

GAME TIME - SCORE --- NAT ---- NAME ------------- ASSISTED --------- PENALTY ------- MIN

```
              (URS) - (TCH)
G   02:05   3  -   0    URS    11 FIRSSOV
P   08:34               URS     6 ROMICHEVSKII                    INTERFERENCE        2
G   13:41   4  -   0    URS    12 MICHAKOV
G   18:43   4  -   1    TCH    10 MARTINEC       21 HLINKA

            4  -   1
```

** 3RD PERIOD **

GAME TIME - SCORE --- NAT ---- NAME ------------- ASSISTED --------- PENALTY ------- MIN

```
              (URS) - (TCH)
G   04:44   4  -   2    TCH    15 CERNY           8 KOCHTA
                                                 11 FARDA
G   09:50   5  -   2    URS    12 MICHAKOV       10 MALTSEV
                                                 15 IAKOUCHEV
P   19:38               URS    12 MICHAKOV                         SPEARING            2

            5  -   2
```

```
- PENALTIES --     1ST 2ND 3RD  TOTAL  TIME      -- SHOTS ON GOAL--          1ST 2ND 3RD TOTAL
            URS     1   1   1     3      6                          URS       18  16  19   53
            TCH     0   0   0     0      0                          TCH       25  22  25   72

                                                  --GOALKEEPER SAVE --
                                                          20 URS    11   9  12    32
                                                           1 TCH    11   1   -    12
                                                           2 TCH     -   7  10    17
```

ATOMOSPHERIC CONDITIONS

```
    HUMIDITY              60   %
    ICE TEMPERATURE      - 5.5°  C
    ICE THICKNESS          4   CM
```

榎田 修

'72.2.13 15:01

INDEX